HISTORY OF ART

MEDIÆVAL ART

HISTORY OF ART

Volume **I**   ANCIENT ART
Volume **II**   MEDIÆVAL ART
Volume **III** RENAISSANCE ART
Volume **IV** MODERN ART   (*In Preparation*)

Harper & Brothers
    Publishers

ELIE FAURE

HISTORY OF ART

MEDIÆVAL ART

Translated from the French by
WALTER PACH

Illustrated from Photographs
Selected by the Author

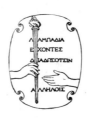

HARPER & BROTHERS PUBLISHERS
NEW YORK AND LONDON

To
My Friends of the Université Populaire
"La Fraternelle"
1905-1909

KHMER ART.   Ornament of a pilaster.   (*Angkor.*)

TABLE OF CONTENTS

THE ENTOMBMENT OF THE VIRGIN (*Cathedral of Senlis*)

INTRODUCTION

(1912)

WHILE the distant civilization of China delays the
hour of its death by turning to its past, while India,
to assuage its fever, spreads a religion across Asia, the
shadows deepen, little by little, over the shores on
which was passed the brilliant and virile youth of the
western world. From the beginning of history, the
ocean of the peoples ebbs and flows from the plateau of
Iran to the fresh and healthful lands that face the
Atlantic. On the plains of northern Europe silent invasions have accumulated reserves of men who will
renew the innocence of the southern peoples when a
too enervating contact with Asia shall weaken their
faith in their own intelligence. We have seen the Phœ-
nicians bring to Greece and to Italy, together with the
science and the ideals of Chaldea and Egypt, the echo
from India of the mystic intoxications through which the
religious thrill of universal life entered the order of the
Occident. We have seen Greece, in the train of Alex-

ander, transmitting its spark of inspiration to the troubled and tired soul of India. Rome, in its turn, is to feel the sensualism of Asia when it brings peace to that land. . . . The movement was exhausting its rhythm little by little. A long repose had to follow the expenditure of energy from which the future of the world had come forth; human nature had to retire into itself to allow its overstrained mind and its perverted senses to forget their conquests and to renew the desire to get back to their natural sources.

From the day when the unity of the Greek soul begins to disintegrate, when two currents appear in the thought of the philosophers and the sensibility of the artists, when Plato and Praxiteles oppose spiritual life to the materialism of Lysippus and Aristotle, from that day the youth of mankind ceased to enchant the world. Their antagonistic tendencies—rationalism that halts the movement of instinct, and sensualism that unseats the will—both lead to the negation of effort. And the skeptic and the mystic open the road to the apostles who come to sow, in the anxious heart of the multitudes, remorse at having lived too fully and an eager desire to purge themselves of the impurity of the body by such an exaltation of the soul that a thousand years will be required by the peoples of the Occident to recover their dignity in a new equilibrium.

It was by the spiritual fusion of metaphysics and morality, by the projection beyond ourselves—who are wicked and corrupt—of an absolute which makes it our duty to repent having been born, that monotheism without compromise was formulated for the first time in the doctrine of the Hebrew prophets. God was outside of the world henceforward, man could no longer attain Him save beyond the confines of his own life. This unity of the divine, which was asserted by the theologians, implanted in our nature that terrible dualism which was doubtless an indispensable trial for all of us, and which still remains so. It was this dualism that caused us to wander for long centuries in search of ourselves. It kept alive for a thousand years, in the depths of our minds, the painful conflict between the solicitations of the senses and the haunting idea of salvation. But it is perhaps, thanks to this dualism again, that we know that our strength lies in the harmony, which we seek in suffering and realize in joy, between our animality—which is sacred —and our reason—which is sacred.

The most expressive and highest manifestation of that harmony — art, the living form which sprang from the marriage of matter and mind to affirm their unity—art had to die at the same time that the nature-creeds died, when the ethical religions appeared, denying its usefulness and precipitating humanity upon paths the reverse of those it had trod up to that time. First, the Jews, who brought into Occidental thought the imposing and sterile spirit of the solitudes, hated and condemned form. The Arabs, born of the same stock, were also to manifest their disdain for it. To change all this there was needed the contact with the soil of Europe, with its bays, its mountains, its fertile plains, its vivifying air, its variety of appearances, and its problems. And it was only after ten centuries of painful struggle, of efforts forever defeated and forever renewed, that the peoples of Europe tore themselves from the powerful embrace of the Semitic idea. It was necessary that India should feel in the very substance of the Buddhistic idea, vibrant within it and creating its strength and its compelling beauty, the incessant action of fecundity and death which causes its forests and rivers to move, in order that it should repeople the temples with its hundred thousand living gods.

After the pantheism of Vedic India and the poly-
theism of Æschylean Greece had attained their highest
expression, and their decline had commenced, there
appeared, in the depths of the great moral religions
which began to claim dominion over the world, the
same despairing sentiment of the final uselessness of
action. Man everywhere was fatigued by living, by
thinking, and he deified his fatigue as, when he loved
action, he had deified his courage. The resignation of
the Christian, the belief in Nirvana of the Buddhist,
the fatalism of the Arab, and the traditionalism of the
Chinese are born of the same pessimistic need for
avoiding effort. For some centuries the Arabs escaped
the consequences of this discouraging idea, but only
because the sole effort demanded from them by the
Prophet was an outward effort, satisfying the essential
needs of their nomadic and conquering life, and because
repose was promised them in death itself, to which they
hurled themselves in the charge of their cavalry, leaving
to the vanquished peoples the task of working for them.
The Chinese, again, escape only through their absence
of idealism and their positive spirit whose energy is
employed, precisely, to fetter and retard action. But
the generalizing peoples of the Occident, the sensual
peoples of India, could extricate themselves from these
consequences only if they profited by the repose that
the doctrines themselves imposed on them. And so
they drove the roots of their instinct deeper into their
earth and fought with all their rejuvenated power
against the spirit of renunciation to which the disciples
of Sakyamuni and of Jesus had dragged the crowds
whose interest it was to listen to them while they hid
the faces of the two men who were all love and therefore
all action.

Now that the ethical religions are a part of history,
now that we have learned that the moral need loses its

power when it presumes to annihilate or diminish the
æsthetic need of which it is only one aspect, we are
sufficiently strong to recognize that Christianity and
Buddhism introduced into the world an admirable
element of passion. In India, Buddhism had never
really assumed the character of radical opposition to
Brahmanism that Christianity adopted toward the
pagan religions. It was not the spirit of one soil and
one race going forth to combat the spirit of another
soil and another race. It was born of the very current
that urged the peoples of India to mingle their soul
with the voices of the universe, and to beseech the
voices of the universe to permeate that soul incessantly; it was an extension in the moral world of the
formidable sensualism whose appeal men could not ig-
nore when that sensualism fused their mind with the
mind of the wild beasts, the forests, the waters, and
the stones. In the Occident, on the contrary, in the
bosom of Christianity, organized into a political system,
the invasion of the human soul by the forces of nature
could take on no other aspect than that of rebellion.
And therein we have the reason why the Christian soul
has stamped a profound imprint on the form of our mind.

By teaching the hatred of life, Christianity multiplied our very power to live when the fatalities of
economic and political evolution in Occidental society
brought them into contact with life, adapted their
organs to new functions, and assured new satisfactions
to their needs. Our senses had kept silence for a thousand years; for a thousand years the sap of humanity
had been turned back to our hearts; for a thousand
years the mind had accumulated, in a frightful solitude,
a world of confused desires, of unexpressed intuitions,
of fevers only partly allayed, which caused the love of
the world to burst forth from the mind when it could
be restrained no longer, and then it appeared with all

the intoxication of the beasts of the forests when released from cages. There is no more magnificent spectacle in history than that of humanity, in its religious
frenzy, hurling itself on form to make it fruitful again.

It is in this spectacle that we must seek for the
origin of the differences that are noticeable when we
consider in their ensemble the manifestations of ancient
art and mediæval art, especially in India and in western Europe. The ancient world had never forbidden
the love of form; it had, on the contrary, arrived
through form—by a progressive, harmonious, continuous effort—at the philosophic generalizations formulated by the sculptors of Athens toward the middle of
the century of Æschylus, of Sophocles, and of Phidias.
Egypt, confined by the theocracy within the metaphysical limits from which it was forbidden to go onward,
had studied man in his structure and had defined for
all time the form of the shadow that he will cast on the
earth so long as the sun shall shine upon him. Greece,
freed from dogma, had scrutinized the relations that
unite man with nature, had found again in the volumes
and gestures of living forms, the laws which determine
harmony, in the revolution of the heavenly bodies, in
the unfurling of the profiles of the earth, in the rising
and falling motion of the seas. It rested with the
Middle Ages of the Occident to render in form the relationships created between man and man by the griefs
that have been lived through together, by the hopes
too long deferred, by the joy of the senses liberated
after centuries of asceticism and of physical and moral
compression. The new spirit manifests itself everywhere by a wild eruption of reveling in matter that
establishes an obscure and magical understanding
between mediæval Europe and mediæval India. Brahman India felt living within itself the soul of Buddha
as Gothic Europe, carried along by its social needs,

felt living again within itself—despite the theologians, the councils, and the fathers of the Church—the loving soul, the pitiful, artist soul of Jesus.

The reawakening of the sensuality of men took on many forms. Among the Christians it had a revolutionary appearance; among the Indians it found its nutriment as well in the moral passion of Sakyamuni as in the pantheist fever of Brahma; it manifested itself against the very spirituality of Islam in the thrust of Berber mosques, in their embroidery of metal and of wood, and in the shimmer of jewels in Persian painting; it attempted a painful escape from the clasp of the fearful nightmare of the Aztecs, bringing together again the strips of flesh that were cut up before men's eyes; it appears in the patience of the Chinese, who, through the language of form, render the entities of their moral equilibrium fit for daily life. But everywhere in the Middle Ages, and whatever the aspect of the revival, the peoples were ignorant of the real object they were pursuing; everywhere their conquest of the life of the universe was accomplished under the pretext of religion, always with the support of the letter of the dogma, always against its spirit. It is this which emphasizes so powerfully, in the art of the Middle Ages, its confused liberty, its drunken and fecund plunge into the fields of sensation, its carelessness as to spoken language—provided that language expressed something, its disordered mixture of feelings springing from the contact of the soul with the world, in the naked strength of instinct. The philosophic idea, which compels all ancient art to seek harmony of form, is rendered useless here by the anchor of dogma, which, outside itself, leaves the rejuvenated and unfettered senses free to seek their realization and permits the love, that is universal at the moment, to release itself from the control of the human will. The admirable logic of the French cathedral builders of the Middle Ages is primarily applied to realizing a practical object, and if the Arab raises over the desert the abstract image of the mind, it is with roses and with women that he fills his cool Alhambras. Immortal Dionysus has reconquered the earth, mingling with his sensual fever the love of Buddha, the gentleness of Jesus, and the dignity of Mohammed; and when Prometheus, through the commune of the Occident, is reborn at his side, Prometheus is unconscious of himself: he also is flooded with mystic intoxication. The Middle Ages have recreated consciousness despite the gods that they adored.

It is always against the gods that the consciousness of mortals is created, even when these gods, as those of the Greek Olympus, express laws that are to be understood in order that they may be obeyed. An inevitable confusion has arisen in us, between the pretext for our beliefs and their real meaning. From the beginning of things we have seen art and religion following the same road, art being willing to move almost exclusively between the dikes of religious symbolism and changing its appearance as soon as one god replaces another. We have never asked ourselves why all the religions, even when they combat one another, express themselves in forms that constantly survive them and that time eventually finds to be in accord as well as a necessity. We have never asked ourselves why the finest creations of the artists do not always coincide with the moments of most intense religious exaltation, why the same religion often remains silent throughout its youth and expresses itself only when it approaches its decline. We have never asked ourselves why the French image makers imprinted their desires on the stones of the cathedrals only after the movement of revolt which assured the

life of the commune against the oppression of the
priest and the lord, why the signs of discouragement
appeared among them precisely during the course of
one century, the fifteenth, when the Catholic faith
knew its moment of the most ardent fever and excitement.   We have never asked ourselves why India
mingled its contradictory gods in the same explosion
of sensual intoxication; why Islam—which has preserved to our own day the uncompromising fanaticism
of ten centuries ago—lets its mosques fall to ruin and
builds no others; why the Chinese artist sometimes
belongs to three or four different sects, whereas the
Japanese artist almost always gives the impression of
belonging to none; why the European raised altars
to a God of mercy at the hour when the Aztec caused
his altars to run with the blood of human victims.   We
have never asked ourselves whether the peoples did
not give to their beliefs the form of their sensations.

We must, however, in our hours of virility, have as
imperious a need of artistic creation as of food and love.
This need sweeps our beliefs along in its triumphal
movement, for there is creation even among those
peoples whose theologians and philosophers teach the
final nullity of effort; their own poets sing the vanity
of our activity in terms that create life.   Christianity
is pessimistic, Islamism is pessimistic, pantheism is
pessimistic.   What matter?   The Christian causes a
sonorous forest of vaults, of windows, of towers to
spring from the soil; the Mussulman spreads the cool
shadow of his cupolas over his incurable inertia; the
Indian disembowels the mountains to make them
fruitful.   Man wants to live, and he demands of those
who sing and carve to show him the way of the true
life, even when they speak to him of death.   It is the
people that makes its gods, whichever they may be.

To be sure, we need a faith.   It is only in faith that

we gather the strength necessary to resist our disillu-
sionments and to maintain before our eyes the image
of our hope. But this faith, which we decorate with
new labels when a new system of metaphysics or of
morality imposes itself on our needs—this faith changes
only its aspect, it does not change in spirit; and as
long as it lives in us, whatever the period in which our
activity takes place, whichever the religion that serves
it as a pretext, the forms of art, even the most diverse,
will do no more than express the faith. It is simply
the confidence that comes after long slumbers, and that
grows weak upon a too prolonged contact with the
mystery which our ardor for life urges us to penetrate.
When a religion arrives at its most harmonious and
expressive degree of development, this faith is not
thereby awakened; on the contrary, the religion is
born of the faith, it is the projection, into the field of
our illusions, of the inner realities which guide and
exalt us. When man is near to self-realization, he
accepts, all at once and in the mass, a great simple
synthesis of everything he is ignorant of, so as not to
be troubled by doubt and anxiety in his search for
what he wants to know. When he has learned too
much, when his faith in himself weakens, his outward
beliefs may last or even become exaggerated, but
at the same time all the expressions of his thought
vacillate. Peoples in action force any religion to bend
itself to the manifestations of their original virtues.
A religion models a people to its dogmas only when
that people no longer believes in itself. Whatever our
paradise, we realize it on earth when we have achieved
self-confidence. To declare this paradise divine, we
wait for centuries and search the world until the hour
comes when life mounts fully in our heart, and the
word "faith" is the religious name we give to energy.

Never before had this energy arisen in the world in

such a violent eruption of intoxicated mysticism. It is this that causes really religious minds, from the moment they cross the threshold of the cathedral, the mosque, or the pagoda, to forget profoundly and completely the rite that is celebrated in the place; it is this that causes them to be absolutely indifferent to the dogmas on which these temples were built; hence, too, their exaltation over the arrested and dead forms of man's religion and over the dead forms in the unlimited field of his relations with his fellow-man. The word "mystic" is still to be defined. If mysticism is that form of despair which urges the human soul, in moments of lassitude, toward external gods in whose hands it abdicates all will and desire, toward gardens which open to the dead alone and offer them flowers that smell of corpses, then the first periods of Christianity were perhaps the only ones to know this mysticism, for at that time a minimum of humanity subsisted in the multitude of superstitions and religious practices. But if mysticism appears under that form of frantic and living hope that hurls itself on the rich fields of sensation and action and gathers into its flesh all the invading forces of renewal and exaltation which the approving world pours into it simultaneously, then it is the creative spirit itself, and its accord with its flesh reveals to it the necessary means. Whatever god he adores, or even if he rejects all the gods, the man who desires to create cannot express himself if he does not feel in his veins the flow of all the rivers—even those which carry along sand and putrefaction, he is not realizing his entire being if he does not see the light of all the constellations, even those which no longer shine, if the primeval fire, even when locked in beneath the crust of the earth, does not consume his nerves, if the hearts of all men, even the dead, even those still to be born, do not beat in his heart, if abstrac-

tion does not mount from his senses to his soul to raise
it to the plane of the laws which cause men to act,
the rivers to flow, the fire to burn, and the constellations to revolve.

And everywhere, or practically everywhere, in the
Middle Ages, the creators had these hours of confused
and limitless communion with the heart and mind of
matter in movement. And what is admirable about
these men is that none or almost none of them has left
us his name. Therein lies a phenomenon, indeed, that
is perhaps unique in history—the very masses of the
people contributing their strength to the life whose tide
flowed in them incessantly; it is a passionate abandon-
ment by the multitudes to the blind impulse of their
regenerated instincts. Antiquity—or Greek antiquity,
at least—had not known this hour, because she had
achieved her conquests in a progressive effort. Here
the peoples recovered, at a single bound, the lost contact with the world; and as the conquests of their
past still lived, though unknown to them, in the potential power that dwelt in them, the return to action
took place in a prodigious tumult. These multitudes
built their temples themselves; the beating of some
obscure heart sealed every stone in its place. Never
has there been such a spurting forth of vaults, pyramids, belfries, and towers, such a tide of statues rising
from the soil like plants to invade space and capture
heaven. From the Dutch Indies and from the Himalayas to the Atlantic, from the Atlas to the North Sea,
from the Peruvian Andes to the Gulf of Mexico, a swift
current of irresistible love passed through space to weld
the worlds that were ignorant of each other. Architecture, the anonymous and collective art, the plastic
hymn of the crowds in action, issued from them with
so deep a murmur, in such a transport of intoxication,
that it seemed the voice of the universal hope, the same

among all the peoples of the earth, seeking in their substance the gods who were concealed from their eyes. When they had seen the face of these gods, the builders of the temples stopped, but with such a gesture of despair that it broke the iron armor within which the theocracies were walling in the intelligence, and decided the individual to make the conquest of himself.

MEDIÆVAL ART

. . . the voices seemed all
to form the same song, so perfect was their accord.
Dante Alighieri

MONT-ABOU

Chapter I. INDIA

I

T the hour when the peoples of the eastern Mediterranean were writing the first page of history, India was also beginning to live a superior moral life. But only the murmur of the Vedic hymns, more ancient by a thousand or two thousand years, perhaps, than the epics of Greece, arises from the confusion of the past. Not a single poem of stone, save a few megalithic monuments whose antiquity is not known, exists to unveil the mystery of the Indian soul before the Middle Ages of the Occident, and it seems nearer to this period than to the ancient civilizations.

It is because the tribes of Iran, when they had left the high plateaus to descend the lengths of the rivers toward the horizon of the great plains, did not find everywhere the same soil, the same trees, the same waters, the same skies. Some of them had to face the unity of the desert, the source of the metaphysical absolutes. Others peopled the countries of moderate size, with scattered vegetation and clear-cut forms, which led them to observe objectively, and brought about the desire to complete in their minds the balanced forces that make up the harmonious universe. The Iranians who had followed the valley of the Ganges had first to give way to the intoxication of the senses. Still keeping within them the silence and the coolness of the high country, they plunged without transition into a world that overwhelmed them with its ardor and fecundity.

Never, in any part of the globe, had man found himself in the presence of an aspect of nature at once so generous and so fierce. Death and life impose themselves there with such violence that he was forced to endure them no matter what their form. To escape the dead seasons, to reach the seasons of fertility, it was enough for him to move northward or southward. Nourishing vegetation, roots, fruit, and grain sprouted from a soil that does not exhaust itself. He held out his hand and gathered up life. When he entered the woods to draw water from the great rivers or to seek materials for his house, death rose up irresistibly, carried along by the waves, as with the crocodile, hidden in the thickets, as with the tiger, writhing under the grasses with the cobra, or breaking down the rampart of trees with the step of the elephant. Scarcely, if at all, in the nocturnal tangle of tree stems, the branches, and the leaves, could he distinguish the movement of animal life from the movement of rotting matter and the flowering of herbs. Born of the hidden fermentations in which life and death fuse, the torrent of sap which feeds our universe burst from the luxuriant body of the earth in healthful fruits and poisonous flowers.

The mingling aspects of generosity and cruelty that nature offered to man disarmed him mentally and

SANCHI (III Century B.C.).   A gate of the Stupa.

physically. The possibility of attaining a moral ideal, to be reached only through the conquest of tremendous forests and multiplied temptations, seemed to him as inaccessible as the brow of the Himalayas which lifted the highest glaciers of the earth into the blue light of

the north. Accepting life and death with the same
indifference, he had to do no more than lay open his
senses to the penetration of the universe and permit
the gradual rise from his instincts to his soul of that
grandiose, confused pantheism which is the whole of

KARLI (II Century B.C.). Bas-relief of the Chaitya.

the science, the religion, and the philosophy of the
man of India.

And yet, when Alexander reached the banks of the
Indus, a great social revolution was shaking the peninsula. A century before, Sakyamuni, the Buddha, had
felt the flood of pantheist intoxication in his inner
life, had felt it invaded by a love whose power swept
him on like a river. He loved men, he loved beasts,
he loved the trees, the stones — everything that

INDO-HELLENISTIC ART. Buddha. (I Century B.C.). (*Private Collection.*)

breathed, that throbbed, that moved; everything, even, whose form could be grasped by the senses, from the constellations of heaven to the grass on which one trod. Since the world is but a single body, it must be that an irresistible tenderness draws together all the dispersed elements, all the different forms which

ELLORA (VI Century).   Basement of the Elephants.

wander through the world.   Hunger, killing, suffering, all are love.   Sakyamuni tenderly offered his bare flesh to an eagle that was pursuing a dove.

Whatever the fatalism and the sensualism of a people, it always listens, at least once during the course of history, to him who comes to pour the balm of love upon its wounds.   The tiger could not be conquered, it is true, the peak of the Himalayas could not be reached, and the sacred rivers that descended from

ELLORA (v Century). Monolithic temple, detail from the life of Vishnu.

it could not cease to roll fever and life in their waters.
And yet the social machinery of the Brahman, the
implacable régime of castes which reflected from top
to bottom the relentless rigor of the energy of the universe, was shattered by the revolt of love. Half a
century after the incursion of Alexander, the emperor
Asoka was forced to follow the lead of the multitudes
and erect eighty-four thousand temples in commemora-
tion of a man who had never spoken of the gods.

How long did Buddhism last in India? Seven or
eight centuries, perhaps—an hour of the life of these
multitudes whose history, as it evolves in the past and
in the future, seems as infinite and as confused as their
swarming in space. India returned, insensibly, to
the Vedic gods; the Brahman, supported by the
prince, rebuilt the social pyramid and swept from the
earth man's hope of paradise. Buddhism took refuge
in the soul of a few cenobites and, beyond the frontiers of India, was to conquer Asia. Thus Christianity,
born of the Semitic ideal, was to conquer the whole
Occident, save the Hebrews. A revolution does not
vanquish the fundamental instinct of the surroundings
that provoke it.

It was from the depths of the Indian nature itself
that the materialistic mysticism had risen again to
stifle all the desires for humanity aroused by Buddhism.
The temples with which the crowds of neophytes
had sown the soil of India brought them, stone by
stone, to submit anew to the ritualization of the primitive beliefs, which did not cease to be source of their
emotions. The Buddhistic monument, properly so
called, has almost disappeared from India. The
topes, the great reliquaries of brick, are perhaps the
only edifices not dedicated to a god having a material
figure. And yet the history of Buddha, the whole of
his life as it was passed among the animals and the

forests, is sculptured on the door. The *chaityas*, the basilicas that were built about the first century, already have capitals composed of animal figures. When Sakyamuni himself appears in the sanctuary, his teaching is forgotten and an instinctive sensualism overcomes the moral needs.

What did it matter to the crowds of India? They needed forms to love. The Brahmans had no diffi-

BHUWANESWAR (VI Century). The great temple.

culty in conquering. Were they even conscious of their victory, and did the miserable multitude feel the defeat weighing upon its hope? Was there a victory? Was there a defeat? Is not defeat the abdication of the real nature that has been developed by our geographical surroundings and the great secret atavism that binds us to the very depths of our history? Is not victory the triumph within us of that imperishable nature through which alone the conception of the life that is native to us can be manifested? Was a single Buddhistic temple destroyed, a single believer persecuted? Perhaps not. In India, the religious spirit dominates dogma. One tide rises after another and, on the shore, leaves seaweed, shells, new corpses, new palpitating lives. Everything is mingled and confused —the Brahman officiates in the Buddhistic temples and venerates the statue of Buddha as well as those of Shiva, Brahma, and Vishnu. A given underground temple, begun in the first periods of Buddhism, continues to be dug out when the Tartars, after the Persians and the Arabs, have imposed Islam on half of the Indians.

II

For the Indians, all nature is divine and, below the great Indra, all the gods are of equal power and can threaten or dethrone the other gods, concrete or abstract—the sun, the jungle, the tiger, and the elephant; the forces which create and those which destroy —war, love, and death. In India everything has been god, everything is god or will be god. The gods change, they evolve, they are born and die, they may or may not leave children, they tighten or loosen their grip on the imagination of men and on the walls of the rocks. What does not die, in India, is faith—the immense faith, frenzied and confused under a thousand names; it changes its form ceaselessly, but always remains the same immeasurable power that urges the masses to action. In India there came to pass this thing: that, driven forth by an invasion, a famine, or a migration of wild beasts, thousands of human beings moved to the north or to the south. There at the shore of the sea, at the base of a mountain, they encountered a great wall of granite. Then they all entered the granite; in its shadows they lived, loved, worked, died, were born, and, three or four centuries afterward, they came out again, leagues away, having traversed the mountain. Behind them they left the emptied

AJANTA (II Century B.C. to VI Century A.D.).   Fresco, detail.

rock, its galleries hollowed out in every direction, its sculptured, chiseled walls, its natural or artificial pillars turned into a deep lacework with ten thousand horrible or charming figures, gods without number and without name, men, women, beasts—a tide of animal life moving in the gloom. Sometimes when they found no clearing in their path, they hollowed out an abyss in the center of the mass of rock to shelter a little black stone.[1]

It is in these monolithic temples, on their dark walls or on their sunburnt façade, that the true genius of India expends all its terrific force. Here the confused speech of confused multitudes makes itself heard. Here man confesses unresistingly his strength and his nothingness. He does not exact the affirmation of a determined ideal from form. He incloses no system in it. He extracts it in the rough from formlessness, according to the dictates of the formless. He utilizes the indentations and the accidents of the rock. It is they that make the sculpture. If any room is left he adds arms to the monster, or cuts off his legs if the space is insufficient. If an enormous wall of rock suggests the broad masses of monsters that he has seen rolling in herds, rearing their heads on the banks of the rivers or at the edges of the forests, he cuts the wall into great pure planes to make an elephant of it. Wherever, by chance, the hollows and the projections occur, breasts swell, haunches tighten and move; the

---

[1] The illustration on page 15 represents a copy of the fresco of Ajanta—Shiva and Parvati—which the Indian Society has kindly authorized us to reproduce. This copy is from the brush of Nanda Lal Bose, a contemporary Indian painter and a pupil of Abanindra Nath Tagore. The school of Indian painting is being reborn, or rather, it continues. It has not ceased to take its inspiration from the Indian myths and legends that it treats—notably in the work of the two masters just cited—with a grave and tender melancholy, and according to the traditional forms of Hindu and Indo-Persian art. (See No. 200 of *L'Art Décoratif*, February, 1914.)

AJANTA (II Century B.C. to VI Century A.D.). Shiva and
Parvati. Fresco. Copy, by Nanda Lal Bose.
(*Woodroffe Collection.*)

mating of men or beasts, combat, prayer, violence, and gentleness are born of matter that seems itself to be suffused with a vague intoxication. The roots of wild plants may split the forms, the blocks may crumble, the action of sun and water may gnaw the stone.

BHUWANESWAR (VI Century). The great temple, a pillar.

Yet the elements will not mingle all these lives with the confusion of the earth more successfully than the sculptor has done. Sometimes, in India, one finds enormous mushrooms of stone in the depths of the forests, shining in the green shadow like poisonous plants. Sometimes one finds heavy elephants, quite alone, as mossy and as rough skinned as if alive; they mingle with the tangled vines, the grasses reach their bellies,

flowers and leaves cover them, and even when their
debris shall have returned to the earth they will be no
more completely absorbed by the intoxication of the
forest.

The whole of Indian genius lies in this never-satisfied
need for setting matter in motion, in this acceptance of

AMRAVATI.   Women in adoration.

the elements offered by matter, in this indifference to
the fate of the forms that it has drawn from matter.
Before the art that reveals to us this genius, one must
not look for the expression which the Egyptian gave
to his metaphysical system, an expression that was
imposed, perhaps, upon the sculptor, but was none
the less real; we must not look for the free expression
of a social philosophy, as among the Greeks.   What
we have here is the dark and troubled expression—
anonymous and profound, but immeasurably strong
for that very reason—of the intuitive pantheism of the
Indian.   Man is no longer at the center of life.   He

BHUWANESWAR (VI Century). The great temple, detail.

is no longer that flower of the whole world, which has
slowly set itself to form and mature him. He is mingled with all things, he is on the same plane with all
things, he is a particle of the infinite, neither more

MAHAVELLIPORE (VIII Century). Monolithic temple. Milking.

nor less important than the other particles of the
infinite. The earth passes into the trees, the trees into
the fruits, the fruits into man or the animal, man and
the animal into the earth; the circulation of life
sweeps along and propagates a confused universe
wherein forms arise for a second, only to be engulfed
and then to reappear, overlapping one another, palpitating, penetrating one another as they surge like
the waves. Man does not know whether yesterday he
was not the very tool with which he himself will force
matter to release the form that he may have to-

morrow. Everything is merely an appearance, and under the diversity of appearances Brahma, the spirit of the world, is a unity. To be sure, man has the mystical intuition of universal transformism. Through transmigrations, by passing from one appearance to another, and by raising within himself, through suffering and combat, the moving level of life, he will doubtless be pure enough one day to annihilate himself in Brahma. But, lost as he is in the ocean of mingled forms and energies, does he know whether he is still a form or a spirit? Is that thing before us a thinking being, a living being even, a planet, or a being cut in stone? Germination and putrefaction are engendered unceasingly. Everything has its heavy movement, expanded matter beats like a heart. Does not wisdom consist in submerging oneself in it, in order to taste the intoxication of the unconscious as one gains possession of the force that stirs in matter?

In the virgin forests of the south, between the heat of the sun and the fever of the soil, faith caused the temples to spring two hundred feet into the air, multiplied them from generation to generation, and surrounded them with ever-growing inclosures, whose position was constantly changed. Such an architecture could not issue from a source less powerful and less dim than the grottos hollowed out of the depths of the rocks. Artificial mountains were raised up, graded pyramids, wherein the thicket of forms moves as if alive. One is tempted to say that there was no plan for the construction of these forests of gods, as they bristle like cactus and evil plants, as they present profiles like the backs of primitive monsters. They seem to have been thrust up from the crust of the earth as if by the force of lava. It must have required ten thousand laborers, working together and by their own inspiration, but united by their fanaticism

and their desires, to build these titanic platforms, carve them from top to bottom, cover them with statues as dense as the lives of the jungle, and support them in space on the aërial festoon of the lacelike ogives and the inextricable scaffolding of the columns. Here are statues upon statues, colonnades upon colonnades; thirty styles are mingled, juxtaposed, super-

MAHAVELLIPORE (VIII Century). Bas-relief on the rock.

imposed. The columns may be round or square or polygonal, in sections or monolithic, smooth or fluted or covered with carving that has an appearance of danger, like masses of reptiles moving in oily circles, like pustules that throb and rise, like bubbles bursting under leaves spread over a heavy water. There, as everywhere in India, the infinitely little touches the infinitely big. Whatever the power of these temples, they seem to have sprung from the earth through the power of the seasons, and at the same time to have been carved out minutely like an ivory sculpture.

MAHAVELLIPORE (VIII Century). Monolithic temple. Bas-relief on a wall, detail.

Forms are everywhere, tufted bas-reliefs are everywhere, from the surroundings of the temples to their summit, on the inner walls, and often on the top of the columns where the whole of humanity, mingled with the whole of animal life, supports the burden of the entablatures and the roofs. Everything may serve to carry a statue, everything may swell into a figure—the capitals, the pediments, the columns, the upper stages of the pyramids, the steps, the balustrades, the banisters of stairways. Formidable groups rise and fall—rearing horses, warriors, human beings in clusters like grapes, eruptions of bodies piled one over the other, trunks and branches that are alive, crowds sculptured by a single movement as if spouting from one matrix. One has the impression that the old monolithic temple has been violently twirled and shot out of the earth. Save in the more recent epochs when he modeled bronzes of astonishing tenderness, firmness, and elegance, the Indian has never conceived sculpture as being able to live independent of the construction that it decorates. It seems a confused mass of buds on the body of a heavy plant.

III

Even out of doors, even in the full daylight, these forms are surrounded by a mysterious obscurity. The torsos, the arms, the legs, and the heads commingle—when a statue itself has not twenty arms, ten legs, four or five faces, when it is not laden with all these aspects of tenderness and fury by which life reveals itself. The depths of the sculpture undulate heavily, as if to force back into the moving eternity of primitive matter the still unformed beings that attempt to emerge from it. We see writhing larvæ, vague embryos; they seem incessant and successive attempts at gestation which start and miscarry in the intoxication and fever of a soil that continually creates.

As one views this sculpture from near by one must

ELEPHANTA (VIII Century). Colossal head.

not attempt to find in it the scientific modeling of the
Egyptians or the philosophic modeling of Phidias,
although Egypt and, to a greater degree, the Greece
brought in by Alexander, profoundly influenced the
first Buddhistic sculptors, perhaps even to the extent
of revealing them to themselves.   Sculpture is no
longer considered in its planes and its passages, save
summarily and by instinct.   It might better be defined
in terms of painting, for in these gigantic bas-reliefs
light and shade play a vital and continuous part, as
if a brush moved over them to soften and caress them.
But Hindu painting, itself, while preserving the qualities of materiality that are in the sculpture, is perhaps
more purified by the mind.   The painting is usually
the work of the monks; Buddhism has left a clear
imprint on it.   And later on it is especially in painting
that, when Islam arrives, the influence of Persia makes
itself felt.   From the great Buddhistic decorations to
the Mussulman miniatures, the spiritualization of the
work sometimes touches the rarest, the highest, the
most human harmony.   One may not assign a place
lower than that of the great classic works to the frescoes of Ajunta, in which the lyrical pantheism of the
Hindus seems to fuse, for an hour, the spiritual radiance
of Egyptian paintings and the moral intoxication of
the old Chinese artists.   By a kind of ethnic paradox
the great painting of India would seem nearer to the
linear rhythms, which are the chief preoccupation of
the Egyptian or Greek sculptors, than Hindu sculpture
itself, for the latter seeks to transfer to stone or metal
the fleeting, flowing modeling of the painter.   When
we compare this sculpture with that of the anonymous
workmen of Thebes or with that of the Athenian masters, we find something in it that is absolutely new,
that is difficult to define—something like the obscure
fermentation in a crucible, as compared with the

TANJORE (XI Century). The Pagoda.

limpidity of a theorem. The modeling aims at movement rather than at form. It is never considered in an
isolated way nor in its abstract relationships with the
neighboring figures. Material passages unite the
figures among themselves; they are always heavy
with atmosphere; the background is always felt;
other figures partly absorb them; the modeling is
fluctuating and billowy, like the mass of the leaves
when labored by the wind. What models the rock,
what rolls it into storm waves, is desire and despair
and enthusiasm. It undulates like a crowd ravished
by voluptuousness and fury. It swells and grows tense
like the torso of a woman as she feels the approach of
love.

   As we have observed, it is the movement and not
the form that interests the Indian sculptor, and so we
do not find him seeking harmonies of relationships or
clearly stated abstractions, but expressive masses
which give an intoxicated, florid image of the whole
world, and no longer seek for an equilibrium between the laws of the universe and the laws of the
mind. By flashes, veiled by obscurity and by torpor,
one can doubtless find everything in this art, overlapping the neighboring element, oppressing it or being
oppressed by it; one can meet with brief jets of consciousness and sudden starts from the most rudimentary realism to the highest idealism. When one
sees them isolated one notes the special quality of the
figures, especially the figures of women, innumerable,
gentle, religious, and yet formidable in their grace,
their sensuality, their carnal heaviness. At every
moment they give evidence of the effort—gigantic,
vague, but often of a mighty fervor—toward a higher
adaptation to their role in humanity. The man of
India loves to see the waist bend under the weight of
the breasts and the haunches, he likes long tapering

Delhi (xii Century). Jain Colonnade. (*Mosque of Koutab.*)

forms and the single wave of the muscles as a movement surges through the whole body. But this hymn
to the more tender forms of beauty is lost in the clamor
of the universe. At one and the same time he can

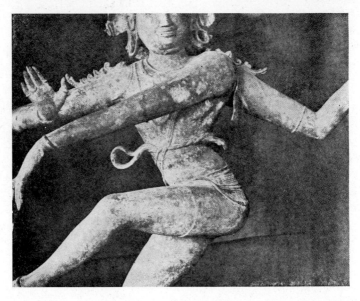

The Dance of Shiva (XII Century). Bronze, detail. (*Museum of Madras.*)

adore Indra, the supreme being; Brahma, the creator;
Shiva, the destroyer; Krishna, the redeemer; Surya,
the light of day; Lakshmi, who is love; Sarvasti,
who is science; and the horrible Kali seated in putrefaction and the clotted blood of his victims. He can
adore the ten incarnations of Vishnu and the crowd of
heroes and monsters of his immense mythology and of
the national epics, Ravana, Sougriva, Hanoumat, and
Ananta. He can invoke Rama, the incorruptible hero
who would have led the Greeks to the threshold of

divinity. Rama is only one idol more in the prodigious pantheon, an idol lost among the gods of fecundity and death. On his walls he can bring together ferocity and indulgence, asceticism and lubricity, fornications and apostleships; he can mingle obscenity and heroism. Heroism and obscenity appear no more important in the life of the universe than the fighting or mating of a pair of insects in the woods. Everything is on the same plane. Why not let instinct spread out through nature with the indifference of the elemental forces and, in its onrush, sweep away moralities and systems? Social idealism is vain. Impassible eternity wears away the long effort of man. The Indian artist has not the time to bring the human form to its realization. Everything that it contains is contained as possibility. A prodigious life animates it —an embryonic life, however, and one that seems

LAKSHMI, bronze (XIV Century) (*Private Collection.*)

condemned never to choose between the confused solicitations of the energies of the will and the energies of
the senses.   Man will change nothing of his final destiny, which is to return sooner or later to the unconscious and the formless.   In the fury of the senses or

GWALIOR (xv Century).   The Palace.

the immobility of contemplation, he must therefore
descend unresistingly into the chaos of the elements.

The withdrawal of the Indian soul from preoccupation with morality, its pantheistic confusion and disorder, cut it off almost constantly from the great
abstract constructions that characterize the aspiration
of the ancient peoples of the Occident.   In India, the
eye does not seize things in their ensemble until it has
taken in all their details.   In Egypt, the desert, the
horizon, and the straight line of the river, as in Greece
the winding bays, the transparent waters, and the
clear-cut crests of the hills, had made of man a meta-

physician or a philosopher, loving the rhythm or the
sinuous continuity that he observed in the universe;
but here it required too many days to reach the mountains, the rivers were too vast and too muddy for one
to see to their depths, the forests were too dense to

BINDERABUND (XVI Century).   A temple.

permit the eye to take in at once the harmonious line
of the trees, the outline of their leaves, the true form of
the creeping animals that appear only in a flash, to
flee from death or to inflict it.   Man is surrounded by
an unpassable barrier of luxuriant life, the eye is dazzled by the ceaselessly broken and mingled colors and
lines of flowers that rain sparkling dust, of vines, of
beasts fantastically marked; one is caught up in the
feverish spirit of the germs of life and death that roll
under the ocean of leaves.   The disorder of the material
world of the Indian intoxicates his soul and brings him

to that pantheistic mysticism that every sensual being can feel rising within him in supreme moments of love, when, through the embrace of the woman who yields to him, he feels the confused and real presence of the universe. In the architecture of India we must not seek that linear abstraction which, by its continuity, expresses the visible rhythm of life; what is sought and found is life itself, gathered up hastily and pressed pell-mell into form. It is part of the quivering skin of the earth from which it was torn. The unity of the world is expressed in it by the heaping up at one point in space of everything that belongs to life, from the densely populated soil to the solitude of the heavens, and from the motionless mountains to the roll of the seas.

IV

However, to the north and the northeast of India, in the regions where the forests are less heavy, where the glaciers are nearer, and the jungle is cut into here and there by great desert spaces, the synthesis was infinitely less instinctive, more abstract, and therefore more sober. It was by this route, indeed, that Greece had entered India, as Rome came later, and Byzantium and Persia which, from the depths of its history, brought the memory of Assyria, of Chaldea, and perhaps of Egypt. With Persia also came Islam, a spiritualizing force that did not love the images and despised the idols. Finally, by way of Lisbon and Venice, there came the Occident of the Gothic age and of the Renaissance. But India is a crucible so ebullient in its heat that for centuries it forced Islam to submit to its genius, to cover the walls of its mosques with living arabesques —lotus, flowering vines, figures of men and of monsters. The Greek statue, hastily imitated by the first sculptors, was forgotten as quickly as it had become known. The disquieting elegance of the works that it inspired was only a prelude to the retaliation soon to be made by a sensuality impossible to restrain. Though captivated for a moment by the unbounded grace and

INDO-MUSSULMAN ART (XVII Century). The Taj-Mahal of Agra.

reason of the Greeks, India was to manifest its own power through the wandering smile of the mouths, through the smothered flame, the enervation, and the ascetic thinness of the bodies. When northern India carried its religion into the south, it also brought with it the pure column that had supported the luminous pediments on all the acropolises of the Occident. But the column was to be overwhelmed by the extravagant growth of the living forests of stone. India assimilated everything, transformed everything, submerged everything under the mounting tide of her ever-moving

force.   Grandiose civilizations passed over her and
sowed her deserts and her woods with the cadavers of
cities.   What matter?   Here neither time counts, nor
men.   Evolution returns upon itself at every moment.
Like a sea, the Hindu soul is eternally mobile, between
fixed shores.   At no moment can one say, here the race
ascends, here is its apogee, here its fall.   In the crucible
some substances melt, others are liquid and burning,
and others cold and hard.   India is the enigma, the
protean, unseizable being without beginning and without end, without laws and without purposes, mingled
with everything and yet alone in the intoxication which
she cannot exhaust.

Thus the aristocratic and more abstract art of the
north, although we may find in it traces of the Mediterranean civilizations, from Chaldea and Egypt to feudal
and neopagan Europe, remains at bottom as Indian
as the art of the Dravidians of the south.   As it rises
from the Dekkan toward the Himalayas, the pyramid
becomes rounder.   In central India its lines become
curves, and though it is still striped like the skin of the
tigers, it is less laden with ornaments and is almost
without statues.   In the valley of the Ganges, the
curvature, upon contact with the Persian dome, is
more pronounced and the vault, built of flat stones in
tiers, takes on the form of the cupola or of the kiosk,
supported by frail pillars hemispherical, ovoid, stocky,
pressed down or swelling out, polygonal or circular,
sometimes bare like those of the mosques, or carved
and capped with turbans like those of the Dravidian
pyramids—the domes look like enormous fat tubercles
bulging with spongy matter.   The form is just such a
one as Indian sensualism has at all times desired.
India, land of ruins that it is, must have seen the complete disappearance, a thousand years before our era,
of edifices that much resembled those forests of bul-

bous domes, temples, or mausoleums that she was still
building in our day. The Ramayana speaks frequently
of "palaces whose white peaks foam into heaps of
cloud."

Even before the domination of the Great Moguls,

Miniature of the XVII Century. (*Private Collection.*)

the Tartar emperors, who came at the beginning of
modern times to impose order and peace on northern

India, the temple of the basin of the Ganges already had, despite its wealth of ornament, a character of equilibrium and of abstract unity that one never finds in the south. The sensualism of the Indians, which caused the southern sculptors to enter the mountains, germinates in the consciousness of the north in trage-

TRICHINOPOLY (XVIII Century). Pagoda of Sriringam.

dies, in poems, in hymns of words and of stone. But if the walls are barer, the forms more peaceful and retiring, if there are longer silences, and if the dome is more abstractly calculated, the temple receives its visitors with more reserve, the mystic intoxication is less heavy. In the south what spoke was the profound soul of India, a wild murmur which we hear throughout the whole existence of this people, and which breaks out spontaneously at every place that it inhabits. In the north the voice of the higher castes dominates the chorus of the people, and does so with infinitely more majesty, power, and splendor because these castes grew from the soil of India like a natural vegetation and because they were able to build up the

TRICHINOPOLY (XVIII Century). Pagoda of Sriringam.
(The Court of the Horses.)

most grandiose philosophic synthesis that man has ever conceived.

The sensual richness of the south, purified by the metaphysical spirit and rarefied by the aristocratic spirit, is found again in the details of ornament in the sanctuaries, as soon as one has crossed their threshold. The Jain temples of central India have pillars as finely cut as glassware, and the arches that carry their forests of white cupolas to the heavens turn into lace under the hands of the sculptors; and yet, despite the over-minute science of the decorators, these buildings express a living faith. In the monarchies of the north, on the contrary, the vanity of the rajahs throws so luxurious a garment over the artists' enthusiasm that its bareness and also the best of its human value are lost together. There are temples stuffed with gods of silver and gold, whose eyes are rubies or diamonds. Drops of fire gleam in the shadows; the royal robe of the tigers, the iridescent plumage of tropical forests, their flowers, and the shining tails of peacocks incrust the sheathing of metal, ivory, or enamel that covers the pillars and the walls with emeralds, amethysts, pearls, topazes, and sapphires. It is an art of externals, and its unvarying magnificence is of a paler light than that of statues in a temple underground. The spirit of feudal India is rather in the great rectangular castles, bare and austere, closed in like fortresses, defended by high towers, and cuirassed with poly-chromed enamel; it is in the palaces of white marble by the silent waters.

V

The Occident of the Middle Ages, the Occident of the fortresses and the Romanesque buildings, is certainly less out of place in the hierarchical India of the

north than in the democratic India of the south. In
one place as in the other, the abstraction descends
from the dominating classes to crush the miserable
classes beneath the petrified symbol of its external
power. But the Hellenic
Occident where, on the
contrary, the abstraction
rose from the masses to
express its inner power
through the voice of the
heroes—the Hellenic Oc-
cident and also the Gothic
Occident would more
easily recognize the trace
of their dream if they
followed the torrent of
ideas that crossed the
mountains, the swamps,
the virgin forests, and
the sea, to spread to the
peninsula of Indo-China,
to the Dutch Indies, and
to Java. The spread of
Indian ideas is witnessed
in the gigantic temples
that cover Java; it is seen
even more in the for-
tresses, the palaces, and
the temples absorbed

KHMER ART. Head of Buddha.

little by little by the jungles of Cambodia, the home of
the mysterious race of the Khmers. They lived in a
country less overwhelming than India, for, despite the
denseness of the forests, the undergrowth was certainly
less redoubtable, the fruits were more abundant, the
rivers more full of fish, and life was easier and freer.
Moreover, the metaphysical and moral life of China had

4

come to give something of its peace to the troubled
and heavy atmosphere of tropical nature. Finally, five
or six hundred years after the disappearance of Buddhism from Hindustan, perhaps about the tenth century
of our era, the Khmer people were still Buddhists, as
were the people of Java. Among the latter the decorative sculpture of eastern Asia, sending forth one of its
most heavily laden branches, causes the monuments of
Java to blossom from top to bottom with bas-reliefs as
mobile as paintings. The moral epic of Buddha unrolls
in them amid perfumed forests crowded with fruit,
with birds, and with beasts, among choruses and musicians who furnish accompaniment to the nonchalant
and lascivious grace of the women that pray and
dance and people the intoxicated sleep of the god with
abundant dreams. But the Khmer people, in its Buddhism, betokened a preoccupation with moral balance
and with harmony that is practically unknown to the
sculptors of the grottos of Ellora and of the pyramidal
temples.

The orgy of ornament, to be sure, never went farther.
This was a necessary result of the still denser, more
flowery, and more populous forests of the country, of
the humidity which is warmer, and of the fever which
is more intoxicating. But the ornament obeys a
splendidly balanced rhythm. Twining lines of flowers,
of fruits, of vines, of palms, and rich plants creep over
the walls from top to bottom, over the sloping surfaces,
over the tops of the doors, and up to the summit of the
four sides of the high tiaras of Brahma which here
replace the Indo-Persian cupola and the Dravidian
pyramid; but the decorative forms marry so well with
the line of the architecture that they lighten it and seem
to lift it to an aërial level of leaves, of winding stems,
of hanging foliage that together form a silent, whirling
rain of petals and perfumes.

KHMER ART. The procession, bas-relief. (*Palace of Angkor-Vat.*)

The Khmer sculptor gives a form to all those things which, as a rule, strike our inner sensibility only through what we hear, what we taste, and what we feel. His carving tells of the murmurs, the gleams, and the odors of the forest, the cadenced sound of marching

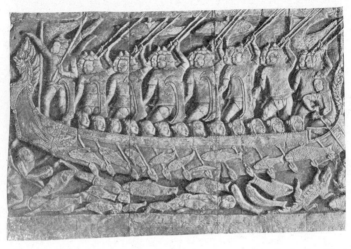

KHMER ART. The rowers, bas-relief. (*Palace of Angkor-Vat.*)

troops, low tones of birds that coo their love song, the hoarse, dull rattle in the throats of wild beasts as they roam through the jungles, and the invisible fluid that circulates in the nerves of the women who dance when the music drones and when voluptuous feeling mounts in their veins. The secret heart of the world beats, tumultuously and regularly, in the crowds that pass under impenetrable branches, whether they sing all together or prepare for massacres or the feast, for death, for justice, or for the building of palaces. And yet, in that inner order which gives these sculptural symphonies so much rhythmical strength, everything interpenetrated without a break. The transmigration of the

thinkers of India causes the rock itself to quiver.
Animal forms and vegetable forms pass one into the
other, vines blossom into figures; reptiles, feet, and
hands sprout and become lotus flowers. What matter?
The luxuriant universe is good, since the divine coun-
tenance of him who consoles appears behind every leaf,

KHMER ART. Frieze of the Apsaras, fragment. (*Palace of
Angkor-Vat.*)

since he loved everything, down to the snakes themselves. The heroes, the elephants, and the tigers that
guard the temples or border the avenues, the immense
cobras with seven heads stretched out, that frame the
pediments or creep along the balustrades, have an indulgent visage and a welcoming smile, despite their clubs,
their claws, and their teeth. Buddha is all love. The
forces of the earth have penetrated him to spread
humanity throughout his being. And so, on the highest
branch of black trees, full of poisonous juices and
swarming from roots to leaves with beasts that distil
death, there is a flower.

The story of Sakyamuni, from his birth to his sleep in Nirvana, flowers on the walls of the sanctuaries. The Khmer sculptor grows tender over the god man of the Orient even as, at about the same time, the Gothic artisan grows tender as he recounts the birth and passion of the god man of the Occident. Everywhere we find smiles of goodness, everywhere open arms, heads inclining on friendly shoulders, hands clasping gently, and the ingenuous impulse toward abandon and confidence. Man is everywhere in search of man. The spirit of evil, Ravana, with the hundred hands from which plants and grasses are born, whose feet traverse forests peopled with animals — the spirit of evil may come upon the scene, innumerable figures of men may struggle under avalanches of flowers, like the spirit besieged by the seductions of the earth. What matter? Against backgrounds of heavy trees, armies march. Rama advances across forests. Man will end by attaining, were it only for a moment, the accord between his social life and his most tyrannical instincts. Neither bestiality nor asceticism. Not only are the heroes of the will surrounded by friendly flowers and the fruits they may easily pluck from the branches that bend over their passing, but there are even gar-

KHMER ART. Decorative figure.
(*Angkor-Thom.*)

JAVA (IX Century?). The musicians. Detail from the life of Buddha. (*Temple of Boro-Boudour.*)

lands of naked bayaderes who await them at the end
of their road, each one different and all the same,
dancing yet almost motionless, as they mark the rhythm
of the music that one guesses, the inner pulsation of the
wave that runs through
them. For the second
time since the origin of
man, intellectual effort
and the joy of the senses
seem to agree for the space
of an hour. Furtive, no
doubt, and more sum-
mary, but also fuller, more
musical, more clogged with
matter, heavier laden, and
moving against a back-
ground of trees and
flowers, the modeling of
Greece seems to suggest
itself here and there.

JAVA (IX Century?). Detail
from the life of Buddha.
(*Temple of Boro-Boudour.*)

Thus, eternally balanced
between its heroism and
its sensuality, passing at
every moment and with-
out transition from the extreme of moral love to the
extreme of material intoxication, from the highest
aristocracy of culture to
the most impulsive satis-
factions of instinct, the Indian soul wanders across living
forests of sentiment and system in search of the law.
In its ensemble, and in spite of its oases of hope and
of cool sentiment, it is pessimistic and cruel. The men
of India have no more need to inflict pain or death than
other men. They are of the true human clay; they

are kneaded with weakness, they are armored with iron and gold, they are swept along to love at one moment, to death at another, according as the air they breathe brings them the odor of the trees, of the oceans, or of the deserts. In every case, here as elsewhere, the

JAVA (IX Century?). Detail from the life of Buddha, bas-relief.
(*Temple of Boro-Boudour.*)

loftiest energy and brute matter wed constantly. The manifestations of instinct, which is hurled with all its strength into the immensity of life, arouse the loftiest sentiment of superior natures. If, after much suffering, the Indian sages rise above good and evil to gain indifference, it is because the crowd, in India, had plunged into the intoxication or the horror of life without knowing either good or evil.

As balance, for them, could be realized only at brief moments in the average life of society, they sought it outside the conditions of that society, in the bosom of an immeasurable harmony, where life and death, whose origins and ends we do not know, mingle their equal powers and know no other limits than themselves. Let life, then, exhaust itself with living until death comes! Let death, in its putrefaction, cause life to flower and reflower! Why should one try to infuse the energies of nature into the harmony of consciousness? Disciplined for a moment, the energies of nature will take the upper hand again, and once more will roll the will and the hopes of man into the confused intoxication of their regenerated youth.

ROAD OF THE MING TOMBS

Chapter II. CHINA

1

IN India, it is still ourselves that we see. If the grandiose pessimism, which makes her plastic language so intoxicating, opens up to us regions in ourselves that we had not explored, it dominates us from the first, because the rhythm of that language relates it, secretly, with all those other languages that express Occidental optimism. In China, on the contrary, we no longer understand. Although it includes a third of mankind, this country is the most distant, the most isolated of all. We are confronted with a method that escapes us almost absolutely, with a point of departure that is not ours, with a goal that does not resemble ours, with a movement of life that has neither the same appearance nor the same direction as ours. To realize unity in the spirit is, doubtless, what the Chinese tends toward, as we do. But he does not seek that unity along the roads where we seek it.

China has not, however, remained as closed as it is said to have been. It mingled with Aryanism incessantly, to the point of producing mixed civilizations, as in Indo-China and in Tibet, for example, where it allowed the rivers of love pouring from the Hindu soul to carry a little of their disquieting ardor into its serious, positive, easy-going, and rather sullen soul. It knew the worlds that were the farthest removed from it, and the most ancient. Rome trafficked with it two thousand years ago; Chaldea, twenty centuries before Rome, taught it astronomy. Nearer to our time, Islam affected it to the point of bringing twenty or thirty millions of Chinese to the god of Mohammed. In the sixteenth century, after the Mongol conquest, Pekin was perhaps the most cosmopolitan and the most open city in the world. The Portuguese and the Venetians sent their merchants there, and the imperial court had artists and savants come from India, from Persia, and even from western Europe.

However, as far back as we look into the past of China, it seems not to have moved. The myth period of its life ends about the century of Pericles, perhaps; the apogee of its vital power oscillates between the fifth and the fifteenth century of our era, its decline begins at the hour when the Occident is about to put its stamp on history. But one must look closely to. distinguish one or another of these phases of its activity. The material testimony of its legendary period that comes down to us does not differ very greatly from what it is producing in our own day, and if its most vigorous effort coincides with that of the Middle Ages of the Occident, the fact would seem to demonstrate only the more clearly—through the insensible passages that attach it to its past and its present—that it has never come out of its own Middle Ages and that we do not know when it entered upon them. In reality, it is the inner world of the Chinese that has never opened for us. It is in vain that we feel their social civilization as more perfect than our own, it is in vain that we

CHANG DYNASTY (XVIII to XII Centuries B.C.). Daiban bowl, bronze. (*Musée Cernuschi.*)

admire the results among them of a moral effort that was as great as our own. We do not always understand them better than we do the ants or the bees. There is the same mystery, awe inspiring and almost sacred. Why are we so made that we can conceive only of our own mode of association and only our own mechanism of reasoning? Whether the Chinese is superior to us or inferior is something that it is impossible for us to say, and the problem, thus presented, is without significance. The Chinese has followed an evolution that we have not followed; he constitutes a second branch of the human tree that separated from the first; we do not know whether their branches will reunite.

The Indo-European world turns, with all its instinct, toward the future. The Chinese world, with all its consciousness, turns toward the past. Therein lies the gulf which, perhaps, cannot be crossed. There is the whole secret of the power of expansion of the Occident, of the hermitism of China, of the strange impersonality of its plastic language. Taken in the mass, China shows no change in time, no movement in space. One would say that it expresses a people of old men, ossified from infancy. It is never to himself that the Chinese looks for his law; it is to his father, to his grandfather, and, beyond his father and grandfather, to the infinite multitude of the dead who govern him from the depths of the centuries. And in fact, it is not the law that he asks, but the recipe for adapting himself to the surroundings that nature has made for him, surroundings, moreover, which change but little.

CHOW ART (VII Century B.C.).
Tripod, terra cotta.
(*Charles Vignier Collection.*)

At first, one thinks of Egypt, of its geological and agricultural immobility, of its impersonal, collective art, hermetical and abstract. But Egypt is restless; it cannot quench the flame that, despite the will of the

HAN ART (from the ɪɪ Century B.C. to the ɪɪ Century A.D.).
Tiger, marble, guardian of the temple of Sniang-fou.
(*Charles Vignier Collection.*)

people, bursts from the heart of the material in which
they worked with such passion. An invincible idealism
crowded them to a horizon which was distasteful for
them to behold. The Chinese also evolved under outside influence, unquestionably, but around the same

HAN ART (from the II Century B.C. to the II Century
A.D.). Bas-relief of Ou-Lang-Tse, print of the stone.
(*Ed. Chavannes Mission.*)

fixed point. He remained practical and self-centered,
narrowly realistic, devoid of imagination, and, in
reality, without desires. Where the Egyptian people
suffers from the domination of the priest and tries to
forget him by exploring life in its depths, the Chinese
accepts without revolt the tyranny—the benevolent
tyranny, we may observe—of the mandarin, because it
in no wise disturbs the doting satisfaction of his tastes.
At least, we know nothing of the immemorial evolutions

which must have led him to that state of mind. Confucius regulated morality once for all; it remained fixed in very accessible formulas and kept to its traditional rut through the unquestioning, dogmatic respect, ritualized and blind, that one owes to one's parents, to the parents of one's parents, to the dead parents of one's ancestors. The upward movement, which characterizes life for us and prevents us from arresting it in a definite formula, crystallized, for the Chinese, into a form which is perhaps not always the same, but through which one gets back to the same principle, a form determined by this principle to the minutest detail. The Chinese is satisfied with it, he has no need to seek any other principle. In reality, if he remains motionless, it is because he has so many native virtues and because his imagination atrophies through never having to exert itself or to struggle. He will receive without difficulty the moral teachings of Buddhism and later on of Islam, because they are practically in agreement with the essential part of what Confucius brought to him. In the religion of Confucius he will find even the belief in Nirvana of the one and the fatalism of the other, and they will cause

ART LATER THAN HAN (III to IV Century A.D.). Ovoid vase with screw decoration.
(*Charles Vignier Collection.*)

5

him to lull into indifference whatever momentary impulses toward revolt he may have.

As far back as we go into the distant childhood of China, we find the race already molded to certain metaphysical abstractions and certain moral entities from which all later forms of expression will descend. The Aryan goes from the concrete to the abstract, the Chinese from the abstract to the concrete. With the Aryan, the general idea is the flower of objective observation, and abstraction is always a thing in process of evolution. With the Chinese, the general idea seems to precede the objective study of the world and the progress of the abstraction ends sharply as soon as a moral law sufficient to sustain social relationships has appeared to the philosopher. In the Occident the symbol comes out of life, and frees itself from life, little by little, through progressive generalizations which are forever broadening, or which start out anew on other bases. In China the symbol governs life and shuts it in from every side.

The ever-changing reality which the Occidental desires, the idealistic conquest which tempts him, and man's attempt to rise toward harmony, intelligence, and morality seem to remain unsuspected by the Chinese. He has found, at least he thinks he has found, his mode of social relationships. Why should he change? When we denounce his absence of idealism, perhaps we are only saying that his old ideal realized its promises long ago and that he enjoys the unique privilege of maintaining himself in the moral citadel of which he has been able to gain possession, while, around him, everything ebbs away, decomposes, and re-forms itself. However that may be, we shall never see him approach form with the desire to make it express the adaptation by the human being of his intellect and his senses to surrounding nature. That

BUDDHIST ART (Wei) (v Century, second half). Kwan-Yn, soft
stone. (*Charles Vignier Collection.*)

is what the whole of ancient art and the whole of
Renaissance art did, but when the Chinese turns to
form, it is with the will to draw from it a tangible
symbol of his moral adaptation. He will always aim
at moral expression, and will do so without requiring
the world to furnish him with other elements than
those which he knows in advance he will find in it; he
will require no new revelations from the gestures
which translate it. Morality will be crystallized in the
sentences that guide him. He has only to treat nature
as a dictionary whose pages he will turn until he finds
the physiognomies and the forms which, in their combination, are the proper ones to fix the teachings of
the sages. The agitation of the senses no longer comes
upon him save by surprise—when he studies the elements of the plastic transposition too closely, and his
science of form, detached wholly from material things,
no longer serves him for more than the defining of
abstractions. His immobile art demonstrates acquired
truth, instead of affirming new intuitions.

To sum up, the Chinese does not study the material
of the world that he may ask it to instruct him. He
studies it when he needs to objectify his beliefs in order
to attach more firmly to them the men who share
them. It is true that he brings to this study gifts of
patience, tenacity, and slowness which are beyond
comparison. The ancient gropings of the first Chinese
artists escape us. . . . One would say that for ten or
twenty centuries they studied, in secret, the laws of
form before demanding of form that it express the laws
of the spirit.

II

In China, plastic expression is a kind of conventional
graphology analogous to writing. The first Chinese
painters were the Buddhist monks who, in the course

of the same centuries in which the Christian monks
were gathering up the debris of the mind of antiquity,
cultivated in their monasteries the only flower of high

BUDDHIST ART (Wei) (v Century).   Grottos
of Yunkang.   The great Buddha.
(*Ed. Chavannes Mission.*)

idealism that blossomed on this immovable soil for
thirty centuries; and note that these first Chinese
painters were also writers.   There were no other
painters than the poets, and they painted and wrote
with the same brush and caused the poem and the

image to comment one on the other interminably.
The ideographic signs which required a lifetime to
learn and which were clothed in a kind of spiritual
beauty that the artists seized in the tenuity, the thickness, or the complexity of the black arabesques with
which they covered the white paper, brought them

BUDDHIST ART (Wei) (v Century). Grottos of Yunkang.
Bas-relief. (*Ed. Chavannes Mission.*)

little by little to handle the brush dipped in India ink
with consummate ease. Whenever their poetry, born
of the same current of feeling as the painting, had felt
the freshness and the calm of the world around the
monasteries, isolated in the upper valleys, the painters
who commented upon this poetry looked upon the
world with an innocence that had never before been
permitted, by their traditional philosophy, to Chinese
artists. Landscape, that instrument of liberation and
conquest, appeared to them suddenly. And at that

BUDDHIST ART (v Century). Bas-relief on rock. Grottos of Yunkang. (*Ed. Chavannes Mission.*)

moment the Buddhist soul found in them its most
serene expression.[1]

Never did the Chinese painters, despite the brevity
of their style, go so far as their pupils, the artists of
Nippon, in the schematized stylization of nature.
Here there was no question of decorating houses or
temples. They illustrated poems for themselves, in
that profoundly gentle and yet profoundly egoistic
spirit of the anchorite who has attained to peace from
the life of the passions. The agitation of the cities
did not reach them. The images, which they traced on
the silk with a minuteness that knew no lassitude, or
which they slowly brought to birth from the dabs of
ink that their brush pressed into the rice paper, often
expressed nothing but the inner peace of the philosopher
as he thumbs the writings of the sages, amid indulgent
trees or at the edge of pure waters. They heard no
other sounds than those of the torrents in the mountain or the bleating of the herds. They loved the
hours when the day is undefined, the glow of moonlight
nights, the hesitation of the middle seasons, the mists
that mount at dawn from the flooded rice fields.[2]
They had gathered a freshness of soul like that of the
morning in which the birds intoxicate themselves.

It is almost impossible to consider Chinese painting
according to that harmonious curve which, in the case
of almost all the other schools, seems to sum up all
the elements of the work: from its beginning, through
the progressive expansion of the elements later on into
a balanced expression, and, later still, to their disorder
and their dispersal. According to the place, according
to the circumstances, the aspect of a century will
change. Here, for example, Buddhistic hieratism will
not appear. There, it will be prolonged up to the
threshold of the modern world, isolated in some region

---

[1] M. Paléologue, *L'Art Chinois*.   [2] *Ibid.*

that lies far away from the centers of life, or, in the depths of some well-guarded cloister, thoroughly cut off from the surrounding world that lives and moves. It sometimes takes two hundred years for a province to accept and to yield to the sentiments of another province, where they have already been forgotten. Among the Tibetans this is constant, but it is also more explicable. Korea, for example, always lags behind China, whereas Japan, which leaps over transitional stages, can imitate at will either a form which disappeared from China ten centuries ago or one that is scarcely born to-day. Tibet is impregnated by India, Turkestan by Persia, Indo-China by Cambodia and Laos. In China itself we find the same thing, according to the dynasty, the school, the region, or the religion. A thing apart, as it is everywhere, and almost immovable in time and

BUDDHIST ART (Wei) (second half of v Century). Kwan-Yn in soft stone. (*Charles Vignier Collection.*)

space, Buddhist art remains distinct from everything that is not itself. It weakens, evidently, in proportion as faith descends, but it still remains distinct and distant, a language symbolic of the infinite and the universal, a spiritual light concentrated in a seated human form and flowing inexhaustibly from all the surfaces of that figure.

If we consider Chinese painting in its entirety and without allowing for its local attempts at emancipation, the artificial survivals from periods when it succumbed, and the general confusion of its development, we may say that some fifteen centuries passed before Chinese egoism consented to tear itself from the contemplative life. Only then could it go down to the torrent where the kingfisher watches for his prey, or furtively approach the bough on which the nightingale, chilled by the dawn, ruffles his plumage as he rolls his last sob, or observe the blackbirds hopping on the snow. It was scarcely before the Ming dynasty, in the fourteenth or in the fifteenth century, that the Chinese painters looked closely at the birds, the fishes, and the flowers, as if to bequeath to Japan, which was asking their instruction, the incomparable science with which two or three thousand years of practical and immediately interested observation had equipped them. With disconcerting facility they disdained, at this moment, the conventional language that had made their art so glorious; they abandoned the disciplined liberty that enabled them to express abstractions of sentiment merely by respecting and exalting the laws of harmony.

Let us turn away from the birds, the fishes, the flowers, the things to be described in their physical aspects; let us for the moment disregard the direct, pure, and clear portraits whose candid penetrating glance astonishes us; let us also forget the embroidered screens and the decorative paintings with their tremulous movement that recalls the flutter of wings. We then perceive what the great painting of China is;

it invades our spirit like a wave of music. It awakens intimate and vague sensations, impossible to seize, but of a limitless profundity; they pass one into

BUDDHIST ART (Wei) (VI to VII Century). Grottos of Long-Men. Guardian of the Gates. (*Ed. Chavannes Mission.*)

another, gradually welling up until we are completely overcome by them. We cannot discern their origin or their end. The forms in Chinese painting have the

appearance of still being partly in the clasp of the
primeval clay. Or one might say that they appear
through a layer of water so limpid, so calm, that it
does not disturb the tones which have been fixed and
immobilized under it for a thousand years. Whether

BUDDHIST ART (Wei) (VI to VII Century). Grottos of
Long-Men, bas-relief. (*Ed. Chavannes Mission.*)

they tell us of a pollen of flowers, of the undefined
shades on the throats of birds, or of the subtle colors
that rise from the depths of ripening fruits, the silk
paintings of China have nothing in common with the
object. They are states of the soul in the presence of
the world, and the object is only a sign—deeply loved,
certainly—which, according to the way it acts and com-
bines with other objects, suggests that state of soul.
The transformation is complete and constant. And
through it, when the Chinese paints or rather evokes
things like the depths of the ocean, which he has
never seen, he does it with a poetry so profound that
it creates reality. Thus. on a canvas the size of a nap-

kin, a heron preens his plumage in the morning mist—
and the immensity of space is suggested. Space is
the perpetual accomplice of the Chinese artist. It
condenses around his
paintings with such slow
subtlety that they seem
to emanate from it. The
masters lay on their
blacks and their reds with
gentleness and power, as
if they were drawing
them forth little by little
from the patina of dark
amber which they seem
to have foreseen and cal-
culated. Children play,
women pass, sages and
gods converse, but that
is never what one sees.
One hears peaceful
melodies that light on
the heart in waves of
serenity.

But serenity, unfortu-
nately, is exhausted as
quickly as is enthusiasm,
for it also is a result of
effort. When the Chinese
artists departed from the
original sources of their

T'ANG ART (VII Century). Tomb
of Tchao-Ling. Mandarin.
(*Ed. Chavannes Mission.*)

inspiration, they resorted to wine in order to attain
the mental state prescribed by the sages, and in the
artificial enthusiasm of the stimulant, in which they
indulged more and more, they discovered their fire, their
joy, their irony, their serenity even, in proportion to
the amount they drank and to the turn of their minds.

In gaining mastery over themselves they destroyed
their own life. From century to century, with the
strange slowness that characterizes the activity of the
Chinese, their painting, which had been taken into the
service of the imperial court as soon as it left the
monasteries, followed the evolution of their other
means of expression. It turned to traditionalism, and
did so with an obstinacy especially dangerous, since,
if painting is to live, it must remain the most individual
of all languages. Here it developed in an almost
unbreathable atmosphere of formulas, of rules and
canons which were written down in twenty thousand
works, codes, histories, lists of practitioners, titles of
pictures, and technical treatises that transformed the
art of painting into a kind of exact science and engendered thousands of imitators and plagiarists of an
ability beyond belief. And so Chinese painting returned
to its origins as a graphic art; it created enormous quan-
tities of models to which the artist could resort for
forms drawn in all their details and all their aspects,
leaving him only the work of grouping them. The
capital vice of Chinese calligraphy, which arrests the
development of the mind by blocking the exchange of
ideas and which carries abstraction into puerile soph-
istry, reappeared in the last expression of the art
which it had endowed with its first technical tool. It
is the form of revenge which the objective world takes
when it is forgotten too quickly. That intoxication of
the spirit known to men who have rid themselves of all
shackles is denied to him who has lost the right to seek
other forms for his equilibrium than those in which his
ancestor found peace.

III

Here we have at once the anchor that holds firm the
soul of China and its pitfall. The architecture of

luxury, the pagodas and the palaces, reveal this in the clearest light. Everything in them is preconceived and artificial, arranged for the demonstration of a certain number of immemorial rules of metaphysics and common sense. The faïence and the enamel of the

T'ANG ART (VII Century). Tomb of Tchao-Ling, bas-relief.
(*Ed. Chavannes Mission.*)

roofs, the blues, the greens, and the yellows, shining in the sun under the veil of dust always hanging over them, exist above all for the joy of the eyes, although each one of them symbolizes a meteorological phenomenon, or the forests, the plowed land, the waters, or some other strip of the earth's robe. And if everything is blue in the temples of heaven, everything red in the temples of the sun, everything yellow in the temples of the earth, everything blue-white in the temples of the moon, it is that there may be established, between the harmonies of the senses and the

BUDDHIST ART (early T'ang, VII Century). Bodhisatva.
(*J. Doucet Collection.*)

harmonies of nature, an intimate and continuous coherence, in which the serenity of the heart fixes itself, becomes immobile, and demonstrates to itself its certitude and necessity. But beneath the great need for unity and calmness, fetishism and magic patiently assert their rights. The placing of the edifice, the invariably uneven number of roofs superimposed on one another and turned up at the corners— a memory of Mongol tents—the little bells jingling at the slightest breeze, the monsters of terra cotta on the openwork cornices, the moral maxims painted everywhere, the scrolls of gilded wood, the whole mass of thorn bushes, arrises, crests, bristling and clawlike forms—everything shows how con-

T'ANG ART (VIII Century). Tomb of Chouen-Ling. Ram.
(*Ed. Chavannes Mission.*)

stantly the Chinese were concerned with attracting the genii of wind and water to the edifice and to the neighboring houses, or of keeping them away. We observe a similar idea in the great artificial parks, where all the accidents of the earth's surface, mountains, rocks, brooks, cascades, forests, and thickets

6

are imitated to the point of mania. It is as if the
Chinese who, outside of the cities, never change the original aspect of their native soil, were expressing the respect it inspires in them by bringing it down to the
scale of human luxury. The Chinese people is more
submissive than religious, more respectful than enthusiastic. It is not that it lacks gods or that it does not
believe them to be real. Those men who called themselves the disciples of the profound Lâo-Tsze, the Tao-
ists, introduced among the Chinese as many divinities,
perhaps, as are born and die every day on the soil of
India. Moreover, all those beliefs that are interpreted
only by the practices of popular superstition grind one
against another and interpenetrate, so that in the same
individual we almost always find them existing side
by side. In reality, whether he is a Buddhist, a Taoist,
a Moslem, or a Christian, the Chinese believes what he
has been advised to believe, without experiencing the
great mystic need to increase, to modify, or to impose
his faith on others. His gods are abstractions of a practical and positive kind: longevity, riches, sensuality,
literature, charity—or they are demons, protecting
or hostile genii, the spirits of the earth, of the sky, the
sea, the stars, the mountains, the cities, the villages,
the winds, the clouds, and the running waters; or again
they are deified scholars and writers. But they have
no other importance. If the Chinese conducts himself
properly, observing filial respect, obeying his ancestors
and the Emperor and the mandarins who represent the
Emperor, if he takes care to place his house in such a
way that the spirits shall not be disturbed and that
their watery, aërial, or subterranean dwellings are
preserved—all of which reveals Chinese mastery of
hygiene, meteorology, and agriculture—he does not
doubt then that these spirits will look upon him with
benevolence. No disquieting thoughts plow the

T'ANG ART (VIII Century). Tomb of Kiao-Ling. Ostrich, bas-relief. (*Ed. Chavannes Mission.*)

depths of his soul. When one roots out desire one kills
remorse, but one also makes an end of the life of the
dream.

What increases, in this age-old habit of discipline
and moral obedience, is patience. The Chinese does
not permit himself to imprint on matter the symbol of
his abstractions until he has scrutinized forms for so
long a time that all of them are defined in his memory
by their essential character. When the flash of intuition illuminates our minds and we need to reach the
law, we do not hesitate to thrust aside the accidentals
that mask it. The Chinese, on the contrary, collects
these accidentals, catalogues them, and uses them in
order to demonstrate the law. His audacities cannot
shock those who know his science. Since his abstraction is fixed, he may express the fact more clearly if he
bends, warps, and twists form in every direction; and
so he makes the wrinkles in his faces so deep that they
must cut into the bone; he arms the mouth with a
hundred teeth, and the shoulders with ten arms; the
head is surmounted with a monstrous skull; the
features grimace; the eyes stick out of the sockets or
are sunk deep in them; he accentuates laughing or
weeping with the most improbable lines; the breasts
fall in folds on the fat of bellies; hips, arms, and legs
are all awry, and fingers are knotted like tendrils of
grape vine. Because of his philosophy he can cause
monsters to crawl on his cornices, unfurl them in the
yellow silk of his standards, and raise them up at the
threshold of his palaces; he has created a whole army
of heraldic dragons, of phœnixes, unicorns, and writhing
chimeras, which are perhaps nothing more than a
vague memory, transmitted by the old legends, of the
last primitive monsters straying among the first men.
In all of this we see the spirit that forces the literary
men to obey a ritual until all their gestures are studied,

T'ANG ART (618–906). Three figurines, terra cotta.
(*Charles Vignier Collection.*)

that causes the historians to deform history in order
to make it fit the outline of their systems, that causes
the gardeners to gnarl the trees and manufacture
flowers, the fathers to crush the feet of their daughters,
and executioners to cut men to pieces. Traditional
morality will destroy life rather than adopt its free
movement.

But also, when life is in accord with morality, when
emotion and will meet in harmony, when the spirits
of goodness, kindness, and justice dwell in the mind
of the artist naturally, what goodness, kindness, and
justice there are in the faces and the gestures of the
gods! The great Buddhas of gilt wood sit on their
beds of lotus, their hands open, their faces illumined
by peace, their whole forms filling the shadow of the
sanctuary with the glow of the absolute which penetrates them. To combat them and make men forget
their serenity, the Taoist priest gathers from life every
engaging expression that he can find—the divine smile
and the dance of women, the quizzical kindness of the
sages, the childlike joy of the saved, the indescribable
and blithe atmosphere in which floats the trinity of
happiness. A strange sweetness emanates from all
those little works of wood and ivory, of jade and
bronze, that people the pagodas and encumber the flat
baskets with the colored-paper signs along the crowded
streets where the refuse of humanity accumulates. In
the heart of this philosophic people the philosopher has
indeed extinguished all of that disquietude which racks
men, but so often causes them to rise higher. What
matter? Situated as they are, they have the strength
of those who know little, but who are certain of what
they know. Their peace is a little stupid, no doubt;
their absence of cares, their absence of dreams, has
something that perhaps irritates one in course of time
and is even unhealthful. But one reads in it such a

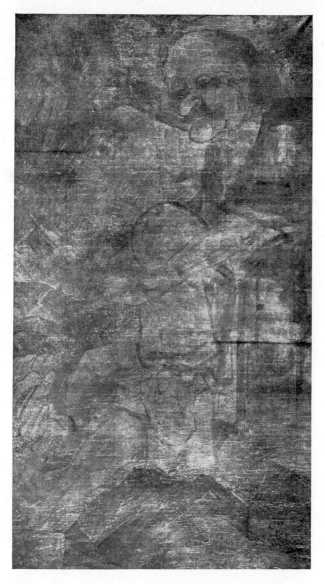

KOUAN-HIOU (?) Lohan, painting (first half of the
x Century). (*Charles Vignier Collection.*)

certitude of honesty that one feels oneself attached to these men. They have given their singular expression to the moral life by studying the incessant struggle that takes place in the depths of human nature and by realizing that it has its origin in the aspiration toward higher levels. The strange thing is that we should see beauty in that struggle itself and that the Chinese should find it in the victory his ancestors won for him in ages past. He expresses his obstinate, unlyrical enthusiasm for those who gave him repose of conscience for all time. And it is the weight of that repose that we feel in his art.

Therein lies the mystery of this soul which is complex on its surface, but infinitely simple in its depths. It achieves a science of form so sure that it can carry the grimace of its logic to a point that we should call impossible; but it can also attain to essential and profound beauty when it is lit up by a flash of emotion or when it is confronted with the necessity of constructing a durable and immediately useful work. We must not allow ourselves to think that their artificial parks are lacking in freshness and silence. We must not fail to see that the whole Orient is in the torrent of strange flowers they cultivate there. They gather into their triumphal symphonies the color of its coral reefs strung with pearls, its sumptuously figured silks that display the red or blue of the heraldic dragons on the imperial yellow which is strewn with flowers of dark and gleaming enamel. It is, indeed, the whole Orient that they give us: the rising and setting of its hosts of powdery stars in the clearness of rain-swept skies. Neither must we allow ourselves to believe that Chinese architecture lacks science and solidity. The fact that the most ancient examples of it do not date much farther back than the tenth century is due to the fragility of the materials. To protect the buildings from heat and rain, the Chinese know what slope and what projection to give to the roofs, which they support by combinations of demountable framework, as powerful and as light as the creations of nature. There is one thing that they know especially well, and therein they are like the Romans, nay, more, they are like all the ancient peoples of the massive continent in which great summits alternate with great deserts, and great forests with great rivers: they know how to give to their work the appearance of style. Whether an airy or a heavy style, it affords invariably a firm and sublime base on which to rest our certitude of having achieved our aim completely. We find this appearance in the utilitarian edifices of the Chinese, in their bridges, triumphal gateways, and gigantic arches, their battlemented ramparts and the immense walls that inclose the plains and climb the mountains. Like the old sculptors of the valley of the Nile, they have animated the desert with avenues of colossuses, whose modeling is so vast and so summary that they seem to be installed in the solitudes for all eternity; the undulation of the sands, as they spread out to the buttresses of the mountains, seems gathered up into their structure, and the sphericity of the sky as it spans the circle of the plains.

IV

If, at about the time that Marcus Aurelius was sending embassies to China, there had not been the strange essay at sculpturing the walls of the temple of Hiao-tang-chan with flat silhouettes that look like shadows on a wall, or if we had not begun our acquaintance with certain archaic figures that date back at least to the beginning of our era, we might still believe, as we did for a long time, that not a stone had been sculptured in this land until the conquerors of the

northern provinces had, in the fifth century, introduced the moral contagion of the religion of Buddha.
Here, as in the Indies, we find mountains hollowed out
and rocks submerged by the great wave that rose from
hearts filled with hope to overflowing. When the flood
had receded, it left behind it colossal figures with pure
faces and lowered eyelids, seated giants whose two
hands lie open across each other; palm branches and fans
are waved over the processions that pass with mighty
rhythm across the walls of the temple, ten thousand
gods, smiling, silent, and gentle live in the darkness.[1]

The cliffs, from top to bottom, were sculptured, the
walls of every rift in the rock became alive, the glow
of the spirit descended from the pillars and the vaults
as they were hewed out along the lines indicated by the
accidents of their projections and their hollows. A
hundred sculptors worked in the shadows to complete
the summary modeling of some gigantic statue; and
such was the unity and power of the creative energy
which animated them, that the divine monster seemed
to issue from two hands and from one intelligence;
it seemed the cry of love that a single breast prolonged

---

[1] The monolithic temples of Ta-t'ong-fou, of Long-Men and of Kong, were
discovered by M. Edouard Chavannes in the course of his admirable and
fruitful explorations in 1907. I thank him most warmly for having authorized me to reproduce the innumerable photographs that he brought back
with him, and of which I have been able to reproduce only a few because of
lack of space. (Note to the first edition.)

Also, thanks to Charles Vignier, I have been able to recast completely
the illustrating of this chapter of the present edition. It is to him that I
owe the information concerning origins and chronology which has permitted me, as far as possible, to get a fresh estimate of Chinese archæology,
a subject that is barely advancing beyond its embryonic stage. I hope that
this rare spirit will pardon me if I do not venture to use the ordinary formulas
in expressing my thanks to him. The distant and slightly ironic character
of the Chinese sages has exercised so charming an influence on the education
of his sensibility that he must not hesitate to recognize a reflection of that
influence in the very affectionate sentiment entertained toward him by
his unworthy pupil in Sinology.

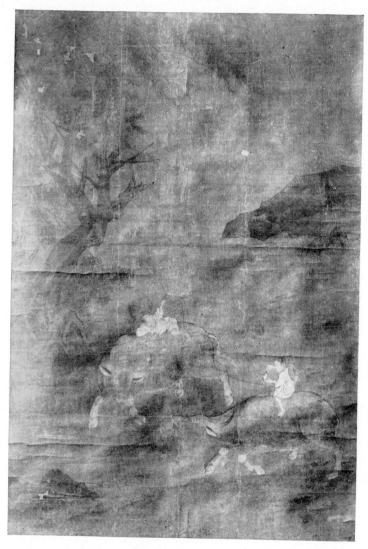

Li Kouei-tcheng (about 910). Children playing on buffaloes, painting. (*Charles Vignier Collection.*)

across the ages. And it is here perhaps that Buddhist sculpture attained the supreme expression of a science of light for which there is no equivalent elsewhere, even among the greatest sculptors. The light does not seem to mingle, as in Egypt, for example, with the planes of the statue in order to render subtle its passages and profiles. One would say that it floats round the statue. The form seems to swim, to undulate in the light, like a wave that passes without beginning and without end. But we have here a specifically Buddhist quality, shared by this school of the northern conquerors with the statue makers of India and Korea, of Japan, of Cambodia, of Tibet, and of Java. It is held in common by all the representatives of this strange international school of Buddhist sculpture, in which the Greek influence is always manifest, through the nervous purity of the Occidentalized profiles, the harmony of the proportions, and the manner in which intelligence sums up and idealizes objectivity. China proper did not share fully in the faith which the invader from the plateaus of central Asia brought within her borders. Doubtless, it was but for an hour that she consented to abandon herself to the supreme illusion of the promised paradises. The most meditative, but, perhaps because of that, the least idealistic people in history had consented only against its will to go with the current that swept all eastern Asia and gave it that impersonal, secret art, of a spirituality so pure that ten centuries passed before China had freed herself from it.

To tell the truth, it was in this land that the wave of Buddhism lasted the shortest time. China reverted quickly to her habits of positivist meditation. Buddhism, with its brief climax of love, was still to give a greater depth and weight to her thought, as happens on the morrow of a passion tender and too clear-sighted.

She turned again toward death, and as the men who
had hollowed out the mountains under her eyes had
taught her to bring out
of chaos the architec-
tured form on which
the light and shade
paint the spirit of life,
she was able to give
to the funeral chant
which she sang for a
thousand years, from
the seventh to the six-
teenth century, a pleni-
tude and a gravity of
accent that had been
forgotten since the
days of Egypt. There
is a heavy, categorical
strain to it as of a set-
tled thing — like the
final conclusion of an
intelligence that has
turned round itself in
a complete circle with-
out discovering a single
fissure through which
doubt could enter.

SUNG ART (960–1260). Water lilies.
(*Charles Vignier Collection.*)

Certainly, we do not
find in the funerary
statues of China that
secret illumination
which mounts from the
depths of the Egyptian colossuses to unite, on the
plane of their undulating surfaces, the mind of man
with the light. The Chinese people, as the masters of
their soil and their culture, never suffered enough to

seek inner liberty and the consolation for living in a constant hope of death. They looked on death with placidity, with no more of fear than of desire. But the fact that they did not lose sight of death gave to Chinese positivism a formidable importance. Meditating on death causes one to see essential things. The anecdote, in which one loses oneself when one is concerned with the adventures of life, leaves the mind forever. The things that interest and hold the majority of men cease to fetter the mind, which realizes that it passes like the daylight between two flutters of an eyelid, and that in the light of this flash it must seize the absolute. And because it perceives nothing beyond life its hymn to death gathers up and confides to the future everything that is immortal in life.

Funerary sculpture increased in grandeur as the power of China increased, and decreased when Chinese power began to wane. From the time of the T'ang tombs to that of the Ming tombs, from the dynasty that represents China at its apogee to that which marks the end of the period, the red and yellow desert that runs in slow waves to the distant mountain chains where copper and iron repose—the desert of China saw the rise of massive forms: men, elephants, camels, rams, horses, and ostriches; some are standing, some lying down—all are motionless and on guard over the sleep of the emperors.[1] The whole plain was a work of art, like a wall of decoration, and the sculptors used the curves, the projections, and the perspective of the plain to give value and accent to the giants of stone. They were seen advancing from the horizon, marching like an army, climbing the hills, descending the valleys, and when they had once arisen for their march

---

[1] These tombs of the first great dynasties, from the seventh to the eleventh century, were discovered also by M. Edouard Chavannes in the course of his exploration.

LEANG ART (x Century). Children playing,
painting. (*Langweill Collection.*)

or parade, they heeded neither the grasses nor the briers that began to grow again as soon as the hewers of images had disappeared. They followed one another

Iron Pagoda of K'ai-fong-fou (XIV Century).
(*Ed. Chavannes Mission.*)

and gazed upon one another; and the crouching lions witnessed also the passing of men laden with tribute —now hidden, now revealed by the undulations of the soil. Separated, absolute and definitive, the lone and silent multitude of forms rose up in the dust, under the sky, as if to bear, to the ends of the earth and to the time when the sun itself should be burned out, the formidable testimony that man had passed this way.

Vault of Kiu-yong-kouan (xiv Century).   Bas-relief.
(*Ed. Chavannes Mission.*)

Starting with the tombs of the T'ang dynasty, from the powerful, bas-reliefs that remind one of an Assyria visited by Greece, the Chinese sculptors, already possessing the most direct vision, condense their science gradually to arrive at a more summary expression.

7

Under the Sungs they were able to conceive an object as a mass so full, so shorn of details and accidents, so heavy and condensed, that it seemed to bear the weight of thirty centuries of metaphysical meditation. Thenceforward they could permit themselves all the stylizations, all the deformations, all the audacities needed for the affirming of the moral truths revealed to China

Wall of Glazed Brick of Ta-t'ong-fou.
(*Ed. Chavannes Mission.*)

by the sages of the ancient days. Under the Mings, at the moment when the artists were about to lay down their tools, when China, then only marking time, was about to let Japan slip from her embrace, to rush into the life of freedom and self-conquest, the Chinese had acquired an imposing virtuosity. They cast enormous iron statues to guard their temples. They decorate walls and vaults with strange figures that form melodic lines undulating in curves which, while irregular, are as continuous and rhythmic as the ripples on the surface of the water. Along the colossal avenues, the grimacing monsters and the chimeras alternate with the massive elephants, the dromedaries, and the warriors as straight and as pure in line as towers.

Thus we reach the same conclusions whether we study this race in the forms farthest removed from the realism of the early ages, or whether we consider the sculptured stones that best recall the living masses one sees outlined against a dusty plain at the approach of evening—the real domestic animals, the herds, and the caravans: we may seek in one type of art as well as in the other for the center of the Chinese soul. It is a soul devoid of imagination, but so firm and so concentrated that it is not impossible that its motionless realism will one day drive back the upward-looking idealism of the Occident and impose itself on the Western races when they have become eager for repose. Chinese art is an immensity. The art workman plays a role in China that is as important in the life of his people, and as permanent, as in Egypt. For thirty centuries he peoples the dwellings of the living and the dwellings of the dead with furniture, carpets, vases, jewels, and figurines. Three-quarters of his production perhaps is still buried. The valleys of his two rivers constitute a mine of art that is doubtless as inexhaustible as that of the valley of the Nile. Also, the forms that it yields vary to as great a degree— from the grave or terrible to the charming, from the pots of bronze that the Chinese buried for centuries so that the juices and minerals of the earth should slowly give them their patina to the swarms of "Tanagras" that issue from the necropolises. These latter are less picturesque, certainly, than their Greek sisters, but they are also purer and more summary; they are conceived with more fleeting contours, more decisive

NANKING.　Stone elephants.

planes, and rounder masses, and they offer a more touching homage to feminine grace, chastity, and majesty. What matter if this infinite art seems paradoxical at first sight? As in the case of that Egypt which at first appeared so monstrous, we are beginning to perceive here the simplicity, the unity, the grand coherence of the strangest conceptions. Under the

Tomb of the Mings (xv Century).
Triumphal Gateway.

grimaces of the statues, under the complicated robes that cover them, under the outlandish cornices of the architecture, the bristling masses of the varnished monsters, and the flaming of red and gold in the sanctuaries, there is present a real and indestructible principle of construction. Sculptural modeling, which is sinuous and balanced among the Greeks, a thing of movement with the Indians, and rectangular with the Egyptians, is spherical with the Chinese. Under the ornaments and the symbolic attributes, under the most disordered coilings and twistings of the monsters, the passage and the plane of the sculptor penetrate each

other in a slow and continual progress, as if to produce
a closed block. In its essential examples, one would
say that this sculpture causes form to rise slowly to
abstraction, that the abstraction descends slowly
toward form, and that lightning flashes from the two
as they fuse, eternal, compact, and pure. At such
moments China, like Egypt, Greece, India, and the
France of the Middle Ages, attains one of the summits
of the mind.

V

The spherical unity of the modeling, which expresses
the immemorial soul of China, is the image of its substance. By its configuration, by its soil, by the race
that peoples it, the Middle Kingdom is a unit. China
and the Chinese form one agglomerate thing in which
the moral and the social solidarity, the passivity and
the impersonality of the crowds, cause their inmost
being to become a mere extension of the country itself.
It is a yellow mass without contours, composed of the
dust and clay of the land: the age-old dust that is
brought by the north winds and that whirls in never-
ending clouds across the disk of the sun, and the clay
carried along by the rivers to cover the earth with
their deposits; the dust and the clay are mixed into
plaster for the walls of the houses, and the houses,
again, and the men with their yellow skin which continues the soil, merge into the entity which we call
China. The yellow earth goes to the very heart of the
cities, and the perpetual exchange of misery, of dirt,
of provisions brought in by the caravans and the river
traffic, gives to the whole mass, and to the life that
runs through to its depths, a slow, compact movement
that never leaves the circle which it first followed.
The horizon is as closely limited as the life, and all the

space and all the duration of the world cohere and are one.

An agriculturalist, or rather, a gardener—for ten thousand years, perhaps—cultivating his square of earth with slow patience and solicitude, accumulating

Tomb of the Mings (xv Century). Triumphal Way. Monster.

human fertilizer for it, getting his food and the food for his family and his beasts out of the smallest space, always bending over his soft soil and often living beneath its surface, his whole skin, his feet, and his hands impregnated with that soil—the Chinese knows its weight, its consistency, its degree of moisture and dryness, its very taste. He hears the dull murmur that stirs it when seed is sprouting. One would say that his whole sensual imagination has concentrated in the desire to handle that unctuous earth and the substances that he takes from it, the fat jade, cornelian stone, crystal, agate, chalcedony, the hard stones whose spots he knows how to utilize, whose veins he knows how to follow, the kaolin and the flint, the white earth, the copper and the tin that he melts together to produce his black bronze. He knows his material so well, he is acquainted to such a degree with its habits and customs and peculiarities, that he can melt or

Tomb of the Mings (xv Century). Triumphal Way. Elephant.

boil it by holding back or by forcing the fire, so as to render it more or less hard, more or less brittle, to vein it, to mix it with other materials; he causes powdered metal that has been liquified by heat to flow through it, or breaks its surface with a crackle. His brass is deeply mottled with the green gold that he runs through it, with yellow, red, or violet gold, and with irised blues that have an appearance of danger, like sleeping waters. As he works his brass, weighty, dense, sonorous, and hard, the metal flattens and swells and takes on the aspect of solid blocks; the incrustations on its rough outside, with all the interlacings of slimy skins, of spines and tentacles, still leave its heavy profile intact and pure. His bloated dragons aroused by the rumbling and writhing of the sea monsters, his snails and his toads swollen with pustules, are brought from within the metal by *repoussé*, and with so sure a stroke of the hammer that the creatures seem to adhere by their own viscosity. The Chinese artist grinds coral

Painting. (*H. Vever Collection.*)

and turquoise into an imponderable powder that he may melt it again and compel it to flow between narrow bands of copper or of gold, and in the enamel made somber by flame his deep blues, his mat greens, and his dull, opaque reds form flowers of blood, thick leaves, and the shining, golden plumage of the birds. On porcelain, finally, he defines his gifts as a painter, for they had never been quite able to become a part of their own time and free themselves from the calligraphic processes to which they adhered in the monasteries.

When he reaches porcelain painting, the Chinese can incorporate the color with the paste and with the glazes of vitrified silicates, and in strokes as fine as cobweb or as broad as petals he projects upon the object to be decorated his childlike gardens, his lakes, brooks, and cascades, his kiosks and bridges, his butter-flies and dragon flies, his beloved and well-fertilized countryside that blooms under the spell of his science of the sky, the winds, and the crops; there are rain-washed azures, there are flocks of birds swept along by squalls, there are clouds, flowered branches, reeds, and aquatic corollas. Here is the flower, here the insect; all the living tissues are here—the wing, the stamen, the antenna, the pulverulent pollen; all the moods of the air are here—its unfathomable transparence, its sudden opacity, its infinitude of shades from dawn to night, from the shower of rain to the dust, and from the pale moonlight to the red of the sun. Against the moving background of the blues, the greens, the reds, the pinks, the yellows, the violets, the whites, and the blacks, he sets the varied stage on which are performed the painstaking, concrete, and monotonous labors of those who cultivate the soil. If he desires to present clear daylight and smiling gardens, his painting is as if drenched with dew, it is as fres has a water color, and it is sharply outlined against the beautiful glazed and translucent backgrounds. If the cloudy sky blackens the surface of the waters, then the branches, the leaves, the dragons, and the landscapes arise from infinitely opaque depths and are seen vaguely, like mosses and plants through the water of a spring. And if a sumptuous evening is the subject which the ceramist has in mind, he lets the flame of his furnace creep over the sides of his vase again, and the variegated enamel gleams amid its wall of gold.

Brass and terra cotta take on the sheen of great, ripe fruits armed with thorns and ready to leave the branch. How heavy, how subtle, and how pure is Chinese form! One might say that it is less a material form, despite its heaviness, than a crystallized sound. The strange, positivist people! without an ideal, it still hears, in the depths of its obscure soul, this clear music. In the cylindrical form, the ovoid form, or the spherical form there is always the circular rhythm of China. Will China always turn in a circle, with the same patient, indefatigable, and slow effort which permits her to keep up the movement that is her salvation and to live without advancing? Or will she break this circle and adopt as her ideal the constant renewal of herself at the crest of the mounting waves of things? Will she not attempt, in this incessant pursuit, to gain the illusion of freedom? It is probable. She is stirring. Her five

MING ART (XVI Century). Divinity offering lichens and chrysanthemums. (*Charles Vignier Collection.*)

hundred million men are going to be swept into the movement of the Occident; they will break our painful, age-old equilibrium, overturn the economic rhythm of the globe, and perhaps, in their turn, impose on us an immobility that they themselves will require a thousand or two thousand years to regain. We know nothing. The complexity of the present and future world is a thing beyond our grasp. Life rumbles, life rises. It will yield up its forms to the men yet to be born, that they may be consoled for having been born.

VIEW IN JAPAN

Chapter III. JAPAN

I

JAPAN, fifty years ago, had not emerged from a social state which recalls that of the Middle Ages. The Daimyos divided up the empire into a few great hereditary fiefs. Between them and the peasants was a warrior caste, the Samurai, and a priestly caste, the Buddhist monks. Above was the Emperor, whom no one perceived, the mysterious intermediary between Heaven and men—and the Shogun, the real chief of the political and military organization, having powers of life and death. To bind the whole fabric together was the steady aim of the Japanese. Here, then, is our mediæval society in its entirety—less sincere and better policed.[1]

[1] It is this mediæval character, retained by social and political Japan until the end of the nineteenth century, which decided me to place this

When the revolution of 1868 caused the feudal
system to fall like a piece of stage setting which had

BUDDHIST ART.   Lacquered wood.   (*Louvre.*)

concealed from Western eyes the true nature of Japan,
the Occident was astonished at the speed with which

entire chapter, as also all the others treating of the non-European arts, in
the volume devoted to the Middle Ages, which should be looked upon as a
state of mind rather than as a historical period. It is to be observed, however, that Japanese individualism tends, from the fifteenth century onward,
as in the Occident, to detach itself from the religious and philosophic synthesis which characterizes the mediæval spirit.

Japan assimilated the external form of the European civilizations. At a bound it covered the road that we had taken four hundred years to travel. The Occident

BUDDHIST ART. Buddha. Wooden statue. (*Louvre.*)

could not understand. It thought the effort disproportionate to the means and destined to failure. It took for servile imitation the borrowing of a method whose practical value Japan could appreciate before

she utilized it, because old habits of artistic and metaphysical abstraction had prepared the mind of the
people for Western ideas. Under her new armament
of machines, of ships, and of cannons, Japan retained
the essentials of what had constituted and what still
constitutes her strength — her faith in herself, her
controlled passion, her spirit of analysis and recon-
struction.

The reproach addressed to Europeanized Japan is
not new. She had been accused of acquiring from China
—and through China from India—her religion, her
philosophy, her art, and her political institutions,
whereas she had transformed everything, recast everything in the mold of a savagely original mind. If one
were to go back to the sources of history, one would
not find a single people, outside of primitive tribes, to
which another people had not transmitted the essentials of its acquirements. It is the wonder and the
consolation of our human nature. By this solidarity,
which rises victorious above all the wars, all the disas-
ters, and all the silences, everyone who bears the name
of man understands the language of man. Chaldea
fructified Assyria; Assyria transmitted Chaldea to
Persia and, through Persia, stretched forth its hand to
India and to Islam. Egypt educated Greece, Greece
animated Italy and, across the Middle Ages, guided
the modern Occident. The Middle Ages of Europe
rejoined the Arabs, through Byzantium and the Orient.
China, which had felt the contact—by way of India—
of Egypt, of Assyria, and especially of Greece—China
carried over all these mingling forces to Japan that the
latter might make such disposition of them as the
teachings of her soil and her passion should dictate.

When, at about the time of Europe's conversion to
Christianity, Korea transmitted Buddhism to Japan
and with it the philosophy and the art of the Chinese

KOBO DAISHI (IX Century). Wooden statue. (*L'Art du Japon,*
publ. by Brunoff.)

and the Indians, the island empire occupied the same position that Dorian Greece did in relation to Egypt and western Asia. Silent, as early Greece had been, Japan did not know, any more than Greece, that she would have found the traces of her ancient life if she had sought the formless statuettes in her tombs. Although Shintoism deified the forces of nature, it had proscribed images. This was doubtless a matter of dogma that was foreign to the soil of Japan and that came, like Buddhism, from one of those ethnic elements —Mongol, Malay, or Ainu—which contributed to the formation of the race. It is certain that Japan accepted it only half-heartedly. As soon as Buddhism had opened its sanctuaries to all the Shinto gods, and fixed their look in bronze and wood, the Japanese recognized the image of their real desires in them.

But so long as the original materials of the race cohered, its artists did not free themselves from the need of Korea, from the immemorial will of the Hindus and the Chinese. The seated gods with the lowered eyes and the open hands are like a block, round and pure and modeled by the light. The spirit that inhabits them flows from everywhere and envelops them in solitude and silence. One feels them as bound up with space, and from all points they seem to gather its vibrations into their fluid surfaces. Are they Japanese, Hindu, or Chinese? They are Buddhist. It is but very slightly that religious sculpture begins, in the eighth century, to reveal the silent germination of the true national sentiment. The development is seen in the work of Kobo Daishi, the old statue maker. In his statues of warrior gods, so radiant with energy, there is something of *arrested* gentleness and of *arrested* violence which is already purely Japanese. He will not surrender his self-control. Whatever his fervor, his anger, and the impulse of his heart, the Japanese,

Priest of the Tendai sect (about the x Century).
(*From The Kokka.*)

when he has attained his true nature, will dominate
the expression of these feelings.

Even when men think they are the masters of those
decisions which seem freest, it is their general and
unreasoned needs which dictate those decisions. When
Japan closed her ports, at the hour when the Fujiwara
came into power, it was because she wanted to grasp

TOBA SOJO (XII Century). Painting, detail.
(*L'Art du Japon, publ. by Brunoff.*)

in herself the meaning of her own effort, amid the
merging currents of the military migrations and maritime exchange. This people does not barter either its
power of withdrawing into itself or its power of expansion. As soon as it perceives that it is too much cut off
from the world or that it has been too active, it bends
all its strength to dissipate rapidly the need for repose
that had succeeded action, or of the need for action
which it gathered from repose. It starts out on new
roads with such a frenzy that it must suddenly stop
to retrace its steps and, turning its back on the horizon,
take an inventory of its conquests. In the ninth and
the seventeenth centuries, it forbade the foreigner to
enter its harbors, once in order to assimilate Buddhism

and again to study in itself the deep echoes of the
Mongol invasions and the first incursions of the Occidental navigators. And it arrives at the decisive stages
of its creative genius at a moment about equally distant from the time when it closed itself in and the
time when it reopened.

II

The archaism that followed the first closing and the
classicism that followed the second both developed in
the same atmosphere of quietude and work. The
political life concentrated in a single capital, Nara for
the Fujiwara, Yedo for the Tokugawa. The people,
which had been warlike until that time, confided the
care of its defense to the military classes, so as to exploit
the wealth of the torrents and the coasts and to clear
the soil in security. And the sudden peace produced
its usual harvests.

Half-effaced symphonies remain to us from these
first ages of intellectual concentration, in which Buddhism, shared but very little by the people, shut itself
up in the monasteries in order that their silence should
enable it to illumine the old silk kakemonos. And
through these works Japan saw within herself the rise
of her veritable realities. At the moment which is
summed up by the work of Kose Kanaoka, for example,
we find a hieratic art full of the spiritual radiance of
Buddhist painting; and this is paralleled by the appearance, in the somber harmony, of its reds and blacks,
of the gold of the backgrounds and the aureoles, to give
a warmer patina. But the new problems—those of the
idea and those of technic—offer no more than temporary obstacles to the nascent spirit of the Japanese
in its manifesting of a vision that was already more
direct, more incisive, and clear-cut than that of the
artists of the continent. Those three obscure and very

Statue of the Jingo Kuago (x Century). (*From The Kokka.*)

slow centuries, when the artists are held in the archaic mold, do not yet, to be sure, permit the Japanese spirit to free itself, since the monastic life in which the intelligence is at work is closed to the life of movement, to what brings enjoyment, to what brings suffering, to what brings understanding. But sometimes, when the

Daibutsu of Kamakura. Bronze statue (XIII Century).

monk quits the cloister, when he comes into contact with the pine forests, the torrents, and the dark seas, prodigious flashes of light bring before his eyes—with a clearness that perhaps is not to be found elsewhere in history—the extreme scope of his genius when freed from limitations. Toba-Sojo, the painter, and Unkei, the sculptor, are already true Japanese. The one has quite left the temples; he roams the woods, collects the insects, and spies on the mice and the frogs; he accords to all the beasts a clear-eyed and joyous friendship, and thereby sees them repeating in their own way the gestures of men—which he finds very diverting. The other, to whom the last sculptures of the Buddhist grottoes of China offered a pretext for releasing the unknown forces that slept in his race, suddenly carries his disciplined violence into the brutal effigies of his warrior divinities.[1] The vision of Kobo Daishi is quite realized with these furious, simple statues—almost pure, but with an inward impulse toward murder and combat.

Between these two contemporaneous works—that of the painter and that of the sculptor, who are so different in aspect—there is, therefore, only an apparent conflict. They meet at the point where the individuality of the Japanese frees itself from the statue maker's art to affirm itself in painting. The abstract art of the metaphysical systems which are present at the origin of every great civilization was drawing to its close. Unkei is the last of the great sculptors. Sculpture, the religious and hieratic art, which always corresponds with a well-defined society, could not survive the feudal anarchy that preceded the Mongol invasion. In proportion as the remembrance of the teachings from abroad was obliterated, the great traditions declined in the monasteries. Civil wars rent the country. Religion lost its original freshness to become an instrument of political domination. While, to the eyes of the people, the Mikado still represented the old Shintoism of their ancestors, the Shogunate, supported by the pretorians, was opposing Buddhism to the traditional cult. Sculpture obeyed the laws of dissociation

[1] M. Edouard Chavannes has already indicated the analogy that exists between the statues of Unkei and the guardians of the gates of the grottoes of Long-Men. See figures on pages 67 and 113. The evidence is clear. How did the Japanese sculptors come to know these colossuses? Doubtless it was because China exported bronzes and wood carvings that were directly inspired from them.

UNKEI (XII Century). Guardian of the temple.
(*L'Art du Japon, publ. by Brunoff.*)

dictated by the state of society. It overloaded itself with incrustations, complicated itself with draperies, and, when it lost the calm of its lines, it lost the whole of its spirituality. It is only in the seventeenth century, when the painted wooden effigies of monks were erected, that among the severe profiles united by

Sesson (died 1495). Dragon. (*From The Kokka.*)

fleeting passages which envelop them with strength and security, the sculptors found again a little of the radiance of the seated Buddhas whose peaceful countenances had for eight hundred years bent over the faithful, and whose fingers, raised in their pure gesture, had taught them wisdom.

Painting, on the contrary, would not have existed without the invasion. The Japanese soul, which had lost its basis of religion and to which Toba-Sojo had prematurely given a basis of popular life, was getting away from its course and becoming anæmic in the service of the nobles. With the Tosa school, founded in the thirteenth century by Tsunetaka, who claimed to represent the art of the ancient archaic master, Moto-

TAKAUBU FUJIWARA (Tosa school). Portrait (end of the XIV
Century). (*From The Kokka.*)

mitsu, its tenacity very quickly degenerated into minuteness, its science into skill, and its fineness into preciosity. When it reached its end in the academic miniatures, in which the court people satisfied their puerile taste for antiquated things, the national spirit had long since been delivered of its atrophying influence. Japan was weary from turning about in the same closed circle, and, having been assailed by the Barbarians ever since her art had emerged from the monastery, being touched by the immeasurable life of the new ideas that invasion brought with it, she let herself go with the wind.

Toward the end of the fifteenth century, when old Kano Masanobu, impressed by the work of the Chinese Josetsu, founded the great school of Kano, he appealed to continental traditions in order to combat the narrow academism of Tosa. In so doing he was following the tendencies that his master, Shiubun, and Sesshiu and Soami and Sesson and Shiugetsu, had already manifested. It was the good fortune of Japan that the Chinese painters of the period were seeking to regenerate their vision by the patient and direct study of animals and flowers. They could inform Japan as to her true nature, tear her away from the religious symbolism for which she was not made, and make it possible for her to follow her individualization along the roads that Toba-Sojo had explored with so much audacity. But the strong discipline of China did not immediately permit the Japanese artists, happily for the development of their mind, to go as far as their astounding precursor. First, they learned the architecture of landscape, they gazed on their country with a religious emotion, they got the appearance of the rocks, the angular trees, the jagged mountains. A rolling murmur followed the reawakening to life, a rude hymn after the silence. Powerful poets of the

Sesson (died 1495). The Tempest. (*From The Kokka.*)

brush, like Sesshiu, Sesson, and Soami, covered their white paper with those summary black dabs of India ink which give us for the first time the effect of things seen in a mirror dimmed by having lain in water. We

SESSON (died 1495). Bird.
(*From The Kokka.*)

see cranes in a sky, ducks in a pond, or the strong lines of a landscape, misty, chaotic, and wooded. Sesson discovered in it fantastic apparitions, dramas of the air and of the lakes —wandering barks, birds at dawn half frozen on the branches, and trees lost in the fog; by his powerful abbreviations he announced Korin. Sesshiu seemed to live with the beasts and to share with indifference their implacable destiny. The violent life of the earth entered him like the breath of his nostrils; he was far from men and seemed to remember the gods no longer. In his somber splashes of ink he gathered up the central forces that issued from the soil of the shaggy, pine-grown hillsides, the sap that poured through branches, the blood that swelled in throats and bellies, the hunger that hardened beaks, the brutal flight that ruffled plumage, the terrible sim-

SESSHIU (1438–1506). Landscape. (*From The Kokka.*)

plicity of natural forms in the presence of instinct, of
space, and the wind.

Kano Motonobu, the son of the founder of the
Chinese school, could now borrow from the continental
painters practically all their subjects, their motifs, and
their composition. At bottom there existed such an
antagonism between the spirit of the islands and the
spirit of the continent—the one resolutely objective
and quite devoid of sentimental partiality, the other
so often employing the aspects of the world for demon-
strating and moralizing—that what Monotobu naturally transmitted to his pupils before all else was the
profoundly constructive action of Shiubun and Sesshiu. He brought to his task the power for synthesis
that only a predestined genius possesses, and, in him,
archaic culture could not fail to establish, on an indestructible base, the powerful sentiment for nature that
the Japanese people had been seeking for five or six
centuries in the depths of its soil, in the seed that expanded it, in the torrents whose every pool it had
explored—whose every stone it had lifted, in the trees
of its forests which it cut down and trimmed for the
building of its houses. Kano Monotobu saw how the
birds polished their feathers in the morning dew and
how the cranes stretched out slender legs as they sank
earthward in their slow flight. Except for some sleepy
creature of the air, its neck under its wing, its plumage
ruffled by the cold of the dawn, nothing would be seen
but the boats lost in fog and in space. . . .

III

This austere vision was very soon to be transformed.
After China, there had arrived the world of the Mos-
lems, of India and Persia, of the Portuguese and the
Dutch. Japan had either to free her mind of the robust

education of the Chinese or else submit to them definitively and surrender her privilege of self-expression.
The Kano masters, on the outskirts of the evolution
of ideas, were turning the continental tradition into
academic formula, little by little, also some of them—
Eitoku, for example, a powerful poet of tree forms—

Soami (xvi Century). Landscape. (*From The Kokka.*)

unfold an arresting personality in the discipline they
observe. Meanwhile, the live elements of the country
strongly concentrated scattered energies in the growth
of audacity and faith which followed the protectionist
edict of Iemitsu, which again closed Japan to the outer
world. In a movement analogous with the one that was
taking place at the same moment in western Europe[1]—

---

[1] It is, moreover, remarkable that the intellectual evolution of Japan
should correspond almost exactly, in its general directions, with that of the
Occident. Its Renaissance is of the fifteenth century, its classicism is of
the seventeenth, its art of pleasure and fashion is of the eighteenth, its
landscapists of the nineteenth.

9

which was realizing its classic expression in France, in Holland, in Spain, and in Flanders at the same

Mitsuyoshi (Tosa school) (xvi Century). Painting. (*Louvre.*)

time—Japan found the moment of equilibrium when the spirit, freed from encumbering ritual, became master of the new rhythm; it could then offer to the

KANO MASANOBU (1453–90). Fishing.
(*From The Kokka, vol. iv.*)

sleepy crowd a safe refuge for ideas ready to scatter over the rich future. A new architecture is to recreate the statue maker's art, and for two hundred years Japan will pour into it the resources of its flora and fauna; before the end of the period, the artists, by their ingenuity, will be compelled to develop from this architecture even the humblest arts of industrial ornament, which will be dispersed among the people, as the dust raised by the fall of the temple descends upon the plain. When, upon the order of the Shogun Iemitsu, Hidari Zingoro built the temples of Nikko, it was in the name of the whole race that this artist, who was an architect, a chiseler, a smith, a beater of copper and bronze, a master of niello, a wood carver, lacquerer, decorator, cabinet maker, and gardener, took possession of the inner realities that Japan was suddenly discovering in herself. These monuments, dedicated to the spirit of the national hero, Ieyasu, fixed in an epitomized and definitive image the desire of an entire people, which thereby freed itself so as to expand in every direction.

On this convulsive soil, where volcanic eruptions, earthquakes, and tidal waves have so often destroyed in a few seconds the great cities that lie between the mountains and the sea, the fall of stone walls would crush men every time that subterranean fire bursts through the crust of the earth. A construction of wood, set up simply, offered no resistance to shocks. And the sanctuaries rose amid the forests of cryptomerias and maples whose eternal youth they called upon to witness their unshakable fragility and to sustain their vigor. The temple is mingled with the forest —which enters into the temple. It is conceived like a picture. Often it leads the traveler to its gates by rows of smiling gods, covered with moss and little flowers, and stretching away on both sides of the road

KANO MOTONOBU (1475–1559). Landscape.
(*From The Kokka.*)

to the horizon. Avenues of closely planted trees, black and straight, conduct one to the very stairways of the porticos. Among the horizontal branches hover the roofs of green bronze; the walls of red lacquer rise among the bare trunks; the somber verdure of the cedars continues through the winter to prolong the monumental harmony into the summer. If among the pines there are some clumps of chestnuts, of alders, or of oaks, the autumn will attune them with the creeping dragons of gold and the lines of gold that wind about discreetly with the ornaments of the cornices. The sound of the bells and the gongs mingles with the sound of the cascades and the sound of the moving leaves. The temple of bronze and of bamboo penetrates to the heart of the thickets, and if heavy trunks and broad branches are met on the way, they are surrounded by walls of lacquer so that they may dwell in the temple, in the center of the inner courts, whence their limbs will stretch forth to rejoin the forest.

And into all the halls, too, this somber forest enters, with all its flowers, all its trees, all its mosses, its springs, its birds, its reptiles, and the frailest and humblest of the insects over which each leaf is spread. Through red lacquer, through gold lacquer, through incrustations of metal, mother-of-pearl, or ivory, the forest spreads out its branches over the blood-red or black partitions that mirror the depths of the dawn or the depths of the night; it lets its petals and its pollen rain into the temple, it sends—flying, creeping, or leaping into the temple—its little beasts, innocent or mischievous, for whom every blade of grass serves as a refuge, which hollow out galleries in the subsoil and whose hum resounds in the sunlight of summer days. Nature is merely an inexhaustible reservoir, swarming with small living forms under the deep mass of the branches, and the artist of Nippon has only to seek there at random to gather the things he uses to decorate the house of man or the house of the gods.

After this moment the Japanese artist no longer

Kano Motonobu (1475–1559). Painting. (*Louvre*.)

thinks of art as having any other function. Thus all the teeming life of the surrounding world is introduced, not only into the religious life of Nippon, but into its everyday life. This is more important, for religion is only a wheel—though a necessary one—in the social mechanism. The life of the world is communicated to the Japanese by the kakemonos, the screens, and the bibelots which furnish his dwelling, the prints which pass from hand to hand, by the flowers embroidered on dresses, by the beasts incrusted on the scabbards and hilts of swords, on combs and on caskets. Only, it is not at random that he introduces this world into his wooden and paper houses. It would have broken down the partitions and torn the windows. He does not forget their calculated fragility or their rigid lightness when he lets in the outside world. He makes all the forms yielding and adaptable to the thickness, to the transparence, to the directions and the colors of the constructions and of the lacquer varnishes or the silks that cover them. He has *stylized* nature.

An erroneous distinction has often been made between the process of reason which consists in stylizing a form and the process of instinct which tends to idealize it. Idealization does not re-form an object; it reconstructs and completes it so as to deduce the most general, the purest, and most hopeful meaning that the object has for man. Stylization adapts it to its decorative function by systematizing the characteristics which appear in practically a consistent manner when the form is studied. The artist saw that all forms and gestures and all architectures in repose or in movement retained certain dominant qualities which defined them in our memory and which, when accentuated by schematic processes, could be applied to decoration with the utmost exactitude. By its power of stylizing the world, Japanese art stands as the most intellectual, if not the most philosophic, of our plastic languages.

School of Matahei (xvii Century). Painting. (*Louvre*.)

Stylization has never been an obstacle to the Japanese artist. On the contrary, it permits him to place his science at the service of a fantasy that knows no limits. It authorizes him to turn into geometrical

A monk. Sculpture in wood (xvii Century). (*Louvre.*)

forms the whole of nature, transposed and recomposed—beasts of silver, pewter, or gold; plants of red or black lacquer; gilded flowers, blue flowers, green flowers; leaves—red or blue or black; nights and days and suns that no longer retain anything of their original colors. But the rigorous logic which brings about order among the sensations out of which the

forms came little by little clothes them in another kind
of reality, distant, crystallized, and magnificent. Their
life exists through their relationships, the object is of
no importance save with respect to the one next to it,
and the higher type of truth is never in a fact, but in
the way of understanding it and of uniting it with the
other facts.

The miracle of this well-formed and precise language
is that it allows the painters of the islands to retain a
personality as clear-cut, as imperious, and as living as
that of any artists of the Occident; the miracle is, too,
that this language is neither transmitted nor repeated
from century to century without contact with nature.
Whatever science and certainty there is in his culture,
whatever the power of his tradition, the Japanese
decorator considers the visible world and takes counsel
from it with unwearying enthusiasm. He is forever
bending over it, and if he composes from memory so
as not to retain anything of the moving form but the
strongest appeal it had made to his mind, he does so
only after having accumulated, like a collector of insects and plants, the tiniest details of knowledge of
that form that he can get from thousands of close
studies, wherein the bird lives again, feather after
feather, the fish with scale after scale, the leaf with
nerve after nerve.

IV

Never was any people more naturally an artist
people, never did such a race draw on a field of sensibility, of enthusiasm and hope as rich as this one.
As in Greece, all the aspects of the universe are gathered
into a small space—mountains, lakes, forests, and
arms of the sea that reach the heart of the land. As
in Greece, an immensity of light glorifies the sea and

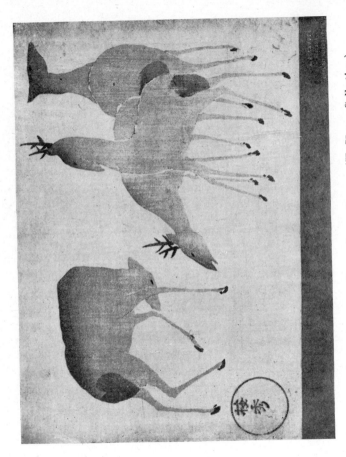

KORIN (1660–1716). Page of an album. (*H. Vever Collection.*)

the sky. More than in Greece, the spring deluged with flowers, the autumn with blood, the torrents carrying along the leaves or the petals which they sweep from their banks, all imprint the face of the soil with the sense of its inner life. All the climates to be found between Scotland and Italy follow one another, from the north to the south, in one continuous gamut upon which the identity of the geological formations imposes an impressive unity.

Not half a century ago, all the Japanese outside of the military caste were fishermen or peasants. Although their soil was hard to cultivate, it was fruitful, and they drew from it enough to feed themselves and, passing their whole life in this great, tangled garden where the tints of the horizon and of the flowers are so varied and powerful, living in the intimacy of the foliage, the snows, the cascades, the fruit trees, and the ever-resounding hum of the insects, they acquired a feeling for the forms and harmonies of the earth that penetrated them and was part of their nature, from the humblest of the serfs to the most powerful of the Daimos. Since the days of the Greeks, no other people in its ensemble was ever an artist to the degree attained by the people of Japan. Not possessing the power of illusion and the ennobling vision of the Greeks, to be sure, the Japanese still recall them in a great number of ways—in the seminudity with which they live their sturdy, healthy lives, in their optimism, in their tendency to deify the forces of nature and to deify human heroism, in the position of woman and of the philosopher-courtesans, in the masks of their theater, and in their sinuous and linear conception of form. It is the land where, in the springtime, husband-men with their children and their women leave the fields and, taking with them provisions for a journey that may carry them twenty leagues from their village, go to see the blossoming of the cherry trees at the edge of a torrent.

What is strange is how this people, always open to external sensations and thus always impressionable and vibrant, still remains master of itself. It resem-

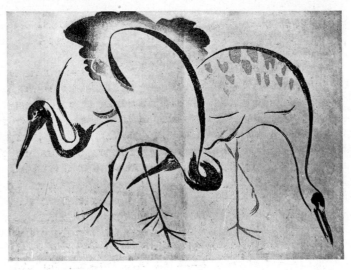

KORIN (1660–1716). Page of an album. (*H. Vever Collection.*)

bles its soil, whose gayety masks the subterranean fire which is always ready to send forth its lava from a hundred volcanoes. It is an affable and smiling people, and if it bursts into furious violence, there is always a methodical guidance for these outbursts. Even its anger is reasoned, its fearful bravery is only a lucid exaltation of its will. Its very emotion is stylized. And its art—whose flight it accurately controls, whose lyric impetuosity it holds in clear-cut, though sometimes abrupt, form—does not abandon itself to the overflow of the marvelous instinct which directs it. Egoistic at bottom, and jealous of keeping its con-

quests for itself, this people seeks to give only a transfigured image of them.

This is the only point held in common by Japanese
and Chinese art, the two being as different as the
indented, violent, gracious islands are different from

KORIN (1660–1716). The Wave. (*From The Kokka.*)

the continent in its massiveness, oneness, and fixity.
From the one to the other there is the distance that
separated Greece, the investigator, the lover of forms
in movement, from Egypt—almost completely immobile and in love with full, subtle, and closed forms.
To the degree that China is a single block, slow in
movement, secretive, and heavy, Japan—nervous, tense
in movement like the twisted cedars of its forests—

is mobile and ready for innovation. The ancestor
worship, which the Japanese retained with the first
ideas of morality that came to them from their neighbor,
was not, as in China, a homage to the immutable, but
the cult of the will power and the moral power with
which the dead had endowed them.[1] Its effect may be
seen in the love of the Japanese for children, who
stand, in their eyes, for an accumulation of energy
greater than their own, because the children see a
larger number of dead when they look behind them.

The world of the Japanese is a moving world.[2] The
flowering of the gardens that they cultivate with a
restless passion has in it something of this mobility,
which we see also in the varying shades of their soil
and in the profile of the mountains—which may
change at any moment as the mists trail in tatters,
now revealing, now masking the roofs of a phantom
city, a lake, a dark stretch of sea spotted with white
sails, a brilliant cone that starts up into the light, the
forests of black pines, and the red forests of autumn.
The soil may begin to tremble at any moment, and the
twilight changes with the fire of the volcanoes. Japanese art will set itself to seize the characteristics of the
object in movement, living, varying its place and
giving, despite its practically constant form, the sensation of instability. It is as far from the mobility of
impressionism, through which the modern Occident
caught the variations of light with so much vivacity,
as it is from the immobility of the Chinese. The
Frenchman, working from nature and adhering faithfully to direct sensation, ended by losing sight of the
characteristics of the object. The Japanese, composing
from memory, sees nothing but those characteristics.
With the former, analysis reaches the point of disso-

---

[1] Lafcadio Hearn, *Kokoro*.   [2] Lafcadio Hearn, *Loc. cit.*

ciation,[1] with the latter, synthesis reaches the point of creating a system.

The need of Japanese art to characterize things is so pronounced that our Occidental eyes cannot always differentiate between a work of character and a caricaturist's system. Caricature appears at the moment

KORIN (1660–1716). Portrait. (*From The Kokka.*)

when the descriptive element tends to absorb the ensemble instead of remaining subordinate to it. But how is that moment to be determined? Character and caricature oscillate around a purely theoretical point which all eyes do not locate in the same place. For a Japanese eye, doubtless, character continues after caricature has already begun for us.

What carries the Japanese artist beyond the mark, perhaps, is the ironical turn of his mind and, at the same time, his miraculous skill, which he does not

---

[1] With Neo-Impressionism.

sufficiently distrust. When, in a flash, he seizes form
in movement, he gives an impression of infallibility,
though one must hasten to add that this applies more
especially to his representation of the smaller animals.
Save in the case of Sosen, a savage and pure painter
who lived in the woods like a wild creature, so as to
surprise clusters of monkeys as they huddle together

Ceramics, enameled and fired earthenware, the piece on the right
by Kenzan (XVII to XVIII Century). (*H. Vever Collection.*)

on great branches and shiver in the snow or the cold
of dawn, the Japanese has not understood the larger
animals so well as he has the smaller ones, for his eye
is somewhat shortsighted and he does not easily grasp
the idea of mass. He has scrutinized the microcosms
so patiently and sagaciously that through them he
has remade the world, as a scientist reconstructs it in
the field of his lens. He has seen the sun behind a
spider web. Beside him, the Occident, in its effort to
bring everything to the level of man and to the general
surroundings of his activity, seems to have neglected
what is at the level of the soil, near our eyes, within
reach of our hands—the things one can see only if one
bends one's neck and stares fixedly at the same point,

only looking up to rest one's eyes after too prolonged
effort. The Occident saw form and lines, certainly, and
colors and their broad combinations, but it never saw
a flower or a plant, it never studied the slight, curling
lines on water or the trembling of a leaf. As it shut
itself up in the house during showers, it did not see how
the rain claws space nor how it bounces from the pud-

EITOKU KANO. A pine, screen. (*From The Kokka.*)

dles on the ground; and when it went out of doors
again when the sun shone, it did not study the dust
that dances in the light. But the Japanese has classi-
fied, as if in a science, the most secret revelations of
his burning curiosity. His eye is a little shortsighted,
he is very meticulous, he squats on his heels to tend
his vegetables, to care for his flowers, to graft his
bushes, and to make war on hostile insects. The life
of his garden becomes the central theme of his meditation, which follows its ironical path through minute
anecdotes and little concerts of rustling leaves. He
has surprised the vast world in its humblest cares.
He has visited the aquatic flowers with the sudden
flight of the dragon fly, circled around with the bee
from the hive to the glycine flowers, pricked the sugared
fruit with the wasp, noted the bend of the blade of

grass beneath the weight of the butterfly. Under the wing shells, as the insect raises them, he has heard the transparent wings unfold, he has observed with passionate sympathy the tragedy enacted by the fly and the toad, and it was in watching the circular muscles roll in the flanks of snakes that he came to understand the silent drama of universal hunger. He has had long vigils over birds standing in melancholy on one long thin leg, and over their motionless intoxication with the freshness of the morning sun. He has seen them stretching out their necks in their rigid flights, and how they wink the round eyes that are flush with the sides of their flat heads, and how their spoon-shaped or pointed bills preen their varnished feathers. He has described the concentric circles that the water spiders make on the pools, he has discovered how the reeds stand waiting when the wind is about to rise, he has felt the agitation caused in gramineous plants and in ferns by the action of dew and by their proximity to a spring. And, having made all these tiny adventures a part of his life, he had only to raise his eyes to the line of the horizon to be filled at once with the serenity of the mountains in the light of the dawn, to feel peace come into his heart with the fall of night, and then to let his dream wander over the immobility of the distance or be cradled by the sea.

V

And here is a strange thing. Although, like the Greek sculptors, they saw around them nude human forms living and moving, the painters of Japan did not always evoke the human form more successfully than they did that of the larger animals, and it is especially when the human form is their subject that we hesitate to distinguish their need for character from their sense

of caricature. . . . Undoubtedly, they are moved on
seeing the roundness of a woman's arm, or the curve of a
breast whose purity seems molded in a cup of crystal. . . .
The glory of the feminine body rises like a poem from
the ardent Koriusai,[1] the painter of warriors and of

MORONOBU (1638–1711). Promenade, print.
(*H. Vever Collection.*)

virgins, to Kiyomitsu (1735–85), to Buntsho (?–1796),
to Kiyonaga (1742–1815), the artists who so often
remind us of the Greek vase painters- and to the
great Hokusai himself (1760–1849), a man who could
draw the fat expanse of the haunches or the globelike
firmness of a bosom and at the same time could understand the upward thrust of the old volcanoes in the
fire of the morning sun, or the rocking of the waves.
Almost the whole art of the eighteenth century, here
as in the Occident, was a voluptuous homage to the
woman in love. Utamaro (1754–1805) is fervent in his

---

[1] Middle of the eighteenth century.

passion for the figures which he describes through the beautiful breasts that offer themselves like fruits, the high, hard necks under the hair that is combed upward, the oval faces under the jet-black masses of the hair that is secured by gold pins; Harunobu (1718–70), who is in love with the young girls he meets in the gardens and on the threshold of the paper houses,

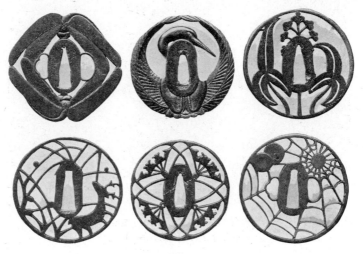

Sword Guards.   (*H. Vever Collection.*)

paints charming idyls in which he associates women and flowers and, through the discreet interplay of the effaced blacks, the burnt-out reds, and the pale greens, gives us glimpses of landscape in which lanterns light up the cherry blossoms that have come out under the snow. The art of these two Japanese would suffice to define the period. But the very strong, very sensual, and very gentle sentiment that even its greatest men had for the beauty of women did not often suffice to conceal the lapses in their expression. Occupied as they were in penetrating the structure of small things,

Masks. (*From The Kokka.*)

did they perhaps not have the time to analyze the human being? When they speak of him their language hesitates and floats, and formula appears. The feet and the hands, the arms and the legs, are singularly deformed and atrophied in ways that are not always very expressive; one finds them approximately the same among all the Japanese artists, as if one painter

Okio (1732–95). Young dogs. (*From The Kokka.*)

had transmitted to the other the patient and meticulous recipe for them.

In the eighteenth century these lapses of expression are rather surprising. The painters who spoke of woman with so ingenuous a love possessed, at that time, a science of line that bordered on abstraction. With Morikuni (1670–1748) and especially with Masayoshi (1761–1824) drawing is no longer anything more than a system, a linear arabesque that silhouettes the movement with a stroke. The powerful modeling of the old masters of India ink is barely suggested by the undulating line whose black accents on the white page give only a slight hint of the succession of the planes and the flight of the contours. The mind of Japan was to evolve fatally toward this prodigious graphology which, by its own realization, satisfies the sensual needs of the imagination in the same way that it is satisfied by the crushed, tapering, or sinuous

Netsukes, wood and ivory (XVII and XVIII Centuries).
(*H. Vever Collection.*)

volutes of the beautiful ideograms. But both expressions lead rapidly to forgetfulness of the external world, to pure abstraction, and to death.

In the full expansion of the Japanese soul, from the fifteenth to the seventeenth century, the understanding of volume, which is to the language of form what philosophic balance is among the teachings of the senses, the understanding of volume by Motonobu or by Korin (1661–1716) enabled the painters to produce their finest compositions. Even when linear arabesque alone filled the white page, even when the graded stroke did not indicate the density and materiality of things, even then their line was so fat and supple, with sinuosities and swellings that responded so well to the moving modeling of the external organisms, that it sculptured the form on the plane of the paper. To grasp Japanese art at the summit of its power we must look to the work of Korin. All the masters of Nippon, from Sesshiu and Sesson to Hokusai, live in that work, *in posse* or as a prolongation. And it comes just at the hour when Japan shuts its gates to descend into itself again and when, in a few years, the teaching of the primitives ripens in the meditative atmosphere of moral unity and of peace.

Masayoshi (1761–1824). Page of an album. (*H. Vever Collection.*)

The school of Tosa and the school of Kano united their conquests to form a definitive bone structure as a basis for Japanese sensibility. Mitsuoki (1616–91) exhausted everything precious and rare that the academism of Tosa could offer to the aristocratic soul of the nation. Tanyu (1601–74) employed his verve and his vigor to free Kano from its last servitude to the

SOSEN (1747–1821).   Monkeys, painting.   (*H. Vever Collection.*)

Chinese. Itshio (1611–1724) struggled joyously against
the Buddhist gods and was the first to go out among
the peasants. Korin could drink at all the sources,
break the fixed traditions to get back to the living
tradition, and bind the new presentiments with the
ancient realizations.

As a draftsman, he covered his albums with those
powerful silhouettes, each one of which specifically
incloses, in a swift line, the whole signification of the
object synthesized, and, beyond the object, all the
echoes that it awakens in the universe that we divine.
As a lacquerer, he seems to do no less than reinvent an
art which, for ten centuries, passed as the really national expression of the Japanese genius; he brought to
fruition within himself the mind of the great lacquerer
Koetsu (1557–1637), and created the great lacquerer
Ritsuo.[1] His brother Kenzan (1663–1743), with Ninsei,
the most powerful of Japanese ceramists, the man
who could render the dampness of grasses and the
freshness of flowers in the fire of his ovens, dipped into
Korin's creations as at a natural spring. . . . As a decorator, he inspired generations of workmen who, a
hundred years after his death, still came to ask him
for motifs, for counsel, technic, and methods of stylization. When he let the India ink or the thick black
varnish flow from the point of his brush, when he
polished his lacquers of opaque gold with powdered
charcoal, it was as if the whole ancient soul and the
whole present-day soul of Japan were suspended within
his soul to guide his hand. He had the power to seize,
in the life that passes, the imperceptible instant that
attaches it to eternal life. A few sparrows on the
snow, a line of turtles, or a tuft of reeds sufficed him as
a subject; a stroke, a shadow from his brush, and the

---

[1] Beginning of the eighteenth century.

absolute flows through his work. He seemed suddenly
to abandon his color and his form when he had barely
sketched them in, as if warned by a prophetic flash

HARUNOBU (1718–70). Young women at their toilet, print.
(*H. Vever Collection.*)

that he should go no farther. A leaf of his album took
on the grandeur of a fresco.

Before transposing the reptiles and the birds and the

fishes and the little mammals and the aquatic grasses into his profound gamut of greens, blacks, reds, and the golds of his lacquers, he had so zealously penetrated the meaning of their animation that it seemed as if that animation was what caused the glistening material to swell. The rolling trot of the mice, the flabby appearance of the toads, the silent flights in the sky, and the undulation of seaweed at the water's edge passed under the glazed skin of his pieces. His heart beat at having understood the enormous force of life that is hidden under the grass we tread on, in the depths of the dark springs in which our gaze is lost, and under the broad leaves which spread themselves out and cast a green shadow. Gold on gold, gold on red, gold on black, red on red, black on gold, the lacquer incrusted with metals seemed, with its creeping forms, its wings, the flowered branches that traversed it, and the pollen of gold powder that rained on it incessantly, an ingot of somber gold in which life trembled.

It was from Korin that there descended upon the later time that wave, formed of the minor industries, which becomes an ever-broadening torrent, and soon gives to any practical object that comes from Japanese hands the character of a work of art. Korin, like every great artist of Japan, remains a workman, and every workman in Japan can become a great artist, whether he is a painter or a lacquerer, a bronze worker or a smith, a ceramist, a wood carver, a carpenter, a gardener, or, like Hidari Zingoro, Korin, and Kenzan, more or less of all of them at once. A close and vast solidarity unites, one with another, all the branches of the most flourishing decorative industry that has ever existed, and it was from the greatest painters that the humblest of the carvers or the engravers got all their motifs. We find in them the spirit of the masters and the same passion, the same skill, and the same power of imposing on matter the direction of that spirit.

Before them, only the Egyptians, when they made the smallest objects, had had the power of giving the aspect of organic life to the minerals of the earth. The fired earthenware of the Japanese has the appearance of animal tissues, or viscera steeped in the sulphur of volcanoes. Their netsukes, the millions of intimate bibelots and mischievous trinkets of which they reaped a sudden harvest in the seventeenth century, are palpitating little things whose ivory, lacquer, or metal our fingers love to caress, as if they were tiny, warm animals hiding in the hollow of our hands. Capable of

UTAMARO (1753–1806). Kitoki taking the breast, print in colors.
(*H. Vever Collection.*)

casting the largest bronze statues that the world possesses, seated colossuses whose raised finger and whose smile dominate houses and forests from afar, these artists have also embroidered in iron and cut it into lace. They found alloys, unknown before, which give to brass the veining of a marble; they mixed and harmonized the metals as a painter amalgamates and

grinds colors and assigns to each its part. Iron, the
bronzes black or green, tin, gold, and silver, are orchestrated as in the processes of the print makers. Mother-
of-pearl and ivory are associated with them, with the
intimacy that the sky and the clouds have with the
form of the earth. The old suits of mail, in which
hammered copper and iron, lacquer and steel, are
bound together by cords of crêpe and silk, look like
great black scarabs. The Japanese have only to open
their windows, and butterflies and grasshoppers,
stamens falling from flowers, leaves torn from trees,
and the broken wing cases of insects enter and fall
here and there, wherever the breath of spring blows
them—on paper fans, on earthen pots, bronze vases,
lacquer scabbards, and iron sword guards. The fragile
life of the ferns and the insects is mingled by the
Japanese artists with social and family and military
life. Even from pools of blood come little creatures of
gold.

VI

It was the period when art resolutely left the temples
and the castles to overflow the street, as after the great
centuries of Greece. It was the period when Matahei,[1]
a direct, sumptuous, and rare painter, turned his back
on dogmatic teaching and opened the way to that
"low school" which expresses with the greatest
evocative force, to Occidental eyes, the everyday
soul of Japan. The genius of Korin, alone and free,
the struggle of Goshin (1741–1811) against a half
return to the Chinese school—favored by Okio (1732–
95), the powerful portrayer of great wild birds—and
above all, the appearance of prints, popularized by the
severe harmonies of Moronobu (1638–1711) and of

---

[1] Middle of the eighteenth century.

UTAMARO (1753–1806). The Mirror, print. (*Louvre.*)

engraving in colors which was invented by Kiyonobu (1667–1729)—all this protected and helped along the activity of the school of the people. Netsukes, potteries, lacquers, inros, and surimonos were sold in every bazaar.

Prints invade the houses of the middle classes and of the common people. Views of the sea, of the moun-

HIROSHIGE (1797–1858). The Shower, print.
(*H. Vever Collection.*)

tains and the woods, the dresses of passing women, pennants, signs, colored-paper lanterns, the whole noisy, bustling, twinkling fairyland of the Japanese, permitted the engravers of the people's prints to expend, in miraculous profusion, the fantasy and power of their genius as colorists, dramatists, and storytellers. Europe came to know Japan by this popularized art, by this infinite subdividing of the central force that Sesshiu, Motonobu, and Korin revealed to their country for the glory of man. It is not altogether the fault of Europe if, in unpacking its boxes of tea, its lacquer caskets, and its bamboo furniture, it hardly

saw more at first than the slightly comical exterior of
the Japanese soul. For only the externals were at
first conveyed by that rising sea of little colored papers
on which stretched out parades of screen figures in
epic posture; gnarled landscapes; warriors streaked

Hiroshige (1797–1858). Road of the Tokaido, print.
(*H. Vever Collection.*)

with blood; convulsive actors; bedizened, painted,
pale women; and artisans, fishermen, reapers, and
children—all a little droll—and multicolored, gesticulating crowds, and evening festivals on the waters.
In that strange confusion the surprised senses of
Europe could for some time discover nothing but
violent colors and disjointed gestures, and it was only
little by little that there came to be perceived a power
of orchestration and a passion for characterizing things
that carried a flood of revealing sensations into the
Occidental mind. How should we, without Hiroshige,
have witnessed the progressive illumination and darkening of the skies over the islands of Japan, how should

we have discovered the limpidity of the great dawns that come up over their horizon lines, the tall, bare trunks of the pines which shoot up from the Japanese roadsides, giving glimpses between of the deep azure of the air and the sea, the somber harmony of the snows, the mass of the waters which are almost black and against which white sails follow one another? He has shown us how the rainstorms drive the birds and bend the treetops, he has shown us the poetry of the blue nights of his country when the trees are in flower, and how its lakes are lit up by fireworks and the lanterns that dance above the wooden bridges; we see the crowded boats and the musicians that play in them. How should we have known Japan without the pure Utamaro who frequented the courtesans and stopped at doorsteps to see mothers giving the breast to their little ones; and without the trenchant Toyokuni, the boon companion of the actors; and without Shunsho, who spread the colors on his prints like streams of flowers; and without Kiyonaga, the reserved lover of the long feminine forms, the bare legs, breasts, shoulders, and arms that look out from amid the discreet harmonies of silk kimonos and half-lit houses; and without Harunobu, around whom women, like flowering reeds, enchant the earth; and without the infinite Hokusai, how should we have assimilated the value of the lines which, outside the realm of all scientific perspective, solely by their expressive force, symbolize the succession of the planes in unlimited space? How could we do otherwise than forget that they no longer knew Sesshiu, Motonobu, and Korin as their models when, to intoxicate our eyes, their flat tints shook out before us the folds and lining of the robes and combined them into orchestral harmonies? We see this clearly, even from our distance, as when one is on a height from which hollows and projections are effaced, one discovers the design of a great landscape garden.

With flowers of green or blue, with flowers of flame, with red leaves and golden leaves, the Japanese embroidered robes in which the dawn rises or the daylight falls, and all the blood of the veins is spread out on them and all the snow of the mountains as it glares in

HOKUSAI (1760–1849). Iris, print. (*Private Collection.*)

the sunlight; the fiery clouds that float in the twilight are on those robes, and the fields veiled in mist—rose, mauve, or azure—and the fruits whose downy skin turns color as they ripen, and the silent rain of glycine petals as they fall on sleeping water, and the pink and white haze of the flowering fruit trees. Tossed upon the robes as the wind might toss them, the Japanese weavers and embroiderers have set frightened birds in flight, and into the folds they have twisted convulsive monsters. In the crinkling silk they have opened up landscapes where leaves and waters murmur,

and—as if seen through autumn foliage—the innumerable suns of the imperial chrysanthemum appear.
The blacks, those deep and absolute blacks that almost
always have a part in their designs, by the stripes or
spots on cloths, or, in their pictures, by the note of the
hair as it piles up in flat coils, or by the fat arabesque
of the powerful ideograms, their blacks are the muted
accompaniment against which the violent melodies
shriek their drama and then grow calm and then
re-echo and die. . . . When the women pass in procession across the prints of Nippon, we do not know surely
whether the flowers, the dead leaves, or the whirling
snowflakes on their silk kimonos were scattered there
by the summer, the autumn, or the winter they have
traversed—or whether it is not just the walk of these
far-away creatures which spreads about them the
summer, the autumn, or the winter. Everything sings
when they come, even violent death. The landscape
responds to them, the landscape with its pink branches
from which the petals will fall like snowflakes, the
landscape where the flowers resist the frost, the landscape with its limpid skies over serene waters, the
nocturnal landscape where women—moving gardens
in themselves—pass against backgrounds uniformly
black.

The sap of Japan, in these millions of flying leaves,
fell like ever-heavier raindrops, but also it got farther
and farther from its roots. The country had been
closed for two hundred years, deaf to the voices from
without—and the voices from within beat against
unscalable walls. Too long deprived of the oppor-
tunity for interchange, which is life, impotent to renew
itself, its soul contracted into itself, grew enervated,
and lost itself, little by little, in detail and in anecdote.
Let us admit as much. The art of the seventeenth
and eighteenth centuries, despite the abundance in

which it spouted forth, despite its verve and its life, seems a little frail and troubled, feverish and caricaturish beside that of the preceding epochs. The

HOKUSAI (1760–1849). Drawing. (*Louvre.*)

great Hokusai himself, the protean poet, the man with a hundred names who filled more than five hundred volumes and twenty thousand prints with his thought, "the old man mad about drawing," the distracted vagabond who gave its climax to the art of the people and scattered the spirit of Japan to the four corners of the heavens, as a great wind despoils the forests of autumn—the great Hokusai himself is an expression of the decadence. He has for his suffering fellow-creatures the unconcealed passion that was perhaps possessed, among us, by Rembrandt alone; he had that powerful minuteness that one finds only in Dürer, and that love of aërial landscapes in which Claude Lorrain and Veronese saw the tremble of their gold and silver; his verve—cynical or terrible or bantering or sinister or harrowing—is the same as that with which Goya tore from the world of forms the swift symbols of the tragedies of his heart. He has the immensity of knowledge and the skill of all the workmen of his nation. A pupil of Shunsho, a lover of Sesshiu, of Tanyu, and of Korin, there was not a fiber of his immeasurable spirit that did not root itself into theirs, to divide and spread in limbs and branches through all the beings and all the plants that he encountered during his very long life—when he roamed through the woods and along the streams, when he breathed the mist of the cascades or crossed some humpbacked bridge to follow the busy crowd till it dispersed in the streets, the gardens, and the houses. He spoke the humblest and the proudest word that has come from the lips of an artist: "When I am a hundred and ten years old, everything that comes from my brush, a point or a line, will be alive." He has described every kind of labor and told the tale of all the days. He did the things that the peasants do, and the workmen, and the fishermen, and the soldiers, and the people of the fairs, and the children. With a tenderness that is now merry, now quite pure, he has set down the story of their games, their trades, and their passions.   He has loved all women, their hard, pointed breasts, and their beautiful arms that flow in such swift, sure lines. He did not have time to tell us everything, though at any moment he would leave the people he was talking

Hokusai (1760–1849). The Rape, drawing.
(*H. Vever Collection.*)

with—roofers laying their tiles, wood sawyers, or ped-dlers—to follow a bee toward a flowering hedge, over which he would discover a gardener at his work. He would lie down in the sun for his noonday siesta, but without any intention of sleeping; he would not make the slightest movement; he would hold his breath; at the slightest vibration he would raise an eyelid; he would follow the buzzing spot until it had settled on his bare arm; he would let himself be stung so as to study the monstrous eye, the sucking proboscis, the metal corselet, and the thin elastic members that the insect is forever rubbing together. When he had gotten wet to the bone while looking so carefully at the rain, he

HOKUSAI (1760–1849). Drawing. (*From The Kokka.*)

was in haste for the wind to come and dry him so that he might see the whirling flight of the dead leaves, the lanterns of the festival, and the feathers swept from wings. If he climbed a mountain and came out above its low-lying mists, it was to get a sudden sight of some peak isolated in crystal space, and, as he came down again, to discover through rifts in the fog the thatched roofs, and the rice fields, and swarms of men under their round straw hats, and junks scattered over an opaque distance. When he had seen the pale moon rise in the black sky over a world empty of forms, he waited impatiently for the red sun to discolor the air so that he might seize the appearance of the world, in the islands of gold spattered with dark touches that sow the inner seas, and the blue or red houses that appear amid the pines, and the wandering sails, and the conical volcano, now crowned with blood, now with silver or opal, now with the violet, the rose, or the lilac that one sees only in half-opened flowers. The oily oscillation of the sea, the glaciers thrusting up above the clouds, the motionless or restless tops of the woods

Hokusai (1760–1849). The Wave, print in colors. (*Louvre.*)

— the whole universe stamped itself on his mind in deep harmonies; he seems to crush blue, green, and blood-red jewels in an air that is filled with watery vapor and that transmits light to things. . . . He commands form like a hero, and at will he is lyrical or philosophical—by turns or simultaneously—and an epic poet and a satirical poet, living in the most frightful nightmares after leaving the most peaceful realities, or while still among them, and passing at ease from the most unhealthful invention to the noblest vision. . . .

And yet, through his swift art, analytical, feverish, and hurried—too anecdotal oftentimes—he is an expression of decadence. One is tempted to say that he foresees the end of Old Japan, that he wants to prepare a living encyclopædia of it, hastening to tell everything about it in direct, immediate notes that strike like lightning, as if to leave its image—complex, multiform, disordered, and immense—to the future.

After him Yosai still addresses a discreet, melancholy, and pure farewell to the kimono-clad women who pass before the backgrounds of flowered branches —and the end has come. The revolution that throws Japan into the path of the Occident brutally extinguishes its art life. It is like a wheat field laid low by the wind of cannons. And notwithstanding, Japan has yielded nothing, abandoned nothing of her soul. She has imposed on the world her right to her life. Now she must find, in the reserves of her silence, all her passion for comprehending and all her power for expressing. The soul of a people cannot die entirely while the people is still living. Already some of her artists seem to be reviving, to be finding again the spirit of their race, broadened and renewed by the thought of the Occident. One day, certainly a great art will be born of that meeting. But the present attempts are premature. Japan has a more immediate and more positive purpose to achieve now. After attaining military strength, let her, therefore, acquire economic strength. In the rise of the energy that leads to action she will surprise the creative spirit that will spurt forth one day. Later, she will be rich. Then poor. And the cycle will begin again.

POPOCATEPETL, MEXICO

Chapter IV. THE TROPICS

I

ALL peoples feel the need, at some moment in their history, to come into that prolonged and fecund contact with the world of the senses from which there comes forth the verbal, musical, or plastic representation of the mind. But each one of them speaks its own language; thus a given people which has composed poems or orchestrated symphonies remains incapable of rising to plastic generalizations of a distinguishing accent. Outside of the French, the Italians, the Spaniards, the Flemings, the Dutch, sometimes the Germans—I hesitate to say the English—the societies of mediæval or modern Europe have left the industrial art of the people only to attempt imitations, more or less disguised, of the great foreign schools. Now all the races, even the most primitive, possess the faculty of decorating pots, carving wooden figurines, making furniture, weaving stuffs, and carving metal. That is to say that any people in Europe which has not, in the general onward sweep of Occidental culture, known how to utilize the stammerings of these rudimentary arts, to make up a language of its own, a living language that expresses

it in its highest desires, must seek to realize them otherwise than by images, which it does not know how to use because it does not love them. Besides, as civilization becomes universal, it perverts the needs of the people's soul, and the manifestations of that soul take on more and more of a mongrel character. To find a primitive art that retains its sap and can impart new and strong emotions to sensibilities that have preserved or regained their first ingenuousness, we must go to those peoples who have remained primitives.

AFRICA. Helmet (Guinea).
(*Guillaume Collection.*)

It is in the tropics or near the polar regions that men, in the heart of modern times, have preserved practically intact the spirit of their most distant ancestors. It is only there that they have not passed beyond the stage of naturistic fetishism and the grouping by tribes.

In one region the heat is too intense; in the other region the cold is too severe. Here the seasons are too distinct and too heavy; there they are too torpid and of too slow a rhythm. Among the peoples of the tropics, even the most rudimentary effort to get food and shelter is practically unnecessary, the effort to rise is too hard, and with the polar peoples the only use of effort is to secure an existence, which is vegetative and precarious, the nature of the country being too ungrateful for the inhabitant to imagine that he could modify his surroundings to his profit. Finally, neither in the one region nor in the other have any great human migrations passed, to renew the race, to bring it the breath of the world outside, because the course of these migrations has been turned aside by the ice, the deserts, the overdense forests, and the too-vast oceans.

AFRICA. Fetish of the Bakoutas, copper and wood. (*Guillaume Collection.*)

The black race is perhaps that one among the backward peoples which has manifested the least aptitude for raising itself above the elementary human instincts that result in the formation of language, the first social crystallizations, and the industries indispensable to them. Even when transplanted in great numbers to places like North America that have

reached the most original, even if not the highest, degree
of civilization that we find in modern times, the black
man remains, after centuries, what he was—an impulsive
child, ingenuously good, and ingenuously cruel; as in
the case of other chil-
dren, all of his acts
spring from immediate
sensation. And yet his
was the only one of the
great primitive races
which, inhabiting a
massive continent in
large numbers, lacked
neither arms nor heads
to modify its surround-
ings, discover new rela-
tionships, and create
new ideas. But this
continent is divided
into twenty sections by
the sands, the moun-
tains, the brush, and
the virgin forests; it is
infested with wild
beasts, it is feverish and
torrid, and is cut in two
by the equator. Its
northern shores, those
on the Mediterranean,
are habitable for white
men, and only these re-
gions have, from the be-
ginnings of history, par-
ticipated in man's great
movements toward the
future.

AFRICA. Bronze from Benin.
(*British Museum.*)

However, if we revert to the earliest times we discover an Africa that was probably identical with what
it is at this hour, and consequently on the same level
with that of the tribes that peopled the north and the
west of Europe—perhaps on a higher level. War and

<small>Africa. Bushman fresco on stone. (*Copy in the Trocadero.*)</small>

commerce created constant relationships between ancient Egypt and the Sudan, and Central Africa participated in the development of the civilization of the
Nile. From that period on, iron was worked in Nigritia,
while the old world hardly knew yet how to work in
bronze, and the African jewelry that is still made by
the Somalis of East Africa, the Pahouins, the Ashantis,
and the Haoussas of West Africa, was brought by
caravans from the confines of Upper Egypt to the
markets of Thebes and Memphis. The jewelry is
heavy, of a thick and compact material, with incrustations of blue and red stones whose opaque glow spots
the circles of mat gold or of somber silver. Geo-

12

metrical figures are dear to all primitive peoples, whether they paint their pots, decorate their huts, weave their clothing, or stripe the skin of their faces or

their bodies; and cutting into the African jewelry in every direction we find again these geometrical forms—short, fat, dense, and pressed closely together. As mathematics, the science of inert forms, preceded biology, so geometrical ornament preceded living ornament, and certain child peoples, incapable of interpreting life, have arrived, in ornamental art, at the highest degree of power. The human mind proceeds always from the simple to the complex, but when the great artist appears to unite the most differentiated living forms through a single arabesque, or when modern science tries to express all its conquests in mathematical symbols, the mind is invariably brought back to primitive sources, the very ones at which instinct slaked its thirst. The result is always the impressive agreement between the most obscure feeling and the highest form of reason.

AFRICA. Great helmet of the Baoules for the Gouli dance (Ivory Coast). (*Guillaume Collection.*)

In general, we need not seek, in the art of the Negroes, anything more than that still unreasoned feeling which merely obeys the most elementary demands of rhythm and of symmetry. When the youthful peoples follow

AFRICA.   The Two Principles (Upper Niger).
(*Guillaume Collection.*)

the instinct which urges them to impose on the living forms that come from their hands a vaguely architec-

tural appearance, an awkward, rough symmetry, they unquestionably obey an imperious desire for synthesis, but this synthesis is of the kind that precedes experience and not the kind that follows it. The sculpture in wood of the Negroes is still very far from the great Egyptian sculpture, for example, whose advent coincides with that of a social and religious edifice of the most powerful architecture. Perhaps it is a first sketch or presentiment of Egyptian art that we see in Negro sculpture—one which may carry us back almost as far as the appearance of man in Africa. From such a beginning may well have come the sudden start for the ascent, through the long centuries in the great fertile valley where the black and white races fuse. Then, after the slowest, the loftiest, the most conscious stylization, after the art of the Nile has sunk into the sands, the Negro again prolongs the immobile inspiration of Africa until our own time. But to him we must not look

AFRICA. Tribal fetish (Ivory Coast). (*Guillaume Collection.*)

for metaphysical abstractions, for he gives us only his sensations, as short-lived as they are violent—an attempt to satisfy the most immediate needs that spring from a rudimentary fetishism. And perhaps it is even because of his fearful candor in showing us rough surfaces, short limbs, bestial heads, and drooping breasts that he reaches his great expressiveness. These sculptures in wood—black wood on which

Polynesia.   Sculptures in wood.   (*British Museum.*)

the pure blues, the raw greens, the brown reds take on
a violence so naïve that it becomes terrifying—have a
simplicity in their ferocity, an innocence in their mood

of murder, that command a kind of respect. Brute nature circulates in them, and burning sap and black blood. Although man is afraid of them, he cannot help recognizing and loving his impulses—rendered concrete in the crawling crocodiles and the crouching gorillas which are sketched by long strokes in the wood and which decorate the doors and beams of his hut or the sides of his tomtoms.

How are we to discover, in the confusion and the ebb and flow of the tribes and the industries of Africa, the stronger currents which would have led, without a colonization of the continent by the European peoples, to a conquest by the blacks of a more enlightened inner world? The Haoussas and the Ashantis, especially, devote themselves to all the basic industries—weaving, ceramics, iron-working, gold-working, embroidery, jewelry, and carving in wood and ivory, and those of the Negroes of the Sudan or of western Africa who yield to the current of Moslem propaganda have a presentiment, on coming into contact with the spiritual spark of Islam, of the existence of a higher life. They frequently surpass the Berber artisan in working metal and leather for articles of luxury. But we must go back farther into the past of this dark land—this land fertilized by blood—and find the traces of a need belonging to a still very confused but strongly affirmed æsthetic order, since destroyed among some of the African peoples, by the immigrations of other black men and the invasions of the whites. Among the natives of Guinea, Niger, the Gaboon, and the Ivory Coast, we find idols, dance and war masks, objects of daily life, and weapons whose prototypes undoubtedly date back to a very ancient period, perhaps an immemorial period, and these works bear witness to a desire for stylization that is not alone very accentuated, but also powerfully original. The plastic synthesis, here, borders on geometry. The ensemble of the work is subjected to a kind of schematic rhythm which permits itself the boldest deformations. but always allows certain expressive summits of the object interpreted to remain. The kingdom of Benin, which was one of the first to receive the Portuguese navigators and in which there developed, doudtless about the end of the Middle Ages, the greatest school of Africa, had admirable bronze workers. By their powerful feeling for embryonic life they became very near relatives of the archaic Chinese sculptors, of the Khmers and the Javanese. They twisted black serpents together to make of the rough and scaly coils in which they writhe the supports for copper stools. Their pots often took on the aspect of a human head and with lines of great purity; other vessels were ornamented with strongly built rude, and very summary sculptures in which the familiar silhouettes of the dog, the lion, the cock, the elephant, and the crocodile are indicated, sometimes with a strong tinge of irony. At this period, in the sixteenth and seventeenth centuries, Africa seemed, moreover, to be emerging from its long nightmare. The Bushmen, contemporaries of the Negroes of Benin, peopled the south of the continent; far from the

POLYNESIA. Sculpture in wood.
(*British Museum.*)

equator, the deserts, and the forests of Central Africa, they lived in a healthier climate where stock raising is possible, where wild beasts are rarer and game is abundant. They could, had they persisted, have given a decisive impetus to the mind of the Negro races. Living more often from rapine than from hunting, their nomadic and adventurous life multiplied their relationships with the tribes and the soil of Africa at the same time that it sharpened their senses and subtilized their mind. On the walls of the grottoes, where they hid the herds they had stolen, they have left frescoes of red ocher in which we see, living again, their hunts, their wars, their dances, and beasts that flee or march in line. The form is only an approximation, but the flat spot is vibrant, and the silhouettes, looking like shadows on a wall, march with a single movement—oxen that are pursued, antelopes climbing a slope, great gray birds crossing the sky.

II

It is the most interesting effort, doubtless, that has been attempted by primitive men since the days of the cave men of Vézère. But this elementary painting seems condemned to have no evolution, to disappear brutally. The warm waters that ended the glacial period obliged the reindeer hunters to flee from western Europe; the Bushmen dispersed on the arrival of the Kafirs, the Boers, and the English; and from day to day the colonization of Australia reduces the number of the aborigines who covered the rocks of the great island with black, sulphurous, red, and blue frescoes which testify to a generalizing spirit whose rudiments are perhaps less visible among the inhabitants of Africa than among certain peoples of Oceanica. Polynesian art, like Oriental art in general, would seem to tend

NEW ZEALAND. War mask. (*British Museum.*)

more especially toward decoration, whereas the character of the art of Africa, like European art, shows itself in a more marked tendency to isolate form in order to examine the activity it possesses within its own limits and within its individual characteristics.

It is true that the climate and landscape of Oceanica offer to the sensibility of the Polynesians resources that are not found in Africa. The dispersal of the race among the thousands of large and small islands, separated by vast expanses of sea, is perhaps the only thing which, preventing the necessary cohesion among the peoples, prevented also a great civilization from being born in the Pacific and from spreading round about. And now it is too late; the conquest of these regions by Europe, the diseases, the alcohol, the morality, and the religion that it brought them have made the Polynesians anæmic, have decimated them and overcome them. The time has already arrived when they are beginning no longer to feel in themselves the poetry of nature which surrounds them and which formed them.

The islands, whose flowered forests spring from seed brought by the wind, cover the blue ocean as the Cyclades of Greece strew the eastern Mediterranean from the promontories of the Peloponnesus to the bays of Asia. Nature is prodigious there—healthy, though sweating with its fecundity, surrounded by perfumes, bursting with flowers, dazzled with its fire-colored birds and its gleaming stones; its forests descend to the water's edge, where they are reflected in the cup of black sapphire incrusted with pearls, where marine monsters dwell in caverns of coral. A beautiful race of men, high of forehead and artists by nature, inhabits the islands; they live in the open air, in the wind from the sea, among splendid forms and the blazing orgy of the colors. The language of the race is harmonious;

dancing and war and music are loved, flowers are woven into crowns and garlands, and when the people gives itself up to love, it is still living with the springs and the sunlight. Its mythology is very near—through its triumphant grace, its perfume of the dawn and of the sky, and through its crystalline symbolism—to the old Ionian legends. Had life been a little less facile,

NEW ZEALAND. Wooden box. (*British Museum.*)

had there been unity among the people, a rich future would have awaited them.

The gods that the Polynesians carved in the soft material of their wood, to be erected on their shores or at the doors of their cabins, are in general more animated than the symmetrical silhouettes cut by the Africans. Perhaps their art is less ingenuously conceived and less severe. There is more tendency to style, it seems, but more skill, and at the same time less strength. The eye sockets, the lips, the nostrils, and the ears become, in the most interesting of these images, the point of departure for long parallel lines, sustained and deeply cut, for spirals and volutes which are the result of the effort to demonstrate religious ideas or to terrify an enemy in war; we find in them a profound and pure agreement between the spirit of the myth and its concrete expression. These are no longer dolls which are terrible only in their candor. They are violently and consciously expressive, with their attributes of killing, with their cruel visages; and the colors that cover them are the symbols of their ferocity in combat and their ardor in love. Whether we consider the grimacing faces on the prows of the long curved boats, or the colossuses sheltered under the branches of the odorous forests—men or monsters daubed with vermilion or with emerald green—we find that all these works have passed the archaic stage represented by the statues of Easter Island, which is to Polynesia what an Egypt still plunged in the original mud would be to a lazy Greece, too much enslaved by the flesh. All are monstrous and alive, all have sprung from the bestial energy unchained by the wild loves and the excited senses of a country drunk with its bursting fruits, its multicolored bays, and the multicolored plumes that rain on it like the sunlight. Long ago, before the white man came to force his somber clothing on the people and to dry up their poetic spirit, the great wooden idols were sisters to the enormous flowers and the birds and the naked men who roamed the woods, tattooed from their feet to their foreheads, painted with red, green, and blue, and covered with great undulating lines that were arranged to bring out the forms, to accompany with their flashes the rhythm of the runners, and to accentuate the muscles of the face in their terrifying play of expression during moments of debauchery and cruelty.

Their purpose was to captivate women, to terrify the enemy, and, through an instinct even more obscure and vast, to play, in the symphony of nature, the role dictated by the great corollas hanging from the tangled vines which bind the giant trees, by the glossy coats of the animals, by the fiery wings, and by the sinking of the stars into the sea. All the primitive peoples of the tropics who go naked in the freedom of the light have, in this way and at all times, loved to paint or tattoo their skins with color—the Negroes of Africa and the Indians of America, as well as the Polynesians. But with the Polynesian, the tattooing takes on a brilliancy, and evinces a care for rhythm and life, that we find nowhere else, save among the peoples that derive from the nations of Oceanica or who have been in touch with them for a long time. For their geometrical ornament, the Japanese substituted figures of birds, dragons, chimeras, women —which are really pictures, through their movement and composition. The New Zealanders, if they preserved in their tattooing the geometrical ornament of their Oceanic ancestors, brought to it a precision, a violence, a will to style that would almost suffice to define them as artists if their plastic genius had not revealed itself by other manifestations.

Wherever they may have come from—the Polynesian migrations

EASTER ISLAND. Colossal sculpture, lava.
(*British Museum.*)

across the Pacific have scarcely more of a history than those of the birds that wander from climate to climate—they retained the ardent sensualism that distinguishes the populations of Oceanica. Like the latter, they loved to set up posts sculptured with atrocious figures, and to decorate their weapons, the utensils of their industries and households, their boxes and vases, with incised painting that ostensibly is there to observe and perpetuate their traditional rites, their practices of exorcism and of magic, but that in reality expresses that human love of form, of line, and of color which inspires us to harmonize ourselves with nature, so as to understand it better and day by day to recreate it with its own elements. But a new and great thing was appearing among them, an art which indicated the rise of the Maoris to a decreasingly chaotic and a more luminous consciousness of their destiny in the world. It lasted until the English, in the middle of the last century, interrupted the development of the natives. They had practiced cannibalism, it is true, but only after they had entirely destroyed the rare specimens of the antediluvian species which still wandered through the silent forests at the time when their war canoes, ornamented with frightful visages, arrived in the great strange islands, which were devoid of all birds, of insects, of reptiles, and which possessed at most a few dwarfish mammals. The Maoris had been in the country only some three hundred years, perhaps, and it was with difficulty that they managed to organize themselves into tribes, which numbered some tens of thousands of men, and in which the births barely filled the gaps made by the massacres of prisoners of war who were offered as a sacrifice to the gods. And notwithstanding, their soul was already escaping from its silence. They had built villages in the center of which the fortified *Pa* contained the embryo of the future city. Four or five communal houses sculptured from top to bottom, schools, museums of tradition and legend, temples, inclosures for sport and for assemblies in which sat the councils of administration and of war. The decorative forms we find here are always violent, to be sure; they tell of killing, they are red with blood

PERU. Painted vases. (*British Museum.*)

and contorted into infernal attitudes, but already they manifest a persistent demand for balance and for architectural rhythm. Must we not, therefore, see, as the dominating influence in them, the majestic landscapes where the activity of the Maoris took place and the effort put forth by the people to maintain that activity? They had passed beyond the dangerous region of the tropical zone. The perpetual spring no longer enervated them. Their islands, like those of Japan, ran the gamut of climate from that of Italy to that of Scotland. They placed their villages beside the opal lakes set in cups of lava, that are surrounded by cold springs and boiling geysers, under the shelter of immense mountains

PERU. Vase, terra cotta. (*British Museum.*)

where active volcanoes alternate with glaciers that descend to the sea; and when the Maoris followed their pine-bordered streams they came upon fiords that reflected the forests and the snows in the shadowy masses of that southern ocean in which no human face had ever seen its image. A great civilization, a great art, could and should have been born there. The mats woven of phormium, hanging at the doors of the huts, shone with burning colors; the rocks were covered with frescoes in which the blue of the ice and the lakes lived again; the villages, built all of wood, with their sturdy houses whose roofs have a steep slope and with their

Photo by Charles Sheeler

NORTH AMERICA. Horsemen, painting on hide.
(*Museum of the University of Pennsylvania.*)

palisades for defense, were works of art, deeply carved with horrible figures which were tattooed like the people themselves and framed in prodigious series of curved lines, of interwoven spirals, of rhythmical coils, thick and fat, whose calculated mazes combined into the form of the human face. From afar, these forests of sculptured wood had the appearance of the arborescent ferns, tufted and slender, which covered the country. There is a little of the decorative spirit of the artists of Japan, but it is more impetuous and barbarous;

13

quite disdainful of the material employed, it lacks that
irony and that minuteness of observation which sometimes dampens enthusiasm. The character of the
works is ferocious. Certain sculptured visages are of
a structure so abstract and so epitomized that upon
looking at them one is reminded of the greatest masters of form, the Egyptians, the Greeks, the archaic
Japanese—and there is, besides, something austere and
trenchant, a terrible purity that belongs to the Maoris
alone.

Certainly, no other people among the Polynesians
has reached so high a level. If there is, between the
races of Oceanica and the ancient inhabitants of
Easter Island, a connection dating back beyond the
range of history, it is the Maoris upon whom we must
look as the most legitimate inheritors of the line, for
the art of the Maoris, as living as that of the Papuans
and the other natives of the Pacific, aspires even more
than theirs to realize those edifices of animated geometry which we can see as the goal of the hieratic art of
the ancestral race. Its island, an extinct volcano, is
deserted. But the rocks are dug out in hieroglyphics
and figures of birds, fish, and men. Finished or unfinished, more than five hundred colossuses stand erect
on the shores or in the center of the dead craters.
They are terrible figures, massive and summary, holding their arms at their sides; almost without a cranium,
they have bestial faces in which the nose is prominent
and dilated and the eyes are wide open; the broad
planes in which they are established look as if they
were cut with an ax, but centuries, perhaps, were
needed before the people could work the basalt of
which the figures are made. Why are they there,
horribly alone, with their faces to the eternal sea, and
what do they mean if it is not our inextinguishable
need to discover ourselves and recognize ourselves in

the rebellious or docile material that our soil furnishes
to us? A seismic catastrophe must have interrupted
the works and isolated them from the world. There
are tools at the feet of the figures, but no other traces
of humanity. Where did those men who erected them
take refuge? Whence did they come? What unknown
sources had slaked the thirst of these forerunners of

NORTH AMERICA. Vases, painted terra cotta.
(*Ethnographical Bureau of the United States.*)

the strange races of Oceanica —with the Indo-Euro-
peans, the most gifted of our planet, and antedating,
perhaps, the peoples of Asia? They were the victims
of their surroundings. The Polynesians had doubtless
come from the Dutch Indies, but that was long before
the period of history and previous to the time of the
Indian civilizations. The present populations of the
Dutch Indies, those Malays who also peopled Mada-
gascar, have not the proud and strong grace of the
Polynesians, nor their free life, nor their ardor in love,
nor their artist mind with its ability to generalize.

The thought of the Malays is timid, their character indifferent; they accept the beliefs that their successive masters from the west bring to them. Their ancient art derives from the art of the Indians, their modern art does not go beyond the monotonous practice of primitive industry. It was doubtless through contact with the sea winds and through their ecstatic abandon of themselves to the great currents of the ocean that the Polynesians escaped from the apathy of such origins and were able to call forth the formidable dream that was interrupted, but whose enigma is offered to us in the giants of Easter Island. Who knows if they did not go much farther and, crossing the islands that have disappeared, carried on by the waves, if they did not bring their dream face to face with the eastern sun whose source was hidden from them by the fiery rampart of the Cordilleras? And did not a gulf open up behind them, perhaps, and swallow up the land of their birth, even within their memory?

III

One can believe such a thing when one tries to recover the trace of the old inhabitants of the dead island. Outside the art of the Polynesians nothing reminds one more of the spirit of archaic Oceanica than the hieratical forms found among the Aymaras of the Peruvian Andes. There, as in the Egypt of the Middle Empire, the architectonic formula seemed arrested. In exchange for the lands distributed to the Incas, their bureaucratic socialism doubtless exacted from them that blind and definitive submission of soul to everything touching the spiritual domain. The Aymaras had reached the point of no longer seeking anything more in nature than motives for ideographs, which they stylized with relentless insistence. Hieroglyphics, carved out and flat, and composite images in which vague human forms appeared among the precise and mysterious interlacings of geometrical figures, framed the monolithic gates of the temples and the palaces. Pizarro melted down and minted the silver and golden statues which the Incas erected to their heroes. Were they of a freer art? Doubtless they were. . . . The Quichua pottery of the same time bears witness to a charming popular spirit. These peoples were good. They loved men and beasts. They looked on them roguishly, but very gently. Almost all their pots, their bottles, their alcarazas for keeping water cold, had heads of animals as spouts, and arms or paws for handles, and the forms are unforeseen, sometimes beautiful; almost always monstrous, they are grotesque, contorted, blown up, crushed

MAYA ART.
Honduras. Stele.
(*Museum of Natural History, New York.*)

in, warped, or paunchlike. Egypt had also reserved the hieratic forms for the face of the sanctuaries, and spent her sorrow in the shadows where, like Peru, she buried her mummies. She also loved to give animal forms to her smallest objects, to finish off pitchers and jugs with the heads of cats, of panthers, of jackals, and

MEXICO. Palace of Mitla.

cynocephali, even as the Peruvians drew out the tops of their vessels or flattened them down into the heads of dogs, of pumas, of ducks, and alligators. But in Egypt there was a purer and a loftier spirit. And if she was sometimes moved by her bent for irony, a very discreet and subtle tendency, she seldom went so far as caricature. Instead of heaping up her cadavers in earthen vases, she stretched them out in troughs of granite. She possessed the cult of form even beyond the grave, and purified the form to the point of abstraction. The wing of the mind had touched it—and our world was to issue from that contact.

But in Peru also there was no lack either of ingenious

social systems or of great dreams. Does not an Aymar legend show the creator peopling the earth with statues which he animates and to which he intrusts the mission of civilizing the world? In no other cosmogony is this profound myth to be found. The old Peruvian poets had felt that it is only when there is a contact between the soul and form that the lightning flashes, and that it is for the artist to introduce into the universe more order, a harmony which is forever evolving and which projects upon the future an anticipated realization of our hope. But the murderous climate and the debilitation of the people, who were decimated by the bloody sacrifices which the priests offered to the sun, upset the prophecies

MEXICO. The stone of the hearts. (*Museum of the City of Mexico.*)

of those who sang the epic of the race and neutralized the best-intentioned sociological teachings. In that torrid and trembling part of America, the most gigantic efforts were to miscarry suddenly, upon the shock of contact with a superior civilization. For in spite of everything, the Spanish civilization was superior, despite the killing and rapine of its envoys and the Inquisition which they brought with them. These adventurers, coming from an old world where the human mind was boiling with the deepest agitation to which it had been a prey for fifteen centuries, these violent

madmen, who had stumbled against this continent in
trying to encircle the earth, represented the conquest
of the future against themselves.

They had only to touch a finger to the rotten fruit
for it to fall from the old tree in which the sap no
longer rose. In Mexico, even more than in Peru, the
incessant ritual massacres had plunged the people into

MEXICO.   The plumed serpent.   (*Trocadero.*)

a dull torpor that rendered them incapable of resisting
the effort of the invader for more than two years.
The sole remaining energy which they recovered was
used to help Cortez in driving the Aztecs from Tenochtitlan,[1] which the latter had held under their yoke for
two centuries. All things considered, the religion of
Torquemada immolated fewer victims than did that
of Montezuma. And for a thousand years, moreover,

[1] Aztec name for the City of Mexico.

such deep waves of men had been passing over this soil that there came over its ancient possessors an absolute indifference as to which master must be paid and to which god should have its tithes of gold and of blood.

Like the Dorians in primitive Greece, like the Teutons in the Italy that was the contemporary of the civilizations of Mexico, all the conquerors had come from the north— the Toltecs in the sixth century, the Chichimecas in the ninth, the Aztecs in the thirteenth. From what direction they had entered, whether from the Orient or the Occident, from Greenland or the Bering Sea, we do not know — from both directions, doubtless. We find all types among the present-day natives or in the old sculptures of Mexico: Mongolian Asia and probably Scandinavian

Mexico. Toltec column.

Europe are represented there, perhaps also the sunken Atlantis. The people had, doubtless, crossed the polar

The goddess of death.
(*Museum of the City of Mexico.*)

regions, carrying with them, in their migrations, some of those Inoits who still inhabit the shores of the Arctic Ocean and who are said by certain scholars to be the descendants of the oldest artist people of the earth, the cave dwellers of Périgord who moved northward with the cold. They had come into contact also with the nomadic Indians of North America, leaving some of their own people among them and taking with them some of the latter to the south. At some periods they had spent winters with the polar races, huddled in their squalid, ill-smelling huts, and, in the dim light, had, with the natives, given rhythm to the interminable polar night by preparing the apparatus for fishing, hunting, and command- the reindeer horn, the jaws of the reindeer and the seal, and whalebone which they engraved with images as precise as the memories of their monotonous life that recommenced each year with the return of the pale sun. At other periods, while moving down the Mississippi, they had drunk water, kneaded bread, eaten meats and fruits from beau-

tiful red vases with broad black spots, which sometimes give to the geometrical ornament the crude
appearance of a beast or a bird. They had slept on
the prairies under tents of hide decorated with childlike
designs of hunted bison, demons, and fearful gods,
which, in their violent coloring and their awkward
drawing, united the most primitive of symbolisms
with the most primitive of writings. In them can be
foreseen the hieroglyphs of Mexican manuscripts and
of Peruvian bas-reliefs, with their geometrical life and
their harsh intricacies like those of a picture puzzle.
With their faces hidden under horrible masks decorated
with striped feathers, beaks, and horns, their bodies
painted in violent colors and covered from head to
heel with multicolored plumes which gave them the
appearance of those monsters with crested spines that
are found in the coal of the Rocky Mountains, they
had danced the terrible war dances that center round
the idea of death.[1] Perhaps even more distant memories moved within them; perhaps there lay in the
depths of their minds some images of the sculptured
rocks of prehistoric Scandinavia and through the
thousands of years of their traditions they may have
preserved, transformed by time and adapted to new
climates, the primeval technic of building with wood
which their oldest ancestor had brought from the
plateau of Iran.[2]

In any event, the ruins which are so abundant in

---

[1] The art of the polar regions and the art of the North American Indians,
among the Eskimos, on one hand, and among the natives of Alaska, Van-
couver, and the United States, on the other, still continues to-day nearly
the same as it has always been. It seems to present the point of relation-
ship with Mexican art—which would be the stylization attained after centuries or thousands of years—that the artistic industries of the African
Negroes have to the great art of Egypt.

[2] Viollet-le-Duc, Preface to *Cités et Ruines Américaines,* by Désiré
Charnay.

Yucatan all bear the trace of these things. The Maya conquerors, who constructed these edifices, probably before the arrival of the Toltecs and perhaps even at the period of the Greco-Latin civilizations, connect the American branch of the Aryas—through their pyramids built with steps on the outside and their buildings with sloping walls—with the Asiatic and European branches which had spread, in the earliest times of our history, over Mesopotamia, India, Egypt, Greece, and southern Italy. And in all the remainder of Mexico, which, in the Middle Ages, was covered with aqueducts, quays, piers, canals, bridges, reservoirs, stone streets, pyramidal temples, terraced palaces, and ramparts, the genius of the white peoples, more or less mingled, more or less resistant, persists—in great purity at times, as among the Yucatecs, or stifled, oftentimes, by theocratic formulas, as at Mitla, or thickened by black or yellow blood, as we find it when we wander on the plateaus where so many races are crossed, where Nature takes back everything to herself, where the woods so often cover enormous ruins that bear on their summit a temple of the Catholic god.

As in India, when one moves from the south to the north, from the confused intoxication of the sensualist peoples to the clear conceptions of the rationalist peoples, here, when one descends from the north to the south, one passes through every stage, from the façades bursting with complicated sculptures to the great horizontal bands—smooth or hollowed out into abstract ornament—which are supported by colonnades and cut by pure edges, as bare as the profile of the soil. From the calcareous plains of Yucatan to the cool plateaus of upper Mexico the way leads through feverish undergrowth, alive with serpents, scorpions, and poisonous insects—a place where the mind could have been dulled by the weight of the noxious exhalations, the eye blurred by bloody mists, so that the various styles of building were fused, as the most bizarre fancies of theocratic pride were imposed on the architects. Primitive India, northern Europe, Asia, and America were mingled, even as their mythologies had been mingled, and disfigured, in the fierce soul of the old Mexican prophets. Nothing can express the burning restlessness of the soul of these peoples, who knew astronomy; who had divided the epic of humanity into four sublime ages — the suns of water, air, fire, and earth- –which represent the struggle against the deluge, the cold, lava, and hunger; who sang the loves of the vol-

The goddess of death.
(*Museum of the City of Mexico.*)

canoes; who adored the sun, the profound father of life, from the tops of the terraces, but who thought it necessary that the walls of the temples which they raised to him be always bathed in human blood, that it should rot on the burning earth, and that at the summit of the temples a Stone of Hearts should offer to the eagles the viscera of the human beings who were sacrificed.[1]

For Teoyaomiqui, goddess of death, for Huitzilopoctli, god of carnage, for Tlaloc, god of water, of forests, of storms, the god who regulated the warm torrents that streamed from the sky for six months, and for Quetzalcoatl, the plumed serpent that was already adored by the Toltecs[2]—from whom the masters of Tenochtitlan received art, the cult of the sun, and the thirst for blood—for all these gods new cadavers were necessary. To consecrate the temples of Huitzilopoctli at Tenochtitlan, eighty thousand prisoners had their throats cut. The bread offered in sacrifice was kneaded with the blood of children and virgins. Their hearts were torn out and lifted up to the god, the pools of blood that spurted from the severed arteries were carefully spread over the image of the god so that it should disappear under a mantle of smoking clots at the end of the ceremonies. Heaps of severed heads were raised as high as the pyramidal temples. There were sanctuaries where one entered through a mouth whose teeth crushed skulls and tore entrails and which one could not pass without walking in blood up to the knees. The priests flayed men to dress in their skins.

From the depths of this horrible red steam that rose everywhere, which got into one's throat, caused a nauseous poison to roll in the veins, and threw a veil over memory, how could the enervated and discouraged soul of the peoples have drawn the forms that sur-

---

[1] I address my warmest thanks to M. Auguste Génin of the City of Mexico for the precious information that he has transmitted to me, when I have not found it in his beautiful *Poëmes Aztèques*. M. Briquet, the photographer at the City of Mexico, is also entitled to my deep gratitude for the zeal and disinterestedness with which he has placed at my disposal a great number of photographic documents.

[2] Toltec signifies "artist."

rounded them, the great laws of living structure from which there issued through Egypt and Greece the civilization of the Occident? Everything that was not death was hidden from the eyes of the people. Only when the sun was at its zenith did it touch the sculptured altar in the well that was hidden in the heart of the artificial mountain. The flat bas-reliefs with which the walls were covered and in which one might, under the brilliant varnish of the greens, the turquoise blues, and the reds, have seen men in plumed helmets hunting the tiger and the boa, disappeared under the blood. The vapor of the slaughterhouse masked the idols. The tradition of sculptured material could not be handed on to mutilated generations, and the landscape at which they

God of the water.
(*Museum of the City of Mexico.*)

looked too hastily was always steaming with rain or else vibrating with sunlight. It is by the intuition for mass, and not by intelligence in the use of profile, that one may compare the stone idols which the bronze tools of the Mexicans drew little by little from the block, with the pure Egyptian colossuses whose planes answer one another, introduce one another, and balance, as the land balances the sea.

The Mexicans scarcely reached and certainly could not go beyond the architectural stage in the evolution of the mind. Undoubtedly, the need for an essential symmetry haunts them when they raise Tlaloc on an ornamented pedestal, his hollow eyes turned to heaven, as he sits motionless with his prodigious expression of waiting and boredom, or when they represent Chacmool gathering the rain in his belly, or the goddess of death dressed in serpents and claws and raising her skeleton face and her horrible, rotted hands. In an effort that one feels to have been a painful one, they attempt the most trenchant expression and, to be sure, they do often attain profoundly moving structural epitomes, in a sudden equilibrium that arrests the tottering of the form and, with the energy of despair, sets it firmly in place. The continuity of the composite monster is then no longer, as with the Egyptian, in the progressive and fleeting undulation of modeling that flowed like a clear water. Like a tropical vegetation swollen with spongy bulbs, with spines and blotches and warts, the Mexican sculpture has its own continuity, as it continues sending forth its thick blood, from the torpid depths where the heart beats, to the fat projections—heads and other parts of reptiles, bare skulls, human fingers, and breastbones of birds that, at first view, seem to be caught there by chance. And yet the work does not break down under the load it bears, for it is brought back to organic unity by a summary but imposing architecture that enables it to retain its sense of mass, whatever the depth of the carving, and that is seen in its living ensemble more than in its abstract planes. Only, the frightful destiny of the Mexicans warned them that they would not have the time to arrive at the deepest meaning of the unity in their art,

GUATEMALA. The tortoise of Quiriga. (*Trocadero.*)

to rise into abstraction, to reach the idea of harmony. They say what they have to say hastily, in confused and violent visions, brief and fragmentary, a heavy nightmare of sadness and cruelty.

Even when they erect whole statues, when they abandon for a day their hieroglyphical combinations of geometrical figures and animated forms, one would say, from their manner of articulating the limbs and of giving an architectural quality to the masses, that they never saw anything but mutilated trunks, dislocated members, scalped heads, skinned faces with empty eye sockets, and grinning teeth. Life exists in these works only by fits and starts, broken as it is in their soul; it comes in brief tremors, and then is stopped short by dogma and by fear.

MEXICO.   Statue, lava.
(*British Museum.*)

In confused forms the sculptors combine sections of living animals, enormous pulpy masses swollen with turbid water and bristling with spines like the prickly cactus.   In Central America, where the earth is soaked with the water of the hot rains, where the vegetation

is heavier, the miasmas deadlier, and the poisonous
thorn bushes impossible to traverse, the dream is still
more horrible. In the sculptured rocks one distinguishes nothing but heaps of crushed and palpitating
flesh, quivering masses of entrails, faces from which
the skin has been torn—a confused pile of viscera from
the sides of which blood seems to run.

By what aberration of art, a thing made to unite
mankind, did it occupy itself so exclusively, among
these peoples, with
the celebration of
slaughter and death
as it so frequently
did also among the
most civilized peo-
ples? Our hearts beat
more regularly and
more strongly when
we follow the Assyr-
ians into their moun-
tains, when they
strangle lions whose iron muscles grow tense and
whose claws tear the belly of the horses. We unite
as if for a prayer around the harmonious groups
on the Greek pediments which evoke the terrible
myths of Hercules, or the war of gods and man, on
the centaurs and the lapiths, or the Amazons works
full of murder, of the blows of falling axes and of
the flight of spears, where fingers clutch desperately
at knives. The lines of soldiers on the arches of triumph of the Romans, the passage of the lictors, of the
legionaries, of the somber imperator with his laurels,
the plod of the captives, and the sonorous step of the
horses fill us with calm and energy. We know on what
heaps of cadavers the mosques and the alcazars are
raised, with what bloody mortar their stones are ce-

MEXICO. Chacmool. (*Trocadero.*)

mented, and yet we love the cool of their shadow and their gardens. We even feel a powerful exaltation before the Indian monsters who drink blood and devour rotten flesh. It is because the spectacle of strength exalts our strength. It is also because we deceive ourselves as to the meaning of our acts and because we like the forms that are necessary to the development of our faculty of bringing about order and of comprehending, even through the composite monsters and the mutilated fragments, as, through combat and violence, we pursue an illusory and distant idea of harmony and of fellowship. We fumble in the darkness and injure ourselves as we collide with the walls. The gateway to the light is never found.

And so we must look for it together, or at the very least we must refrain from striking down those who are passionately seeking it in the depths of the shadows. In Mexico, in Peru, the slaughter of the peoples was at every moment sweeping away thoughts that were necessary to the development of other thoughts, and so, one by one, the roots of the future were cut as fast as they grew again. If war can at times exalt and even reveal the creative energy of a people, systematic massacre extinguishes all energy. The arrival of the Spaniards in the New World, which brought the most implacable of the European races face to face with the most implacable of the exotic races, was a terrible con-

ALASKA (XIX Century). Handle of a spoon, slate. (*Museum of Natural History, New York.*)

frontation and one that was providential in history. Spain, to whom the attainment of its unity had given a century of creative velocity, was, because of the Inquisition, to perceive the need that man has for man in order to realize himself. It was not to be long before the moral desert should reach across Spain, as it was beginning to reach across America when that land had made a material desert of itself by burning its cities and by throwing its broken idols into the lake of Tenochtitlan.

A medallion, enamel on gold. A saint. (*In the Svenigorodskoi collection, Metropolitan Museum of Art, New York.*)

Chapter V. BYZANTIUM

I

BYZANTIUM carried along the world of antiquity to the end of the Middle Ages. As it guarded the gates of the two continents and the two seas, as it was at the center of the eddies of the fallen civilization, it fed its violent and troubled life with the slow death struggles of the ancient peoples. For a thousand years it defended, against the human inundations from the north, the east, and the west, the spirit of law that was Rome, the habits of trade, of politics, and of speculation of the Greeks, and the cruel luxury of the monarchies of the Orient.

The cult of wisdom would doubtless not have felt itself very much at ease under the cupola of Saint Sophia; Athens would not have recognized, in the stiff idols that decorated that church, the freedom of her religious naturalism, nor her respect for the living form in the atrocious mutilations that Byzantine justice inflicted on the condemned. The uncompromising

realism of Assyria would have found no savor in the
images of the books of prayer, and the kings of Nineveh
would not have comprehended the revolutions fomented
in the hippodrome and the changes of government
effected in the antechamber or the bedroom where the
purple of the Empire was forever dyeing itself with
fresh blood. The Rome of the Republic would not
have recognized its legionaries in those fat soldiers

ROME. A repast, fresco. (*Catacombs.*)

cuirassed with gold; it would not have tolerated the
continual retreating of law before imperial caprice or
the intrigues of the eunuchs.   However, under the
fermentation of the vices, the orgy of the games, the
cries of the massacres, and the convulsive autocracy
that was obliged to obey the orders of the populace,
the law of Rome was here, the opulence of Babylon,
the curiosity of Athens—and the only focus of light in
the dark night round about.

Christianity, which the Greeks of Rome were propa-
gating in the night of the catacombs by means of the
image, could not purify or extinguish the light that
came from the roaring fire, which was burning away all
that remained of the sap of the ancient world in the
poisoned fruits. The crowds that had responded to

ROME. Portrait of a deceased person, fresco. (*Catacombs.*)

the appeal of the apostles of Galilee had rendered possible, through the renunciation of their revolutionary
instinct, the coming of a social régime harder than its
predecessor; and the Byzantine autocrat, in order to
assure to himself their support, adopted the letter of

RAVENNA (v Century).   Mausoleum of Galla Placidia, interior.

the new order and enjoined the priests to change the
names of their gods.   That was all.   The Sophists had
misled the philosophic spirit.   The Byzantine concilia
codified sophism.

The schism of 1054, which separated the Church of
the Orient from the Pope, was the consecration of the
political schism which had been separating the Orient
from the Occident since the division of the Empire.
Each half of the ancient world, thenceforward, took
its course alone toward transformation and recasting.
The mold of Rome is offered to the barbarians at the

ALMENNO S. SALVATORE, (*Bergamo*) (v and vi Centuries). San Tommaso, interior.

risk of being broken under the pressure of their desires. Hellenism modified by Asia dominates the Orient through Constantinople until the Orient enslaves it through Stamboul. The orthodox icons are to represent the dying Greek idolatry as the Catholic icons, some centuries later, will represent Latin idolatry in its rebirth.

When we open one of those psalters that the Greek monks illuminated in the depths of their cloisters, between the sixth and the tenth century, we soon see it was of the dying idol of Greece that Christianity had asked the consecration of its own life. The whole history of the Jewish people is conveyed in these illuminations and takes on, under the names of the new divinities, the appearances of Greek mythology. David is Heracles when he fights, and Orpheus when he sings. The great goddess, with her beautiful arms, her beautiful face and breast, is always there in the idyllic landscape of the Alexandrian romances. At the time when Byzantium was young, Alexandria was still alive, and the growth of the one and the decline of the other mingle their voices confusedly. Asia, through Sassanian Persia, transmits to Byzantium the spirit of the high plateaus and the land of the rivers. But because of its Greek character, the city is above all sensitive to what the artists of the delta of the Nile have to offer it. They create the image of Hellenized Egypt—that profound portrait in which one looks into the limitless depths of the eyes that have lost their health; and with this revelation the Greco-Egyptian artists teach the decorative industries, mosaics, and painting, such as we see in the garlands of foliage, of fruits, of amours, and of animals that the painters of Pompeii also used to decorate their walls.[1]

---

[1] For the multiple origins of the art of Byzantium, see the *Manuel d'art byzantin*, by Charles Diehl.

In the illuminations of the manuscripts there is evidently nothing left of the freshness of the world that once went mad with the joy of its self-discovery. But it is the Greek spirit that is here. Man approaches the god with a free attitude; all of life finds its goal in him, as in a center of attraction, and the organization of life

RAVENNA (vi Century). Nave of Sant' Apollinare Nuovo.

is a natural one and well balanced in its elements. If this spirit is less apparent in the great painted idols and in the shining mosaics that decorate the convents and churches from top to bottom, it is because there is less of suppleness in the material, because the surfaces to be covered make severer demands, because a decorative scheme is more necessary, and because the artist is under closer surveillance. Sometimes, upon contact with the soil of Italy, at Ravenna, especially, the images turn into pictures full of movement, and figures pass

among the trees, among the herds, on the sea, or on
the shore. Almost always they are stiff, ranged in

RAVENNA (VI Century). Capital. (*Sant' Apollinare Nuovo.*)

parallel lines, and possessing no more of the humanity
of the Greeks than that expressed in the timid inclina-
tions they make, one toward another, bending their

heads and necks as if to recall the undulation of the great wave that once flowed over the pediments of the old temples. And yet, the soul of antiquity survives in the great, simple gestures, the silence, the calm glances, the indefinable nobility and majesty that descend from the agony of the past. The soul of antiquity survives through their mere existence, because the people can pray before them, because they have invaded the altar, the chapels, and the reliquaries with the gold and the silver and the ivory from which they are cut and the jewels with which they are incrusted. During a century and a half of imperial ordinances, of ecclesiastical interdicts, of revolts and carnage, when the great sculptures of Asia and Greece lie broken in the sanctuaries everywhere, no menace, no persecution will drive them out entirely. Dogmatic in their immobility, Asiatic in their material, they remain Greek before all else, because they express something which, while it may be transformed, vitiated, bastardized, cannot disappear—the instinct which urges a people to demand from the forms of nature the education of its spirit.

II

They are Greek, also, because, despite their fixed attitudes, despite the barbarous splendor that surrounds them and stiffens them, they radiate a profound sense of harmony. They are the troubled instinct, the living seed of a magnificent flower at the bottom of a plague-ridden pool; their fearful splendor is that of those blue or green flies incased in shining metal that breed on rotting meat. The spirit of Phidias has returned to earth and found its way to the charnel house, where life is blindly asserting itself anew. The whole glorious life that hung suspended in the pediments of the temples, swinging from one horizon to another, seems to have gathered itself in the depths of these Byzantine images. Even the formation of the heads denotes atrophy; life wells up in the great eyes that look out into space, into the darkness, and into the decomposition and the morbid fever in the soul of the people.

RAVENNA (vi Century). The Magi, mosaic, detail.
(*Sant' Apollinare Nuovo.*)

The inner spirit of the time makes its true appearance as these strange beings look down from their walls and try, in the prodigious fermentation that is taking place in man's consciousness, to reconcentrate the energy scattered piecemeal over all the pathways of the mind by the decadence of Hellas. The Byzantine idols have regained the immobility of the statues which, before the time of Myron and Phidias, characterized the concentration of all Hellenic effort as it prepared its conquest of an imposing and fugitive equilibrium. But

RAVENNA (VI Century). Women bearing offerings, mosaic. (Sant' Apollinare Nuovo.)

the calm of the Dorians and the smile of the Ionians
have left them. A dread anxiety dwells in their fixed
eyes and around them; instead of the great daylight
and the limpid space, there accumulates, in the darkness of the chapels, those magic phosphorescences that
steal over heaps of waste and over poisoned waters.
The world of Greece, despoiled of the rhythm which
had risen so quickly from the depths of its desires to the
summit of its will, returns to its origins, to demand of
an intoxication, in barbarous harmonies, the meaning
of its new presentiments. In the penumbra, inflamed
by the heavy glow that falls from the mosaics, one sees
but vaguely the motionless processions that carry one
—as across a long forgetfulness—back to Panathenaic
friezes, and one would imagine oneself in the heart of a
Hindu temple all covered with peacock tails petrified
in the light. Never did the heavens or the waters have
these blue, concentrated, opaque depths, knowing no
other limits than the smoky dream that extends them
to the infinite. The reds and the greens had never
shone with a more liquid splendor to dye the fields of
the earth and the broad mirrors of the sea. Never had
fire and gold mingled more harmoniously to give an
added glory to darkening suns or to envelop prayer
in greater voluptuousness. All the colors of the universe seem reduced to a few essential hues, deepened,
intensified, made somber through being piled up in
limpid glazes and through crystallizing in space the
vague harmonies that float across our minds and
harass our desires.

Seen through the reddish mist caused by the incense
and the ten thousand lighted candles, the Christ Panto-
crator, the Virgin, the apostles, and the saints crowned
with gold and dressed in shining robes, seemed far
away. High up, the great flattened cupola held the
nascent dream within the temple, which the half

cupolas at the angles and the three terminal apses connected with the soil by a series of wavelike steps—as the foothills of a mountain chain lead from the peaks

RAVENNA (VI Century). Interior of San Vitale.

to the plain. In the ancient temple everything combined to associate the meaning of its external form with the line of the mountains and the surrounding horizons; now it had turned inward, and Greek naturalism was brutally accommodated to the taste of peoples who had been enervated by Oriental life. Whatever the gathered force on the outside of Saint Sophia, whatever the weight of its round domes, it was by the luxury within that it held the crowds and stupefied the travelers to Constantinople who spread afar the glory of the Greek Empire.

Never did material luxury such as this bind popular sentiment to the letter of a religion which claimed to represent pure spirit. The veined marbles, the polychromed mosaics, the great paintings on the vaults and the walls, the pendentives which permitted the heavy circle of the cupola with its constellations to be inscribed exactly in the square of the building, the silver barrier of the sanctuary, the altar of gold, the tribune of gold, the six thousand candlesticks of gold, the swarm of incrusted gems which covered the gold of the tribune and the altar with a stream of sparks, the censers, crosses, enameled statues, reliquaries, tiaras, and diadems, the rigid, embossed robes in which living idols—the emperor and the patriarch—were held motionless: the whole was like an enormous sphere of diamond, shot through by flames, a resplendent vision suspended from garlands of light. The promised paradises were realized here below.

And yet when the temple is quite bare, as at Périgueux, for example, or when the mosaics, by their tone, are so incorporated in the edifice that, in the warm and reddish penumbra, one sees nothing but what properly belongs to the thick walls, the sturdy and massive pillars, nothing but curving lines, vaults, arches, and semicircles, a strange sense of harmony comes upon one little by little. The virtue of numbers, that mysterious power that is ever present and active in great architecture, on which all the masters depend for authority, which they always invoke and never formulate—the virtue of numbers is imposed with a formidable, monotonous, and musical authority. Yes, the flattened cupola prevents the dream from rising, but the dream turns and re-turns upon itself unceasingly, in closed coils, in a moving geometry that reproduces, summarizes, petrifies the gravitation of the heavens. The golden spheres turn in their round. Sophistics, which had taken refuge in the councils, and mathematics, which had been exiled, fuse in a pure flash, to inclose architecture in the obedient orbit of the silent worlds.

III

Here, doubtless, is where we must seek the highest expression of an epoch when barbarous luxury crushed intelligence, when the latter was reduced to shutting itself up in the solitary enjoyment of harmonic mysteries which were transmitted from one to another by the initiated. Outside the circles of the adepts, the art of Byzantium was never fully developed, for it was enchained with gold, rendered motionless by dogma and by bureaucratic regulations which fixed the social and professional life of the corporations and the artists, down to its smallest details. Even so, the rise of Byzantine art to its heavy flight was interrupted for more than a century by the edicts of Leo the Isaurian and of his successors who proscribed images. The cult of the icons triumphed only after a hundred years of proscriptions, killings, and furious vandalism. When the images reappeared, the tradition was shattered, the root of the effort was cut, the artists of Byzantium were dispersed by exile into the near-by Orient, into Italy, and as far as Spain and France. If Byzantine art survived, it was because the illuminators continued their work in the monasteries right through the iconoclastic periods; it was because a renewal of energy followed the effort that Constantinople was to make in

ISTRIA (VI Century). The Visitation. (*Church of Parenzo.*)

throwing back the Slavic invasion and the Mohammedan invasion; above all, it was because, with the
Crusaders, a great current of life traversed the country.
During the two centuries that this current lasted, it
filled Byzantium, Salonika, and Syria with those

Rome (ix Century). Church of Saint Praxed. Mosaic.

basilicas with the polygonal towers—so poor on the
outside, with their flattened, tile-covered domes, with
their indigent and dry material, but so rich in their
interior, where, from a blue and green darkness, elongated figures look down out of great eyes. This new
life installed itself in the cradle of Venice, penetrated
to the heart of the Arab caliphates, to Bagdad, to Abys-
sinia, where it still persists, invaded Christianized
Russia to combine there later on with obscure Asiatic
influences which the Mongol invasion brought from
Persia, from India, and even from China. It is through

this other current that we explain the icons with their gems and gold, and also the golden cupolas, blown up and bulbous, flattened or elongated, spindling or twisted into rhythmic curves. Everywhere in Europe, up to the hour when the French soul—after having concentrated in the springs of its inspiration all the

Rome (ix Century). Bas-relief of S. Maria in Cosmedin.

currents that had come from the Greek, the Hindu, and the Arabian Orient, from the Scandinavians and the Romans—began, in turn, to pour itself over the Occident, everywhere, for three or four hundred years, the stiff arabesque of Byzantium was found—its flat, symbolic animals, its wheels, its crosses with splayed arms and its bas-reliefs that have the appearance of thorn bushes. In the capitals of columns, in the embroideries of metal, of stone, and of wood that cover the balustrades, doors, and caskets, in the enamel

sheathing of reliquaries, sacred vases, and censers, and
in the rigid folds of priestly garments, we witness the
steady invasion of a monotonous and systematic art of
ornamentation. Its character of monotony and system
is the evident mark of the persistence of Greek genius
—forced by intelligence to formulate a harmony which

ROME (IX Century). Bas-relief of S. Maria in Cosmedin.

flees the heart of the artist to dwell in the mind of the
theorists. But with this characteristic we must consider the profusion of the ornament, which is the evident mark of the persistence of the Romanized genius
of Asia, compelled by sensuality to express a richness of
impression which the mind of the theorists cannot tear
from the heart of the artist. The overabundant flavor
of Roman decoration fuses, in a stiff and dull, but
impressive, ensemble, with the feeling for balance and
selection that characterized Greek decoration. The
merchants of Byzantium inundated the world with

carved ivories, gold objects incrusted with enamels and
pearls, cloths of gold, and golden reliquaries set with
uncut polished gems.   In these objects, which were for
use in the church and which were exported in such profusion, we see how the hard patience of the carvers and

BYZANTINE-ASIATIC ART.   Sculptured parapet.

the lapidaries succeeded in overcoming the moral passivity of the barbarians.   Through the Byzantine
artisan a semblance of tradition was kept up everywhere; what was left of the effort of Rome and Athens
was communicated unconsciously to the sensibility of
the new peoples; an indefinite and floating, but real,
transition was established between Europe and Asia,
between the spirit of antiquity and the spirit of the
Middle Ages.

When man's energy for an ascent is exhausted, when
a social and political group becomes the motionless

center of gravitation for a world, it is historically necessary that revolution or invasion renew or destroy that
world. All the blood sweated by the Middle Ages and
all the gold that was heaped up were suffocating Constantinople. Other centers of light were growing in

PÉRIGUEUX (x Century). Nave of Saint-Front.

power. Islam was approaching its summit. The Crusaders, from the end of the eleventh century onward,
were hurling Europe upon the Orient in troubled torrents. The barbarians of the west fell on the fabulous
cities of the east as the barbarian of the north had
marched on Rome. A hundred years after they had
pillaged Jerusalem, a city of the Infidel, the Franks
pillaged Byzantium, a Christian city. Europe breaks
down the rampart that protects her from Asia.

There was in the fourteenth century, indeed, after the
fall of the Frankish Empire, a last outburst of energy
which spread the art of Constantinople over Rumania,

MONREALE (Sicily) (XII Century). The Cathedral.

Serbia, and Macedonia. The mosaics became more living, more full of movement; the world moved; Giottesque Italy, after having undergone the influence of Byzantium, affected Byzantium in its turn. Great painting was perhaps to have emerged from the confusion of the primitives and to prepare, as it did at the

SALONIKA (XIV Century). Church of the Holy Apostles.

same moment in the Occident, the reign of the individual. But here the effort was too old and had been too often repulsed, the Greek rhythm that was prolonging its echo in other countries was giving way under the pressure of Asia, which was overflowing at every point. It was too late. Even if the Turks had not taken Constantinople, men would have seen that the hour had struck. Manuel Panselinos, who, about the beginning of the sixteenth century, is to cover the convents of Mount Athos with frescoes, seems completely, even too completely, Italianized. And about the end of the same century Theotocopuli flees his

Greek island, leaving behind him nothing but the letter of Byzantium and bearing off its spirit alone, in the sumptuous envelopment of Venetian painting. He sublimated the opulence of Venice in the flame of a heart that is unique in history, that was capable, by its sole action, of making fertile the stormy and solitary soul of Spain. It was too late. In reality, when Mohammed II planted the standard of the Prophet on the Golden Horn and installed Islam in Saint Sophia, the crisis was ending and no event could have modified the issue. In Palestine, in Egypt, in Sicily, in Tunis, in Spain, in France—everywhere about the Mediterranean, the two mystic currents born of the old Semitic ideal had been clashing for three hundred years, repulsing each other at some points, mingling at others, and revealing to each other, despite themselves and unknown to themselves, the resemblance of all men and the unity of their desire.

THE DESERT

Chapter VI. ISLAM

I

HE two religions confront each other.
The drama begins, and we must observe
that the ideas which Islam was bringing
to the Occidental civilizations and the
results of those ideas were more numerous than those which Christianity had,
up to that time, offered to the civilizations of the Orient.
Islam, which in a savage burst of disinterested faith
had launched forth, poor and free, upon the conquest
of the earth, having no homeland save its tents and the
infinity of a dream which it pursued in the gallop of
its horses, in the wind that carried the burnooses and
the clouds of dust—Islam, throughout the Middle
Ages, was the true champion of the never-attained idea
which, the more we seek to grasp it, plunges us only
more deeply into the future.

When Justinian had closed the schools of Athens and had driven the artists and scholars from the Empire—at about the period when Gregory the Great burned the Palatine library—it was with the Sassanian King Chosroes that almost all of them took refuge. History has magnificent strokes of chance. The Arabs, masters of Iran, found there the treasures snatched from the shipwreck, and it was these that permitted their scholars to initiate the new Europe into the thought of antiquity. While the shadows were growing thicker over the Occident, the caliphs were opening universities, digging canals, tracing gardens, reviving the study of geometry, geography, and medicine, creating algebra, and covering the conquered lands with caravanseries, mosques, and palaces. Against the black background of the history of those times we see their works as in a dazzling fairy tale, a great heroic story from the *Thousand and One Nights*.

The miracle of the Arabian mind is that it remained itself everywhere and dominated everywhere without, of itself, creating anything. Anarchic, nomadic, and a unit, as little bounded by moral as by material frontiers, it could, through that very fact, adapt its genius to that of the conquered peoples and at the same time persuade the vanquished to allow themselves to be absorbed in the unity of that genius. Coptic in Egypt, Berber in the Moghreb and in Spain, Persian in Persia, Indian in India, Islam allows the converted races—in Egypt, in the Moghreb, in Spain, in Persia, and in India—to express, according to their nature, the new enthusiasm which it knew so well how to communicate to them. Wherever it established itself, it remained master of the people's heart.

When Abu-Bekr proclaimed the holy war after the death of Mohammed, the first conquerors of Syria and Egypt installed their immobile dream in the

Cairo (vii Century). Interior of the mosque of Amru.

Byzantine or Coptic churches which they came upon
in their path. The earlier consecration of the edifice
did not matter much to them. They were at home
everywhere. They covered the mosaics and the frescoes with a coat of paint, hollowed out a mihrab in the
wall facing toward Mecca, and lost themselves in
ecstasy, their eyes fixed on that spot. When, in Egyptian, Greek, or Roman ruins, they found ancient
columns, they assembled them haphazard, often with
the capital downward, all mingling like trees in the
same living unity. On three sides of the inner court,
where the fountain for ablutions brought to the dried-
out soil the eternal freshness of the earth, their parallel
rows of columns carried ogive arcades which supported
the flat roofs common to the hot countries. The outer
walls remained as bare as ramparts. Egypt recognized
its dream in that of its conquerors.

But enthusiasm creates action and incites to discovery. Three centuries have passed, the era of the
conquests has closed. Islam extends, *via* northern
Africa, from the plateau of Iran to the Pyrénées. The
nomad enjoys his conquered domains, arouses the
energies that had grown weary there, and consents to
animate with his spirit the plastic genius of the vanquished peoples, who have become fanatics. All the
oases that sow the deserts of Africa and Spain transform themselves into white cities, are surrounded with
crenelated walls, and behold, springing up rapidly,
palaces rich in shade where the emirs come to seek
the cool after having crossed the sands. When the
horde or the caravan has marched long days in the
reddish and moving circle whose edge is never reached,
it is no longer the bouquet of palms that it sees when
the burning air that vibrates and rises has hung a
vision in the sky: it is a pink or bluish haze wherein
terraces, rounded needles, and cupolas tremble behind

an imponderable veil. The Moslem soul, even at the
hour when it thought it had gained control over itself,
never grasped more than a mirage, a cool shadow,
spread for an hour between two sheets of flame over
which the conquerors passed.

CONSTANTINOPLE. Saint Sophia (532), with Turkish minarets.

When their great drive was ended, when the dream
which had always surged like a wave before them found
itself stopped by the sea or by barriers of mountains
or by the walls of Byzantium or the squadrons of the
Franks, it had to find some other escape and, the horizon being closed, it had to move upward. Now it
stifles under the Byzantine cupola, it spreads and
stretches out under the ceiling of the Egyptians.[1]
The heavy semicircular arch of the basilicas has already
become the broken arch that launches upward. The
spherical cupola will likewise take on ascending lines.

[1] Al. Gayet, *L'Art Arabe.*

It will find again the old Assyrian forms that Sassanian Persia had continued until the times of Islam. The slender ovoid dome carries the eye upward until we get the illusion that the dream of the builders is gliding with its forms and follows its fleeing curve to escape at its summit; the base of the cupola is strangled so that its point of support may be masked and the

CAIRO. Tombs of the Mamelukes.

mystery of the suspended infinite be realized. Beginning with the fourteenth century, the columns disappear and the bareness of the great naves evokes the desert, with its circular horizon and the vault of heaven—the only repose for the eyes as they look upward. Outside, above the vertical walls that are as naked as the soil, one sees the cupola rising in purity, accompanied by the flying minarets from which, by the voice of the muezzins, the words from above descend at the hour of prayer.

The mysticism of the nomads had found its resting place. Only the Turk, who mirrored his heavy soul in the dull tones of Persian faïences, retained the Byzantine curve with the flattened cupola, invisible under the clumps of black cypresses from which shoot up the pointed roofs of the cylindrical minarets. It was without knowing it that he inherited the glory of Byzantium; he did not see the torrent of the white, blue, and pink stones streaming to the sea, lighting up in the morning, and dying out at evening, nor the domes of gold which, till the fall of night, retained the flame of the twilight. But, aside from the Turks, the Moslem architects, from Egypt to Spain, attached themselves by instinct to the upward-springing forms of the windows and cupolas, and here their mystic aspiration was not limited, even if, with the changing direction of their genius, they changed the distribution of the domes, the disposition of the naves, or the type of the minarets, which are now round, now square, now octagonal—smooth or damascened. The Egyptian mosques remained as bare as the spirit of the desert; the mosques of the Moghreb and of Spain crossed their arcades of black-and-white arch stones and gave a double rise to their rows of cylindrical columns that are like thickets of palm trees from which droop the long leaves. The great mosque of Cordova, dating from the time of uncompromising faith, is almost a dark forest. In its shadows, made denser by the perspective of the silent shafts, one feels the presence of a terrible infinite that is impossible to seize.

II

The Moghreb artist varied the form of the arcades and gave diversity of aspect as between one hall and another, one alcove and another, in the mosques and

especially in the palaces, the alcazars and the alhambras of Andalusia, where one's enervated fancy wanders from the halls of red and gold, black, emerald, or
turquoise blue to the great colonnaded courts, to the
paved gardens where the perfume of the lemon trees,
the mimosas, and the orange trees weighs on the stifling air, and to the motionless shadows under which
basins of marble offer to the yews long mirrors of pure
water in which to dip their image. Empty of animate
forms, the mind of the Moghreb artist sought restlessly
to break the monotony of its plastic visions by com-
bining familiar lines and twisting them in every direction. The semicircular arch drew its points together,
curved itself into a horseshoe, was narrowed, fore-
shortened, splayed, loaded with stalactites, with cells
like those of a beehive, and was fretted to a greater or
less extent with festoons and lacework. And when
the formula was exhausting itself there came the arabesque that bit into the stone, carved into openwork
the plaster moldings wherein the stained-glass windows
were incased, and invaded the rectangular framework
of the arcades. It sent its winding flame even to the
inner surfaces—blue, red, white, and gold—of the
niches and vaults that offered an escape from the
world outside, from the sun and the soil whose torrid
uniformity heightened the charm of the multicolored
paradises stretching out in the cool shadow and the
silence over the perfumed waters and the soft divans.

When linear ornament had attained its full sweep,
it invaded the mosque, like the alcazar, from the base
of the walls to the top of the cupolas. Disdainful or
ignorant of the form of a world that offered little to
attract the eye, the Arab had the time to pursue, to
combine, to vary, and to multiply his arabesques.
In the interlacing rosework, the polygonal ornaments,
the stylized inscriptions, all the ornamental motifs

issuing together from a vague and subtle imagination,
ecstasy, doubt, serenity, and distress were expressed
by the obliqueness, the verticality, the waviness, the
detours, and the horizontality of the lines. All the
ornamental motifs corresponded with the obscure and
complex ensemble of man's feelings and were developed

CORDOVA (VIII Century). Interior of the great mosque.

to the point of mingling, superimposing, and juxta-
posing themselves in squares, circles, bands, ovals,
and fans. They passed without apparent effort—like
the soul itself—from exaltation to depression, from
reverie to logic, from rectangular forms to rounded
forms, and from the fantasy of the unrestrained curves
to the severities of the geometrical figures. Everything
that detached from the walls, the *nimbars*,[1] the banisters, and the gratings, was embroidered with interlacing

[1] In Moorish architecture the term for the niche in the mosque indicating
the direction of Mecca.

lines; stone and plaster were perforated, wood was inlaid, plaques of bronze, silver, and gold were carved. . . . An immense system of tapestries and embroideries seems to be spread over the walls, to cover the arcades, to distribute the light from the windows, and some-

CAIRO. Detail of the façade of the Kalaoum Mosque (1284).

times to fall on the cupolas and the graded minarets where the interlacings and the arabesques became more and more complicated. The whole thing became like a hanging fairyland, like cobwebs in the great garden of space, dust, and sunlight.

The arabesque had had its hour of concrete life. Geometric ornament, into which it was to evolve, is never born spontaneously; it realizes, in the brain of

GRANADA (XIII Century). Hall of the Abencerrages in the
Alhambra.

the artists, the final stylization of a motif from nature, just as the mathematical formula is, for the scientist, the form of expression which a truth derived from experience must take, and thereby grow inert. The

arabesque was born of the twining together of flowers and leaves, as we first find it around the arcades of the old mosque of Ibn-Touloun at Cairo, when, after the end of the conquest, the imagination of the Arabs was less tense and had the leisure to become complicated and the desire to become subtler. It took on a far rarer quality when the fourteenth century had fixed its law of decoration. And this progressive passage from the living line to the ideographic line, from the ideographic line to the geometric line, sharply defines the spiritual direction of this art. When the regular polygon made its appearance in the *répertoire* of ornament, the Arab geometrists tried to deduce from it general principles which would permit them to extend the system of the polygon to the whole of decoration. Arab art, from that time on, became an exact science[1] and allowed the reverie of the mystic to be inclosed in the hard language of perfectly bare abstraction.

Mosque of the Aljafería, decorative detail. (*Museum of Saragossa.*)

Born of the desert, where there are no forms, where space alone reigns and has neither beginning nor end, Arabian spirituality found its supreme expression in the

---

[1] A formula drew from the polygon and brought back to it all the geometrical motifs of decoration.

arabesque which also has neither beginning nor end.
The eye cannot come to rest on it. It is like those
voices of the silence that we hear and follow in their
interminable round when we listen only to ourselves,
and when our feelings and ideas are enmeshed confusedly in a kind of languid pleasure which we experi-

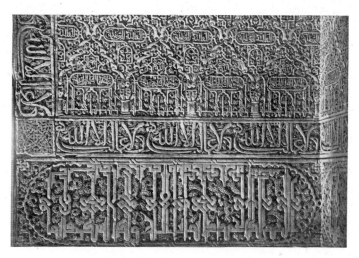

GRANADA (XIII and XIV Centuries). Ornaments of the Hall
of the Ambassadors in the Alhambra.

ence when we allow our consciousness to become
closed to the impressions of the world. If the reverie aims to reach some conclusion, if the metaphysical abstraction seeks to clarify itself, it can
find no other language—since it has remained outside of life — than the mathematical abstraction
which compels the mind to move in an absolute of
convention.

It is singular that the most precise of the languages
that we employ, the most useful to our modern civilizations, should also be the one which—when we seek dis-

interestedly the pleasure of its abstract creations—
should awaken in us only those sentiments that are
most lacking in precision and most impossible to seize
upon. It is singular that this instrument of pure
mind should serve only our most material needs, and
that, when used to explore the spiritual world, it should
be the most impotent of all in penetrating its mystery.
All-powerful when we desire to know what motionless
matter is, it is of no use whatever as soon as we seek
enlightenment regarding living matter in its activity
and its evolution. If it is an incomparable weapon for
a mind that dominates it, it is dead for a mind that
can be dominated by it.

Art, like life itself, is in a constant state of evolution.
If scientific certainty is perchance substituted in the
soul of the artist for the desire for that certitude which
not only torments him but gives him strength, the need
for effort is destroyed within him, and enthusiasm
weakens because static realization has replaced the
constant renewal of desire. When mathematics is
introduced into the domain of the artists, it should
remain in the hands of the architects as an instrument
whose purpose is to define and determine the logic of
the edifices they construct. But architecture cannot
pretend to do more than adapt a building to its utilitarian function and suggest, by the direction of its
lines, the most powerful, but also the vaguest, of the
great collective sentiments. It is not the prerogative
of mathematics to monopolize form and thereby inclose it within a wall of pure abstraction. When it
prevents sculpture from developing and the painted
image from being born, it condemns the people which
it expresses to remain slaves to the temporary form,
which they had given to their idea; it condemns them
to die.

What endows it with its greatness endows it also

with its weakness. It is slain by the realization of its purposes. It does not renew itself, since the individual cannot break the definitive formulas in which, by its own will, it had inclosed itself. The mosque and the

GRANADA (XIV Century). Patio de la Alberca
in the Alhambra.

Arabian world grow motionless together, exactly at the moment when the Occidental peoples are emerging from the collective rhythms. It is in the hope of a discovery half seen that men gain the power they express in their work, and from this moment on the mosque builders begin to lose courage.

Mosque of the Aljafería, detail. (*Museum of Saragossa.*)

If the desert reveals to men the unity of mind, it is also responsible for the mind's forgetting the few forms that are presented. From the desert came the antisocial and anticivilizing conception of the two irreconcilable worlds of the immaterial soul and the material body. After the death of a people that has failed to discover and to express its accord with the external universe, there remains nothing of that people, however great its courage; the spirit which men follow is that which knows how to animate with its life the forms of that universe. It is the rocks, the water, and the trees which, through the spirit of the Greeks, made the Occident fertile. Every time that history hesitates, we look to the pediments of the temples where men recognize themselves in the gods.

III

The Arab, it is true, never compels the artist to refrain entirely from representing animate life, and sometimes it trembles furtively on the walls of the palaces and mosques of Spain and Morocco. Like all the monotheistic peoples who have been modeled by the desert, he was only obeying his instinctive repugnance for everything that is living form. Religion represses instinct only during periods of decadence. During periods of strength, instinct sweeps religion along with it in whatever direction it chooses. In Egypt or in Syria, Mohammedan art had the nakedness, the sadness, and the grandeur of the desert. In the depths of the cool grottoes of the Moghreb and of Spain, where the caliphs came to listen to the pholosophers and to breathe the odor of the lemon trees after their cavalry had reaped its harvest, Mohammedan art seemed to work with blocks of gold ground in clotted blood. In India, it allowed the whole flood of the world of matter to invade the mosque. On the plateaus of Iran it was like a field of flowers.

Persia no more resembles the sandy plains of the eastern Mediterranean than it does the Andalusian or

CAIRO (XVII Century). Interior of the Bordeini Mosque.

Moroccan valleys, which are forever contested by hard shadow and by fire. To the west, in the upper regions which border the central desert, high above the dust, three thousand meters above sea level, and thus so much nearer the stars, the air has the transparence,

PERSIA. Young men making a sacrifice, miniature.
(*Private Collection.*)

the limpidity of glass. In the breath of the wind the
white meadows and the pink meadows there are mottled
like watered silk, and from spring to autumn the broad
strips of poppies and the fields of grain run the gamut
of all the uncertain color tones, from tender green to
golden yellow. The skies, where the pigeons fly, and
the clouds have those delicate tints that one can
observe in the earliest blossoming of trees. The cities
are deluged with roses.[1]

When one approaches them their assemblies of
domes, ovoid, swelling, or twisted, and their long,
straight minarets that emerge from the groves of
cypresses and plane trees, seem like memories already
blurred by uncertainty. In turquoise blues, burnt-
out pinks, pale greens, and dulled yellows the mirage
has taken on the appearance of an aërial water color
painted with vapor on the fleeing horizon that is known
to artists who have followed the path of the caravans
from oasis to oasis. Near-by one sees crumbling walls,
cracking cupolas, minarets whose decoration of interlacing black and white is scaling off. It is ruins that
are before us. But they are the ruins of a recent period.
The enamel that clothes them, the old Chaldean enamel
that ancient Persia had made known to China and that
China brought back to Iran by the Tartar hordes —
the enamel has kept its glassy brilliancy under the
coating of silicate that covers the brick. Violets, blues,
and browns, ivory whites, lilacs, yellows, and greens,
shine in these enamels, pure or in combinations that
make rosebushes and anemone or iris flowers over
white inscriptions and arabesques of gold. The pulpy
flesh and the pearly surface of the flowers marry and
swell the living garlands that here replace the abstract
arabesque in which the inventive faculty of the Arabs

[1] Pierre Loti, *Vers Ispahan.*

found its expression. Under the high ogive of the
doors framed with a crust of enamel, the dim glow of
turquoises, amethysts, and lapis lazuli makes a creeping
phosphorescence; under the inner crown of the domes
whose rounded softness knows nothing of the mystic
impulse of the desert, the ornaments shaped like

PERSIA. Elephants fighting, miniature.
(*Musée des Arts Décoratifs.*)

honeycomb drip with stalactites. Sometimes the
interior of the cupolas sends forth flashes from plates
of glass combined with prisms.

It was in an ancient and forgotten period that the
people spread on the walls the Persian carpets resem-
bling dark, plowed earth into which crushed flowers
have been pressed. In their place shone enameled
brick when, at the end of the sixteenth century, the
great Abbas suddenly caused the monumental fairyland of Ispahan to be built. The Persian school of
painting which was born at that moment had only to
listen to the counsels of the men who gave the wealth
of decoration to the enameled mosques in order to

reach, through Djahangir, through Mani, and through
Behzade especially, the highest living expression that
Mussulman art has known. The whole industry of the
potter, everywhere most ancient and most durable,
brought its necessary contribution to this art also.
The Persian pot is already painting crystallized in
fire. Its decoration, which is not very rich in images,
is doubtless the richest of all in its ever new stylization of the summits of sensation. Nothing remains of
the world of the senses save what is profoundest in
color, what is most immaterial in the object, most
fleeting in the form. Neither the sky nor the sea nor
the flowers are painted there, but beds of flowers break
through with their freshest corollas, great stretches of
sky with their pearliest billows of cloud, and the immensity of the seas with their shining surface. In
spots, in creeping lines, in drops, in clusters, and in
mottlings, the most elaborate and elusive principles of
the flowers, the sky, and the sea are evoked according
to the changes in the harmonies with which they fill
the memory. The rare painting of Persia arrests this
fugitive splendor in every form depicted. The school
flowers suddenly, to fade quickly, and to die in two
centuries because it had given out too much perfume
and brilliancy. It was like an enchanted dream in
which for an hour there were blended the passionate
sensuality of India, the mannerism of the Persians, the
slow science of the Chinese, and the great fairy dream
world of the Arabs.

Rolling its treasure from the deserts of Arabia to the
happy islands of Japan, and from the Moghreb to
India, Persian painting is like a deep ocean made up
of all the ingenuous desires of the flesh, all the frankness
of its intoxications, all the puerilities, the smiles, the
wild and touching fancies of the primitive peoples
suddenly carried beyond the rosy gates of the paradise

BEHZADE (Persia). Man painting.
(*From Les Miniatures Persanes.*)

253

of art! . . . It was an Eden where tigers trod on meadows full of flowers, where men and women in robes of silk— green, red, or blue—men and women with delicate noses, little mouths, very long black eyes, and oval faces, were seated in a circle on beautiful embroidered carpets. Trees in bloom rose against backgrounds all of gold. For the Persian there could never be enough flowers: there are flowers on those lawns of almost black green which make one feel that living water is near; there are flowers among all the leaves, flowers on the carpets, flowers everywhere, enormous flowers whose trace is to be found even on the little cups of coral and of porcelain from which the ladies and gentlemen with golden spoons dip the candied flowers. In landscapes of red, green, or gold, whose natural symphonies take on the quality of a deep and precious velvet, nervous, delicate black horses with curving necks pass at a gallop, each bearing a proud rider, a falcon on his wrist, a brilliant aigrette on his turban. Multicolored birds fly in the trees—they are genii who talk with men, far better than those golden birds with topaz eyes which flew and beat their wings about the throne of the Byzantine autocrat. Magical palaces open their gates of light and their porticos of lace; their enameled or damascened walls are embroidered with gems; their ceilings are of crystal; silent carpets lead to thrones of gold where golden peacocks spread tails of emerald; there are gardens with vases of por- phyry and jets of water where the sun lights up opals, graded white terraces, and cupolas, pink, azure, or milky. Even in the depths of the night they gleam like the snow at dawn. When evening came, one listened to musicians on the blue waters, one breathed the odor of the fruits that gleam in the black heart of the trees. The djinns descended among men with baskets of rubies and baskets of topazes, and the

rising moon was like a pearl fallen from the necklace
of stars that encircles the sky. . . . All this is painted
with subtle strokes, with brilliant tones that die out
in their harmonies, with the tremulous purity of the

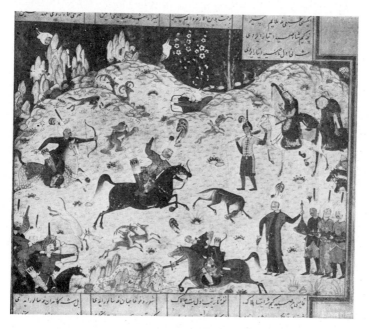

PERSIA (XVI Century). The Hunt, miniature.
(*Bibliothèque Nationale.*)

shadows, and with the unchanging light of the day.
Here are all the Thousand and One Nights dreamed of
by the old story-tellers who, from evening to morning,
talked inexhaustibly to the gay travelers seated in a
circle under the tent.

Here are strange races, veritable masses of contrasts;
and the deeper they plunge into the desert, the farther
they live from the cities, the heavier the sun that beats

upon them, the more marked and surprising these contrasts become. Here are men who wear robes of green and red silk under burnooses of white wool, and who cover the harness of their horses with gold. They forge weapons and incrust them with gems; they keep their water pure in damascened copper. They know only silence and melancholy contemplation, or else frenzied laughter and uproar. They forget their natural sobriety to enter suddenly on a round of incredible feasting. They despise death, they despise life. Among them a state of ecstasy follows hard upon crises of unbridled sensuality. Their paradise of abstractions is peopled with women. Their terrible fanaticism is unequaled by anything but their terrible inertia; the flight of time is nothing for them, and they let their temples crumble with an indifference as marked as the ardor which they expended in building them.

The excessive climate, the great contrasts of nature, and the life of the nomad have created this ignorance of—or this disdain for—the balance of soul that we love. The oasis is too cool after the sands, the water is so sweet to the burnt lips, the cities offer to the wanderers such hot pleasures and such gold! The rich man shall have a hundred wives and the poor man shall have none, and so there is a gap that can never be filled between the metaphysical absolutes and the worst bestiality. But the races of the Occident fill this gap by exploring all the roads that must be traveled in order to rise from and by means of sensual life to the threshold of the heroic life. With these races of the Occident we must number some of the Oriental races which belong to the same ethnic groups as the European peoples. It was, doubtless for this reason, that the Persians—whose mind was less spacious, perhaps, but certainly more curious than that of the Semites—

Turkish (?) Art. The Repast.
(*From Les Miniatures Persanes.*)

never swerved from their historic role, which is to
carry on forever into the future a little of the immemorial civilizations of the country of the rivers. It was
for this reason again that in Persian art there was no
break in continuity between Sassanian Persia and Mussulman Persia, and that the carpets and the vases
continued to be made in the same workshops. Because
of their racial quality, also, the Persians recovered
from the Tartar invasions and outlived the Arabs in
their period of greatness by three centuries. It was for
the same reason, also, that the idol worshipers of
Byzantium will one day be justified by the moral history of the world, as they triumphed, ten centuries
ago, in their struggle with those who were opposed to
the idols. A resolutely spiritual religion must, doubtless, do without images, even at the risk of declining,
at the risk of dying; but what we need to know is
whether it is better for us to cultivate pure spirit or the
images. It is a weak defense of the iconoclastic emperors to show them as encouraging art whenever it was
separate from religion. Art is one; its growth increases
with the growth of a living faith, regardless of the way
in which it is clothed or labeled or of the role in which
men try to arrest it; and if religion dies of freedom, art
lives only through its introducing into the world a little
more freedom each time it manifests itself. To forbid
art to drink at any one source is to dry up all the sources
at once.

If idolatry did not save Byzantium, it was because
Byzantium was not a beginning, but an end, a rotten
fruit of the Greek tree. But it was idolatry which
made Egypt and Greece and India, which unchained
the great Gothic revolution and the Italian and Flemish
Renaissance, and which, later, at the threshold of our
own time, aroused sensualism, transformism, and the
admirable, vital investigation of the whole last cen-

tury in Europe. All durable civilizations are born of
idolatry, obliged, as they have been, to demand that

PERSIA (XVI Century). Carpet, fragment.

external nature surrender to them the inexhaustible
treasure of her teachings in order that they may give
reality to the images that are within them. We cannot
demand that humanity live in the desert forever,

when we see that even the peoples of the desert seek the oases.

We may not believe that among idolatrous peoples the superior minds have freed themselves from idolatry: they have freed themselves by it. It is they who, by it, by the living relationships that it revealed to them, have introduced reason into the world, not as an end in itself, but as an incomparable instrument for analysis and for the liberation of the individual. The peoples who recognize nothing but the spirit are the only ones who have never been able to detach themselves from the metaphysical idols which the blankness of the desert imposes on their meditations, because they have been powerless to seize upon their thought and confront it with life.

Moreover, far from arresting the dream, the image offers it a point of support, which enables it to keep within the limits of human reality, and at the same time the dream is broadened because the relationships which the image reveals to it cause other relationships to be suspected, other images to be desired; and so men draw from realization—always a dead thing—the ever-living hypothesis. Idolatry leads to experience and through it to action. When we have lost our equilibrium, it is to the idols that we turn to invoke them to teach us form and life once more. Science is the aspect that our eternal idol worship wears at the present time. Idolatry saves the world when nothing but a little invisible dust is left of the great unbalanced dreams which have been lived by the prophet-peoples fashioned by the desert.

ROUEN

Chapter VII. CHRISTIANITY AND THE COMMUNE

I

THE Semitic spirit, at the decline of the old world, tried to conquer Europe through the apostles of Christ, as it was to take possession of western Asia and of Africa through the knights of Islam. But through the desert, the bare sky, and life without movement the religion of Mohammed remained near to its sources. It could easily retain its original form and spiritualize everything, even to its

TRANSLATOR'S NOTE.—The following lines from the *Encyclopædia Britannica* will explain M. Faure's preference for the words "ogive" and "ogival" as against the more common but less precise word "Gothic," in speaking of the architecture dealt with in this chapter and the next.

"A very great step in advance was made by the invention or application of diagonal ribs under the intersection of the plain groined vault. This

expression in plastics. Europe offered to the Jewish
idea an outline less suited to it. The contact with the
cultivated land, with the woods, with the running
waters, with the clouds, and with mobile and living
form, was to impose on the religion of Saint Paul a
sensuous and concrete form which turned the idea
from its original direction, little by little, and was to
bring the peoples of the Occident back to the course
of their natural destiny.

It is true that the impress had been made. The
Jewish apostolate, through the power for penetration
which it derived from its disinterested faith, carried
with it a disappointing dualism, but at the same time
it peopled the inner solitude of the masses who had
been forgotten by the civilizations of the past. Its
pitiless insistence on justice fortified the social instinct
in them. And it is thanks to this that the Greek spirit
and the Semitic spirit slowly brought about in the crucible of the Occident an accord of which Æschylus had
the presentiment and for which Jesus had the desire.

Had Christianity remained as Saint Paul desired it
and as the fathers of the Church defined it, it must
needs have turned its back upon the plastic interpre-
tations of the ideas which it introduced. But as it
wished to live, it obeyed the law which compels us to
give to our emotions the form of the things that we
see. In Rome, while it was groping in the shadow,
trying to tear its doctrine from the confused mass of

---

association of strengthening ribs in a cross form to each bay of the structure
forms the *ogive*, the characteristic form from which the alternative name
of Gothic, 'ogival,' has been derived. . . . The word 'Gothic' was applied
by Italian writers of the Renaissance to buildings later than Roman. What
we now call 'Gothic' the same writers called 'Modern.' Later the word
came to mean the art which filled the whole interval between the Roman
period and the Renaissance, and then, last of all, when the Byzantine and
Romanesque forms were defined, Gothic became the art which intervened
between the Romanesque era and the Renaissance."

the old myths, graven and painted figures were appearing, from the first century onward, upon the walls of the Catacombs. They announced new gods, to be sure, but their form remained pagan, even Greek, most often, for it was the Oriental slave who propagated the religion of Galilee in Rome. Grown clumsy in

CAHORS (XI Century). The cathedral, detail.

the hands of the poor people, the art which, above the street level, builds thermæ and amphitheaters, which covers villas with frescoes and gardens with statues, hesitates in the darkness underground. The soul of the people will not be silent until the day when official Christianity emerges from beneath the soil to take possession of the Roman basilicas and decorate them with pompous emblems. It will require ten centuries of seclusion before it finds its real expression and compels the upper classes to return to the deeper life and to embrace the hope which has been set free.

The organization of the new theocracy, the repeated invasions of the barbarians, hunger, torpor, and the frightful misery of the world between the fall of the

Autun (xi Century).   Capital from the nave of the cathedral.

Empire and the time of the Crusades, did not permit any people of western Europe to take root in its soil. In return, although every human tide carried away the new cities built on the newly made ruins, the tribes descending from the north succumbed, little by little, to the domination of the moral unity inherent in the Christian idea for which the trappings of the ancient civilizations offered an imposing framework. Over the heads of the peoples in their unhappiness, the instinct

POITIERS (XI Century). Church of Saint-Pierre.

of the military chiefs, who had rallied to the letter of organized Christianity, brings them into alliance with the higher clergy, whose spirit, through contact with the warrior class, becomes more and more harsh. When Gregory the Great, some years after Justinian, ordered the destruction of what remained of the old libraries and of the temple of the ancient gods, he consecrated the accord of Rome with the barbarians. The soul of antiquity was dead, indeed. The monarchies of the Orient gather up its last echoes, the monasteries stir up its dust.

18

The religious communities had remained, up to the Crusades, the only isles of light in darkened Europe. The cloistered luxury of a chosen few, a hothouse civilization, was the representative of sixty centuries of effort, of sensibility, of living realizations.   Thebes, Memphis, Babylon, Athens, Rome, and Alexandria

Moissac (xii Century).   Abacus of a capital of the cloister.

were contained within the four walls of a monastery, in old manuscripts thumbed by the hard men who opposed the necessary counterpoise of the Rule, to the frightful impulses of a world that had fallen back to the primitive state.   But it was around these walls, in these out-of-the-way valleys, away from the great highways which saw the massacres that, here and there, the people of the countryside were assembling to shape the future.   The north of Gaul during the Merovingian period had no other centers of activity in the chaos of manners, races, and languages that hov-

ELNE (Pyrenées-Orientales) (XII Century). Belfry of the church.

ered over this agony of the burning cities and the ruined harvests.

In the south, on the contrary, tradition was still profoundly alive. The aqueducts, the arenas, the thermæ, and the temples were still erect in the landscape that is silvered by the forests of olive trees. The amphitheaters still opened their pure curve to the light. The sculptured sarcophagi were in their accustomed place, bordering the roads shaded by the plane trees that are whitened by winter when it despoils them of their leaves and that remain white under the dust of summer. On this burnt earth of southern France, which outlines itself against the sky with the sure lines that one finds again beside the bays of Greece, Gallo-Roman art united quite naturally the positivism of Rome, Hellenic elegance, and the fresh vitality of the Gauls. It declined but little, if at all, upon the passage of the Arabs, who were adopted by this burning soil. Nothing could arrest its fever. Under its violent sun, the blood of nomadic Asia mingled with that of Greco-Latin Gaul. It was a strange, cruel, perverse world, but one of intense, irrepressible life; its ideal was one of equality and it was freer and more extensive than the remainder of France when the division of the empire of Charlemagne had separated it from the north, which was beginning to discuss its problem of Frankish or Norman domination.

When an orgy of love and blood craves the excitement that results from the nervous tension of the higher culture, when morbid sensuality and exasperated intelligence arise from the same ground, the lightning that flashes from their meeting sets fires burning, and their flame leaps high into the air, fed by all the winds that blow, by the dust they bring, and by the debris of green wood and dead wood alike which they hurl into the blaze together. A hybrid

and convulsive art emerges from the earth, a trifle
frail, but so glowing in its intensity that its onrush
leaves a groove that cannot be effaced. The trail of
fire passed over Provence, surrounded Toulouse, and
ascended to the plateau of central France. The antique
columns were set up again round the nervous and
clumsy bas-reliefs that were painfully inscribed within
the rigid curve of the portals. Byzantium and Islam
deposited their ferment and their spark in the heart of
the material that still retained its memory of the
Romans; and the Crusades brought back to the stones,
stirring in their new animation, a disordered tribute of
memories of Greece and the Syrian world, and, with
these, the more distant echo of Persia and India.
When the Clunisians set to work upon the stones,
about the eleventh century, and erected them according
to Norman and Scandinavian ideas, which we see also
in the heavy jewels that bear the trace of the oldest
traditions of Asia, the great Romanesque style crystallized suddenly, to become, in the hands of the
monks, the purest architectural expression of organized
Christianity.

II

The church built on the plan of a cross evolved from
the old basilicas; stiff and thick-set, it has to make an
effort to lift up toward heaven its two burly towers,
vibrating with their bells, but unshaken by the wind.
If the heavy arch that weighed on the central nave
did not crush down its supports, it was because the
other naves were loaded with lengthwise vaults supported by enormous walls which suppressed the empty
spaces where the openings for windows would have
been. The farther the nave was extended, the thicker
the walls became, and the deeper became the darkness
in the sanctuary, daubed with red and with blue. The

short painted pillars there, with their capitals cut into by crude forms, seemed to bear the formidable weight of a sky filled with eyes that judge and with gates that close on paradises seen but for a brief moment. The edifice was like a crouching monster whose over-heavy

MOISSAC (XII Century). Detail from the western door.

spine bore down on its thick paws. In the center of the silent cloisters, which cut out a square of shade in the light of the south, the soil might crack with drought, but there was cold under the vaults. From these gathered forms, from these clear-cut façades, where the firm semicircle of the arch opened between massive columns, there radiated a naked strength which affirmed the elegance—austere, brutal, and categorical—of a caste in possession of undisputed power. It is the exact image of a fixed Catholicism—the authority of the Councils seated on rock. No outlook on life is

SAINT-AMAND DE COLY (Dordogne) (XII Century).
Interior of the transept of the church.

afforded—the soul alone has the right to life, on condition that it never breaks through the continuous circle of stone in which it is held by dogma. Rome has cemented the thought of Saint Paul in the material of the churches.

When the uncompromising morality of this rigid world, clad in rough cloth and iron, was ready to quit the pages of the manuscripts and the pulpit of the temples and to show its symbolized face to the multitude, when the four animals of the Evangelists consented to have grow up beside them a new world of animate forms that descended the length of the columns and escaped to the very tympanums of the doors and invaded their lintels, Saint Bernard was the only one who perceived that an era was about to end. The monks could no longer close their eyes, when once the day had touched them with its light. Once life had begun to penetrate dogma, there could be no question as to the final result, even if a few centuries were still needed before life should be released by the compact and closed mass of doctrinary Christianity. In vain it opened its hell, sent stiff, devouring monsters to crawl upon the stones, unchained horrible battles between the absolute virtues and the irreducible vices, divided the world into definitive truths and definitive errors: life, poor and bruised, but regaining its mastery little by little, was introducing its subtle

Souillac (xii Century). A pillar of the church.

Vézelay (XII Century). Figures in the tympanum of the church.

connecting passages between each of these pairs of moral entities in order to animate them and to unite them.

It was clearly impossible that in this universe which had been closed for ten centuries, the monk sculptor of the Romanesque churches, the theologian armed with a chisel, should discover any more, at first, than a meager type of nature—emaciated, compressed, and suffering, like himself. Long figures, which make a tragic effort to break the mold of the Byzantine, were flattened against the new façades, mechanically expressing an arrested symbolism. The only men, precisely, who reserved the right, at that moment, to express form and life were the heirs and guardians of a theology that had not ceased for a thousand years to look upon and to condemn form and life as contemptible appearances. For the same length of time, the people had been crushed between the material invasion of the barbarians and the moral invasion of Christianity. It had resigned itself, in the promised hope of a future life, to the hazards of its actual life, and, when it fled the devastations of its countryside, it found no other refuge than its feeling for the supernatural.

But despite everything, and contrary to the life and the ideal which they had accepted, the artist-monks were expressing, in those primitive sculptures that were invading the porches of the churches in ever denser crowds, the first sudden perturbations of the needs of their time. A singular force was mounting very rapidly within these works. In close-growing vegetation made up of these rough forms, there circulated something of the sap and the energy which, in the same centuries, were lifting up the wrought stone of the Dravidian pyramids and the Cambodian temples. A dull rhythm, a heavy and vigorous rhythm—like that with which the flood of the springtime carries its wealth of buds up out of the soil—runs through these rude figures, these heads, and bodies that are hardly more than squared off, and which are elevated in a single movement. A puissant grace, a candid and robust charm hesitate in the stone itself. Clear-cut planes define the elementary movements that incline one face toward another face and cause one hand to reach out toward another. They seem to obey the silent music which groups numbers into constructions and into figures, according to the summary but essential appearance that reveals them to us when our minds are strongly aroused. It is a rough expression but a fervent one that results from this dramatic meeting of Christian symbolism at its highest tension and popular realism in the innocence of its dawn. The breast of the world was dilating slowly, but with an irresistible effort that was to burst its armor. There had been no invasion for a century or two. Born of war and living by it, the feudal lord carries war to the surrounding countries. Gaul, to which the military chiefs had been leading their hordes for so many years, became the central hearth for the fire of expansion and conquest. About the closing years of the eleventh century, the one during which the Romanesque church allowed its compressed life to burst its shell, the Norman barons

CHARTRES (XII Century). A saint. (*Cathedral*.)

passed into Sicily and into England, and the first
Crusade hurled the French barons upon the Holy
Land. Feudal brutality emigrated for two hundred
years.

III

Then the native soil, that which the peoples knew no
longer, their roots having been torn from it in every
generation by some human tempest—the native soil

CHARTRES (XII Century). Angel. (*Cathedral.*)

rose to the heart of its races. At the same time, the
profound movement which cast the mystic and miserable Occident upon the rich Orient, sent flowing back
upon the Occident the life of wonderful lands, of other
faiths, of other legends, of other customs, and the
powerful, confused sensation of a material world and a

world of the soul broadening while changing in appearances, and of a universe that would not be contained within the limits of revealed religion.

The earth quivers with pride. Almost at the same hour, appear the Republic of Florence and the Uni-

BEGADAM (Gironde) (XII Century). Apse of the church.

versities of Palermo, of Bologna, of Paris. In the very bosom of the Church there are born spirits more religious than the Church, and they subject dogma to a courageous examination. Abelard, the Christian, denies original sin, contests the divinity of Jesus, exalts once more the dignity of the senses, and tries to establish—from antiquity to the Middle Ages, by the impartial study of ancient philosophy and of the doctrine of the fathers—the unity of the human spirit. Four years after his death, his disciple Arnaldo da Brescia proclaims the Republic in Rome. Such a life animates men's hearts, which Catholicism, carried along with it, discusses, interprets, criticizes—and the dead letter recoils before the living spirit. For the first and the last time in its history, Catholicism follows that profound movement which, from time to time, reveals to a privileged people the conquests it has made during its silence. At the hour when it looks into itself to observe the rising flood of life, it does not perceive what is happening in the strongest cities of northern France. Sometimes supported by the monarchy that feels them to be a bulwark against the lords, Le Mans first, and Cambrai, then Noyon, Laon, Sens, Amiens, Soissons, Rheims, and Beauvais transform themselves into free communes by the refusal to pay taxes, by proscriptions, and by insurrection, sword in hand. Those were the days when the cadavers of bishops were dragged through the streets.

It matters little that the incentive of the movement toward the commune was the material interest of the people. Opposed to the spirit of the Christianity of the Councils, which made obedience the fundamental principle, the spirit of France, which, by way of the Renaissance and the Encyclopædia, was to reach the Revolution—the spirit of France revealed itself in this movement with a youth and a strength that it never again possessed. For two hundred years it gave to the cities of the Ile-de-France, of Picardy, and of Champagne, a richly flourishing civilization, confused in its appearances, but of an inner rhythm so powerful that it constrained feudalism to take refuge in the country, where it brought about the Jacquerie two or three centuries later, and—under pretext of exterminating heresy—to fall upon the cities of the south, whose culture and growing free spirit it crushed. This was the terrible ransom of the liberty of the north. The foci of energy were still too scattered on our soil, the

CHURCH OF COULOMBES (XII Century). Detail of a column.
(*Louvre.*)

antagonism among the provinces was too sharp for the
people to be able to feel solidarity in itself everywhere
and in a co-ordinated effort to overthrow the political
powers which it still needed to protect itself against
the enemy from without.

Filled with the eager life that had been restrained for
so long a time the French Commune assigned to each

ARLES (XII and XIII Centuries).　Façade of Saint-Trophime,
detail.

person the work for which he was best fitted.　It was
an association of strong corporations representing
every stratum of society, wherein individual tempera-
ments obeyed no other rules than those of the spontaneous harmony we see in the woods—made up of a
hundred thousand trees which plunge into the same
soil, are watered by the same rains and fertilized by the
same winds.　The Commune entered history with a
power that gives it that character of necessity which
we now recognize as the "Greek miracle" and the
"Jewish miracle."　The art, formidable and one that
expressed it, was born with it in France, and died with
it there.　It was the French soul delivered into its own

SAINT-GENOU (Indre) (XII Century). Capitals of the nave.

keeping for the first and the last time. The peoples
whom it penetrated with its vitalizing force could
accept it and adapt it to their needs—they could not
touch its inner principle without, at the same time,
ruining its national and social significance. Between
the Vosges, the English Channel, and the Loire it was
really life, order, truth. It was the barn and the
farm and the house of the cities which silhouetted the
lacework of its carving and its pinnacles against the
sky, the narrow house of earth and of wood bordering
the round-backed bridges and the tortuous lanes. It
was the thick wall that bit into the rock, the high wall
as clear-cut as consciousness, the haughty refuge that
dominated the sea, the egoistic abbey where slow lives
wore away, to the rhythm of the hours of the church
services. It was the little country church around
which a few huts were gathered at the foot of the
curtain wall under the dungeon that, for ten generations of men, prevented the long and fertile contact of
those who lived in its shadow with those whom it confined. It was the great cathedral. It was strength, it
was the dream and the need, the belly, the heart, and
the armor. The same spontaneous harmony was
everywhere, issuing from the desire of the people and
burning out at the same time that it did. The crenelated towers, proclaimed, to be sure, in the face of the
productive commune, the apparently antagonistic
principle of the right of conquest. But with it they proclaimed the same principle of life: they were built by
the master mason who directed the work of the cathedral. And the cathedral was born with the communes,
grew during their time of maturity, covered itself with
statues and stained glass, and then languished and
ceased to grow when they declined and died. Noyon,
Soissons, Laon, Rheims, Amiens, Sens, Beauvais—
wherever we find a great commune the great cathedral

appears, vast and bold in the proportion that the commune is well armed and well established, and in proportion to the vitality of the communal spirit.

The cities of France, during two centuries of relative
peace, had torn down their walls. Their houses spread
all along the rivers and the roads; the neighboring

Le Thoronet (Var) (xii and xiii Centuries).   Cloister
of the abbey.

forests were cleared away. In observing the new organs
that grew little by little from the re-formed social
body—to build dwellings, to pave the streets and
stretch chains there, to bring vegetables and wood from
the country, to kill animals and shear them, to tan
leather and forge iron—men saw that their common
interests in these activities increased their strength.
The concentration of the social forces made possible
the birth of that wonderful hope which is born spon-

taneously in an organism, when all its elements harmonize in the mind which is directed toward a practical purpose that lies within reach. All the guilds
together felt that from their instinct there was germi-

Mont-Saint-Michel (xii Century). The gallery.

nating an ever-growing imperious desire which, for its
satisfaction, demanded the creation of a central organ
that should summarize the effort whose power and
necessity were expressed in the ensemble of the Commune. The church of the clergy was too narrow and
too dark, the crowd that was rising with the sound of
a sea begged for a church of its own; it felt in itself
the courage and the knowledge necessary to build
that church to its own stature. Its desire was to have
the whole great work of building pass, with the material
and the moral life, from the hands of the cloistered
monk into those of the living people. No longer should

the poor folk who lived in the shadow of the monasteries enter in fear at the hour of the service to hear the voice of the Church in the darkness of the low vault.

SAINTES-MARIES DE LA MER (XII Century). Apse.

The Church should be the common house, the storehouse of abundance, the labor exchange, and the popular theater; it should be the sonorous and luminous house which the flood of mankind could invade at any hour, a great vessel, capable of containing the whole city, the ark filled with tumult on market days, with dances on feast days, with the sound of the tocsin on the days of revolt, with singing on church days, with the voice of the people on all days.[1]

Some of these great temples, to be sure, spring from the pavement amid the silence of the crowds—in Paris, in Bourges, in Chartres, where the communal spirit did not conquer. But Bourges is a city royal and under the sword of the king; its workers, enriched by the court, escaped the power of the feudal lord. Without anxiety or remorse, the cathedral of Bourges spread out the holiday splendor of its porticos at the base of its enormous, irregular mass. In Paris, also a city royal, Notre Dame covers itself with statues and magnifies the light of the day by the rose windows of its transepts at the moment when the citizens and the merchants strive for freedom. At Chartres, whether the vision of the pure façade and the spire dominates us or whether, on passing through the nave, we are gripped by the sensation of poignant mystery, we know well that we are in the presence of an obscure tragedy of the heart. The prodigious harmony has something disenchanted about it, something in which one divines the torment of an imprisoned conscience. How could Roman austerity tolerate in its shadow the radiance, given forth by the sensuous glory of the race of statues which guards the enigma of the nave? Here theocratic will clashes with popular desire without either one becoming aware of it, and from the unconscious conflict there spurts up an invisible flame—the dull,

---

[1] The greater part of the ideas expressed in this chapter have already been defended with profound logic and authority by Viollet-le-Duc in his *Dictionnaire d' Architecture.* It must be said, however, that his writing suffers from an excess of laical narrowness.

CHARTRES (XII Century). North portal of the cathedral.

mystical, agonizing beauty of a great idea that contains the secret of a world and cannot formulate itself.

IV

Everywhere else the multitude is master of the works. The honest master builder, to whom the Commune and the Bishop turn, knows practically nothing save his trade. Behind him is the confused Byzantine-Romanesque tradition which he possesses imperfectly; before him is a problem to be solved: to build an edifice vast enough to contain the inhabitants of a city. He knows his material well, the stone of France, powdery, watery, and easy to work. He has his compass, his water level, his plumb line, and his square. Around him are good workmen, of the same spirit as himself, filled with faith, not in the least disturbed by worry as to social questions or by doubt as to religion. He possesses that clear good sense, that free and direct logic, which later brought out of the same soil such men as Rabelais, Montaigne, Molière, La Fontaine, Rameau, Diderot, and Voltaire. A new function appears, so complex that it absorbs the life of the century. For the new organ to adapt itself to it, nothing more is needed than that the master builder consent to be a man of his time, like the least of his companions.

Whatever the force in the ascending movement of the French churches, whatever their lyrism, their perfect intelligence lies too deep within them to make its impression at once. Their whole form is determined by the ogive window that hides itself proudly in the upper shadows of the nave. It has not revealed to us the subtle passage that leads a French or a Norman mason to isolate in the Romanesque church the projections from the ribbed vault and to raise its lateral edges by means of the angular window which the Crusaders had seen in the Orient. But it was that window which overcame the round arch and the vertical weight that crushed the vessel. Everything is to radiate from the ogive—the drop of its diagonal ribbing on to the columns that spring up to separate the three naves, the entire vault that is inscribed in their intervals, and the flying buttress that carries off obliquely the thrust of the vault. Everywhere else one finds the immense expanses of glass through which the light penetrates. . . . The logic is that of the skeleton, wherein all pressures are balanced and transmitted; it is the image of the absolute transported into the perishable order of the scattered elements of life. Between the flying buttress and the vault, the edifice is like the carcass of a gigantic cetacean suspended in space by

CHARTRES (XII Century). The month of July. (*Cathedral.*)

iron hooks to permit the light of heaven to traverse it in every direction. It seems to float in the air.[1]

Gothic architecture was opposed to leaving anything in darkness. Indeed, it died of its love of the light. Sens, Beauvais, Laon, Soissons, Amiens, Bourges (in spite of its five naves) are full of light, like our modern markets of iron and glass. But in these cathedrals there is, of course, the necessary framework which made some dark places; there is the stone skeleton work of the rose window, the leads which hold the stained glass, the wire netting which protects it, the

---

[1] The ogive, of which an example is cited in England, at Durham, about 1104, appears for the first time in France, probably, about 1115, at Morienval, near Soissons and Noyon, between the Ile-de-France, Picardy, and Champagne, where, through Saint-Denis and Notre Dame, Amiens and Beauvais, Rheims, Laon, Sens, etc., it saw the birth of the most numerous and most beautiful architectural works consequent upon it. Who discovered it? Several master builders, perhaps, each one contributing a new idea, from the association of which the ogive was born spontaneously. Here is one of the most surprising characteristics of the Middle Ages in the Occident, and one that it shares with hardly any other art than that of ancient Egypt and India. Of all the image makers, scarcely a name has come down to us, and if we know who some dozens of architects were, it has required patient researches or chance to bring forth their names from the municipal account books that slept in our archives. This is an anonymous art, and, consequently, it is collective and disinterested, it is the *social art*. These men thought of nothing but the accomplishment of their task, and not one of them dreamed of laying claim to being the father of the most original creation in architecture since the vault of the Assyrians.

Guillaume de Sens, who was one of the greatest of the constructors and who was brought to England to build the nave of Canterbury, passed as the inventor of the ogive for a long time. He was, doubtless, one of the first to apply it to the construction of an edifice—the cathedral of Sens—whose whole structure it determines. But it seems to have received almost as complete an application, for an ensemble, with the building of the choir of Saint-Denis (1144), and in some churches of a transitional character dating from that period—Noyon, Lisieux, Le Mans, etc. In any case, it was in the Ile-de-France that, before the middle of the twelfth century, the architects systematized a process of construction which permitted Jean d'Orbais to build Rheims, Robert de Luzarches to build Amiens, Pierre de Montereau to build the Sainte-Chapelle, and a hundred others in every part of France and Europe to erect buildings of a unity of structure that is absolute and of a variety of aspects that is inexhaustible.

CHARTRES (XII Century). Head of a man. (*Cathedral.*)

dirt of centuries, due to all the old dust that has heaped up. . . . When the cathedral is dark, it is because the master builder has miscalculated his effort, because he

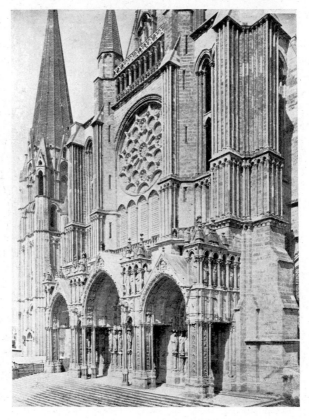

CHARTRES (XII and XIII Centuries).   South transept of the cathedral.

expected the building to yield more than it could, because he wanted to crowd too many people into it, as in Paris, where galleries press down on the four lateral

CHARTRES (XII and XIII Centuries). Transept of the cathedral.

naves.   The object of the stained glass was not to
darken the nave but to glorify the light, whose glow
scintillated with the richness of powdered jewels.   And
this glass was used not only in the churches but for the
rooms of the châteaux and for the houses of the middle
class.   The memory of the carpets hung up in the
mosques filled the minds of the men, who were returning
from the Orient, with visions transfigured by enthusiasm and regret.   They opened the side of the wall to
set into it a translucent painting, a fresco shot through
by flames, illumined by the heavens.   The stained glass
offered to the pale light of the north its flaming matrix
so that the sun should give a warmer caress to the
stone that rose everywhere.   Its azures, its dark blues,
its saffron and golden yellows, its oranges, its vinous
or purple reds, and its dark greens streaked the nave
with the blood of Christ and the sapphire of the sky,
with the russet of the autumn grapevines, and with the
emerald of the distant seas and of the meadows round
about.   In the depths of the chapels of the apse, where
the spot made by the candles caused the darkness to
tremble, the light of the windows weakened only to
accumulate around the sanctuary, the agonizing vague-
ness and the voluptuousness of its mystery.   When, on
one of those gray days of the Ile-de-France, one enters
Notre Dame to wait for the sun, one knows when it has
come out by the blond inundation that suddenly invades
the nave, renders it aërial and golden, and little by
little touches and makes dazzling the very ribbing
which, under their rigid palm ornaments, suspends the
shadow of the forests.   At evening, when the darkness
is almost nocturnal in the vast interior whose vaults
one sees hovering high up like the wings of a great bird
of the night, one thing alone remains luminous—the
glass of the windows.   The dying light from outside
spatters the black pillars and the pavement which has

SAINT-YRIEIX (Corréze) (XIII Century). Nave of the church, detail.

disappeared, with a fiery shower, more intense and more glowing in proportion as the darkness increases. The rose windows gather up the last reflections of the sun that has set to illuminate the shadows with them.

Everything that gives the cathedral its meaning, everything that determines its aspect—the irresistible

PARIS (XIII Century).   Vault of the nave.   (*Cathedral.*)

rise of its lines, the balancing of the curves that raise it above the cities—everything is brought about by the desire for light; and the desire for light increased among its architects at the same time that they became more familiar with the handling of its curves and its lines.   Never did an edifice so truthful proclaim its function with such simplicity.   At every point the bones were just beneath the flesh; each one recognized its role: there was not a recess, there was not a projection which did not justify its presence.   The fixed framework of the exterior, the immense parallel arches which start up everywhere to suspend the central nave or to radiate to the apse, carry the building up into space and cradle it there, like the articulated members of a

PARIS (XIII Century).   Triforium, wall, and vault.
(*Cathedral.*)

gigantic animal. Every one of its organs, from the haughtiest to the most obscure, participates in its power—the humble ornament, the flower that varies a plane that would be too bare without it, the slight bas-
20

relief that gives movement to a profile, the small belfries that load the pinnacles to increase the strength of
the piles which catch the thrust of the flying buttresses,
the niches for statues hollowing out the buttresses
wherever there is no pressure, the gargoyles that spout
the rain water away from the building so that it shall
not gnaw the stone, the long grooved columns on the
body of the pillars themselves, giving to the supports
of the vaults that nervous and sustained spring which
causes them to spread out at their summit with the
ease of a sheaf.

Nowhere else has sculptured ornament become so
much a part of the edifice. In India the statue is incorporated in the building because both, at the same time,
grow out of a pantheistic conception of life which sweeps
the builders and the statue makers into its own head-
long movement. Here, not only does the unity of conception, of traditions, and beliefs carry in the same
current all who share in the work, but every statue,
every carved column, every branch, or fruit on the wall
is there to give more balance and solidity to the ensemble. The ornament gives animation and movement
and carries off into space everything that would serve
to rob the cathedral of mobility and to bind it to the
soil.

Bare in the beginning, at Sens, at Saint-Denis, in the
first tier of the cathedral of Paris and at Soissons, bare
as a race abounding with life, the cathedral was covered in a century with the forms which this race had
found on its pathway. The porches, the tympanums,
the lintels, the galleries of colonnettes, the high towers
—sonorous organs raising in a single flight their thickets
of close-set stones, everything became part of the miracle, and this whole soil, which had been barren before,
sprouted with trembling bas-reliefs, with the carving
of the foliage that seemed ready to burst with sap—

Tour (Calvados) (xiii Century). Belfry of the church.

and in a thousand powerful statues quivered the life
of a people.   In the mist or in the sunshine, the world
of the painted images caused the façades, from their
severe base to their sweeping towers, to partake of the
movement of the black streets into which the neighboring countryside penetrates unceasingly, with the
hucksters, the traders, their horses and sheep, with the
boatmen and the market gardeners who bring vegetables and wood to the city.   On days of prayer, the
people ask the stone symbols for the human significance
of the mystic emotion that pervades the multitude of
pure and gentle beings which surround the cathedral
of Chartres.   On rainy days, people take refuge under
the porches of Notre Dame—the three porches inscribed
in the bare wall, which is not more sober and simple
and firmly built than they, and the stories that the
image makers in their sheltered workshops have been
telling for a century are discussed by the citizens.   On
feast days and in fine weather, people stop to look at
the way in which the façade of Amiens is blossoming,
as if the reapers and the vintagers on its doors were
covering it with vine branches and sheaves—from the
embroidered galleries to the flames of the great rose
window.   On fair-days, people at the top of the towers
of Laon would see the oxen bending to their work in
the fields.   On coronation days, or at times of royal
pomp, when the processions defile between the rows of
narrow houses where the tapestries hang, people follow
the harmony and the tumult of the marchers and are
engulfed with the latter in the five porches of Bourges
that shimmer with their painted sculptures; while at
Rheims, the sculptures are carried on up to the summit
of the cathedral, from which there pours the incessant
torrent of the forms and colors of nature.

But inside—not an image.   The nave would lose
something of its sonority, its grandeur, its light.   The

vault, the generating principle, is bare, and only the capital of the columns is permitted to flower. The long, slender shafts, the long ribbing that ascends and descends to outline the stained glass of the windows, the absolute lines that converge and that answer one

FLAVIGNY (Côte-d'Or) (XIII Century). Capital, choir of the abbey.

another, the pure radiance of the rose window—everything has the abstract force and the nakedness of the mind. And everywhere it is function that determines form. The armed castle is a church turned inside out, its exterior bare for purposes of resistance, and covered with frescoes and carpets within, well supplied

with carved wood furniture and with forged iron for
the delight of the eye and for repose. The only French
cathedral in the ogive style, whose exterior is bare and
whose form presents a hostile mass, was built at Albi
in a spirit of defiance and combat—it is a fortress
rising in a block to surround the sanctuary of the spirit
with armor. In the south, the Roman majesty of the
wall is retained, and even, at certain moments, en-
hanced. Especially in those places where the Romanesque spirit and the ogival spirit fuse, at Saintes-Maries
de la Mer, at Aigues-Mortes, at Albi, at Agde, at the
Château of the Popes in Avignon, a sublime art will
appear. In the rhythmical alternation of the massive
wall that mounts straight upward and of the offset
inscribed directly in its thickness to make openings for
the superimposed windows under the proud ogive at
the top, it is so lofty, so bare, so measured and sober
that, beside it—whether a church or a fortress—the
Romanesque temple seems crushed or heavy or frail
and the French cathedral seems overloaded with the
decoration on its exterior.

In the architecture of the ogive, as in the Romanesque
architecture, several schools have been isolated. And,
in fact, it is as easy to distinguish in one's first glance
at the ogival building, the sobriety and the measure
of the Ile-de-France and the Valois, the gayety, the
animation, the truculence, and the verve of Picardy
and Champagne, the square and rugged force of Brit-
tany, the profusion and complexity of Normandy, as,
in the Romanesque construction, one can distinguish
the patience of the workmen of Poitoux, the gathered
power of the Auvergnats, the tense elegance of the men
of Provence, and the vigor and the fineness of the men
of Périgord. It is also easy to recognize the meeting
of the two great styles in the stately eloquence of the
Burgundians. But in one group as in the other and

despite the general tendency which, in the south, gives predominance to the spiritual, abstract, structural, and didactic element and in the north to all the gradations of the living, anecdotal, and picturesque element, despite the predominance, in a word, of sculpture in the north and architecture in the south, a constant inter-penetration of local styles, of epochs, and of influences

PARIS (XIII Century).   Grapevine.   (*Cathedral.*)

from without transforms the whole land of France into a forest of stone designed and worked, and to compare with it there is perhaps only the growth that India brought forth from her miraculous soil. And we may add that Indian art and the art of the Khmers and the Javanese, and Byzantine art as well as that of the Arabs, and the art of Greece as well that of Rome, by direct or indirect connection, by reason or intuition, by the contact of thought or by chance, seem to gather here from every place on earth to summarize and co-ordinate themselves for a century in the ever-alert sensibility and the ready intelligence which characterize France. From one end of the land to the other, a wonderful variety of sensation and expression becomes easily a part of the spiritual unity of will and faith. Whether the Romanesque temple is carved like an ivory or whether it is simple, whether its tower is square, polygonal, or round, solid or open to the air by its juxtaposed windows, whether the belfry rises straight as a cry or whether it curves like the line of a lamentation, whether the apse is circular or whether it forms a polyhedron, whether the arches are multiplied on the moving surface or barely indicated at the summit of the straight walls that are as fierce as ramparts, everywhere the majesty and the force of the doctrine impregnate the expressive surfaces with the savor and the rhythm of life. Sometimes, on the ogival façades, the great silent planes are displayed almost bare between bare buttresses or, on the contrary, the buttresses are fluted like organ pipes, as if to accentuate their vertical flight toward the sky, and the façades are covered by a lacework of leaves and branches. Sometimes the porches are inscribed in the walls, at other times they bristle with pediments, spires, and pinnacles. The rose windows may be circular or flame-shaped, the number and the disposition of the towers vary endlessly—now they are cut into by high windows, now designed with clusters of colonnettes like wheat sheaves, or again they pass by insensible transitions from the square to the polygon and from the polygon to the conc. But everywhere the flood of the animated forms and innumerable aspects of life permits the logic of the function and the rationalism of the mind to appear freely. Even—and here the miracle is perhaps more surprising —when three centuries and four or five styles have mingled the Romanesque and the Gothic in a simple monument, the whole indivisible world of sentiments and sensations that it presents enters in a mass, and forever, into the immutable order of the mind.

BAGÉ (Ain) (XII and XIII Centuries).   Belfry of the church.

V

In reality, when France was covering with living flesh a framework so logical that it fixed the form of the monument in its every detail, she was still pursuing

Laon (xiii Century).   Capital in the triforium.
(*Cathedral.*)

the conquest of herself.   The French mind is of all the most structure-loving, but the structure must be simple in the proportion that its surface is mobile and rich in gradations, it must remain close to her soil, to her

AMIENS (XII to XIV Century). The cathedral.

rivers, and to the winds that cross her skies. The men of this land have always loved to give to matter the image of their visions. The first engraved and carved objects which the world knows appeared on the territory that extends from the Atlantic to the Pyrenees and to the Cévennes. The Gauls beat, forged, and molded bronze before the arrival of the Legions. The Greco-Latin genius became vibrant each time that it touched this soil.

And yet before sculpture had departed from the cloister entirely, the saints, both men and women, had been far-away gods whom the people could barely see at the summit of the ecclesiastical hierarchy. Once they had gained the street they lived there. The local god, the god of works and of days, the god of the fountains and the woods, the genius, who participated in all the acts of the agricultural, social, and industrial life of the people, joined the company of the saints— without any one perceiving it. Sculpture was suddenly invaded everywhere by a moral sentiment, which was as familiar and as penetrating and as simple as the living activity of humanity always is; and, without visible connection, this sentiment continued the oldest memories of man. Its actions were those of confession and protection and health, and their attraction was irresistible. Hands sought other hands and found them, faces bent toward other faces, from which emanated the gentleness that men show toward each other when they need one another. The virgin, deified against the desire of the clergy, carried her child in the crowd and showed him to the poor people.

Surely, those were good Christians who sculptured those round torsos, those flanks, swelling with child, which are lifted up by the bulk of the little one, those long limbs, nervous or full, under the woolen dress, and those good smiling faces which they copied in the workshop from the women who brought them their soup. If all they really loved in Christianity was its tender human myths, they accepted without question its belief in the supernatural, and, in consequence, they were not too severe with themselves for the acts which they committed. As long as they did their work well, they con- sidered that their sin of gluttony had the advantage of renew- ing their strength and that their sins of in- continence compen- sated for many other disagreeable things. The churchmen were no more offended than the laymen by the in- genuous wantonness of the stories which the popular imagina- tion never ceased to bring forth. We must remember that in these centuries, morals were not very edifying.[1]

School of Rheims (xiii Century). Angel, detail. (*Louvre*.)

Almost all of the priests themselves had concubines, and not one of them made a secret of it. Life was too rich in re- juvenated strength to be restrained by any dikes. The man of this time brought to the service of the church his greatest and his simplest love; but it was the spirit which he adored, and the very power of his faith set free his power of action by rescuing him from

---

[1] See in Lavisse's *Histoire de France:* "The Thirteenth Century," by M. Langlois.

the letter of the law. There was many a nudge of the
elbow, many a slap exchanged during the preaching,
and sometimes it was the priest who got the drubbing.
And now it was no longer monks who continually
represented the virtues on the lintels and the tympanums. Much more frequently it was the virtues,
with the enchanted smile of a feminine face, that welcomed the poor people. It was thought very natural
to see demons pushing into the caldrons a gesticulating
troop of soldiers, bishops, and kings, all shuddering
with fear. The people, in France, was too sure of itself
not to pardon injuries, for it said what it thought with
perfect candor, and although its hell was more comic
than terrifying, it opened the gates, in its malice, to
those who did not respect the task the accomplishment
of which they pretended was their sacred mission.

The Almighty seldom appeared in the statuary of
the churches. The poor image makers did not aspire
that high. They were unable to create that which they
had not seen. They did not lack imagination, certainly, and even a vague, universal, and confused
culture. But their imagination moved within limits—
immense and multiform, be it said—of the life that
surrounded them, and their instinct as artists was too
imperious to permit their theological and legendary
culture to furnish them anything but pretexts for the
manifestation of that instinct. Our Lady the Virgin
stepped out of the stone alive, because the image of
maternity, in this period of superabundant life, was
everywhere. And if the saints and the angels surrounded the portals, it was because those who suffered
saw faces of kindness and faces of hope bending over
them daily in their distress.

The Church, in the course of its defensive organization, had turned aside, to the profit of its external power,
the impulsion of sentiment from which Christianity

had sprung. The France of the thirteenth century restored this impulsion of sentiment in the full life of humanity. Under the pressure of this inner force, the

RHEIMS (XIII Century). A knight. (*Cathedral.*)

old world of theology cracked everywhere. Christianity, which until then had dominated life, was dominated by it and carried along in its movement. Moving on a higher plane than that of the Semitic idea of Saint Paul, who had prepared life for its explosion by forcing repose upon it, contrary to the discipline of Rome which, for a thousand years, had been raising dikes to protect it against the anarchical forces from without,

RHEIMS (XIII Century). Winter. (*Cathedral.*)

life once more joined in the fraternal spirit of Him who was born in a stable, who was followed by troops of the poor, who received adulterous women, and who spoke to the flowers; it did so because man was emerging from a social state harder than that of the old world and because an insurrection of virile tenderness was becoming the universal need.

The civilizations of antiquity wept at their decline. Their sorrow has seemed declamatory and grimacing because life was leaving them. The Middle Ages, in which life was rising, mastered their suffering. They were happy, as happy as the old world in its full sweep upward, and for them pity was never more than one element in the generated energy of life. They did not even realize how courageous they were when they stretched out their two hands to all who asked for them. Without any effort, they found, in the fulfillment of their daily task, the social principle of Christianity, which the fathers of the

RAMPILLON (Seine-et-Marne) (XIII Century). Detail of the base.

Church had sought in a theocratic organization that was momentarily necessary to protect the growth of the new peoples, but that was a drawback to the manifestation of their original thought.

21

This social character defines French sculpture.
When we see it from our distance, to be sure, when we
see it in its ensemble from the twelfth to the fifteenth
century, it strongly recalls the progression of the
schools of antiquity from archaism to academism,

ROUEN (XIII Century).   Base and shafts of a door of the
cathedral.

with their passage through a point of equilibrium
wherein science and sentiment, rising to their loftiest
certitude, shine from the same focus.   Romanesque
art has the smiling strength and the rhythmical stiffness
of the sixth century of Greece; the art of the thirteenth
century is calm and mature like that with which Phidias
and his precursors affirmed their complete self-pos-
session.   Afterward, in France as in Greece, virtuosity
—descriptive, naturalistic, and picturesque—gains the
upper hand little by little.   Doubtless, the essential

difference is that Gothic sculpture does not tend above all to the realization of that balance of volumes by which the statue makers of Olympia and of the Parthenon passed from one form to another form, from one

RHEIMS (XIII Century). Caryatid. (*Cathedral*.)

idea to another idea, without leaving a trace by which the mind could follow the course that had been taken: it had to enter, with the sculptors, into the consciousness and the need of the universal harmony. When Gothic sculpture seizes this balance, we seem to be in the presence of an isolated attempt; a solitary in-

dividual seems to have made his impressive appearance
in the midst of a murmuring throng. . . . The Greek
artists almost invariably spread out the inner life of

RAMPILLON (Seine-et-Marne) (XIII Century). The
Carpenter. Altar screen of the church.

the stone in rhythmic waves over the whole extent of
the planes, to make all the figures participate in the
cosmic equilibrium. The Frenchman almost invariably
concentrates it in a bowed forehead, in a raised chin,
a shoulder, a dress, an elbow, a haunch or a knee,

RHEIMS (XIII Century). Figures from the porch. (*Cathedral*.)

which often breaks the line that one anticipates, so that we may see more clearly the direct, actual, and simple meaning of the action that he wants to express. . . . In the sculptures of Olympia and in the Fates of the Parthenon there was, doubtless, the dawn of a modeling similar in spirit to the Gothic. But the desire for harmony dominated everything.

The contours of the Gothic statue are less defined than they were among the Egyptians and less subtle than among the Greeks. They are more varied and more living, for the light changes more frequently and is more diffused, and above all because they express a world of moral needs which neither the Greeks nor the Egyptians could feel. Never had shadows and lights been distributed with such an understanding of their psychological value. Never had the material been worked with an emotion so concrete, never had a more profound, a more complete, and a more gentle radiance emanated from it, from the full and broadly treated forms which exhibit the material to our eyes. Never had the necessity for effort been accepted with a more joyous soul by a youth with more courage to live its life, though it was better prepared than the younger races for the misfortune that awaited it. Certain statues of Rheims remind one of the Apollo of Olympia, by the rise into the light, from which their brow seems to emerge. The pure spring water that issues from the rock of Hellas seems to flow over the sides and the limbs of the statues of women, which watch over the portal above the transept of Chartres. Once more, men have lent their heroism to the gods.

It would be erroneous to conclude that even the greatest master builders and image makers among the French had ever possessed philosophic ideas so elevated as those of the sculptors from whom the Greek thinkers derived the life of the mind. But outside of the geographical conditions which so sensibly differentiated northern France with its humidity and its coolness from the arid and burnt land of Greece, life

Séez (xiii Century). Splaying of the door of the cathedral.

had been harder in the Middle Ages than in the century of Pericles, war and misery had made it more necessary for the masses to bring about an active solidarity, and man was more profoundly necessary to man. Moreover, these different conditions of natural

and social life revealed themselves unexpectedly in the
atmosphere of sentimental legend that Christianity
created little by little. It is indubitable that the Greek
sculptor who tore the ancient world from its exhausted
rhythms, was intellectually as superior to the mason of
the cathedral, as the "Prometheus" of Æschyus or the
"Antigone" of Sophocles is to a thirteenth-century
mystery play; but it is certain that the mason of the
cathedral easily rejoined him in the universal eurhythmy, because he was an element of the monumental symphony which the instinct, common to a
whole throng, causes to spurt from its heart.

VI

The entire people in the Middle Ages, with all
that it knew, all that it desired, and all that it confusedly dreamed, built its temple, the house of its
reality and its hope, as it was building up at the same
time, through the freedom of the Commune, its right
to live, the right for future ages to conquer through
thought. It was not, as has been claimed, that each
inhabitant of the city and the country contributed his
stone to the pile. But the corporations which worked
at it, the carpenters, the masons, the stonecutters, the
glassmakers, the plasterers, the leadworkers, and the
painters, all plumbed the lowest depths of the people
whose forebodings and needs they drew forth whole-
heartedly. The master builder laid out the plan, and
distributed the work; then each man, with his instinct
for independent action, animated a capital, sculptured
an image, framed in lead the holiday splendor of a piece
of stained glass, and set in line, between the diagonal
ribbing, the little stones cut by hand that suspended
the vault a hundred or a hundred and fifty feet above
the soil. The cathedral lived so completely the life of

its builders that it changed at the same time they did, and one generation would erect a tier in the pointed style on top of a tier of round arches, while another would abandon the arm of a transept already half

The descent from the Cross, ivory (XIII Century).
(*Louvre.*)

constructed, would add a crown of chapels, change the profile of the towers, multiply or leave them unfinished, or would set a rose window flaming at the front of a Romanesque nave which had been relieved of its vault. The cathedral rose, sank, and spread out with our feelings and our desires.

Hence its close, rich unity wherein, as in a crowd or

in nature, all the different forms derived their solidarity
from the current of the same sap. Hence the liberty,
the sweep, and the violence, and the sweetness of the
hymn which these innumerable voices chanted and with
which it still trembles. It was an Encyclopædia,

TROYES (XIII Century). Gargoyle. (*Church of Saint-Urbain.*)

chiseled with love from the stuff of which France is
made. The Bible story and the Christian myth,
translated into active life, were lost in the rising tide
of the expressive forms which told, with their thousand
mingling voices, everything that was contained in the
soul, now mischievous, now naïve, now lyrical, now
genial, of the men who had heard these voices awakening within them. The good knights were bringing
back the dragons and chimeras from the Orient. The
newly acquired strength of the imagination made more
concrete the figures of the vampires and the man
wolves, the moralizing beasts, and the talking beasts
of the old fables in verse. As the image makers had
not seen the legendary kings, saints, or bishops, they

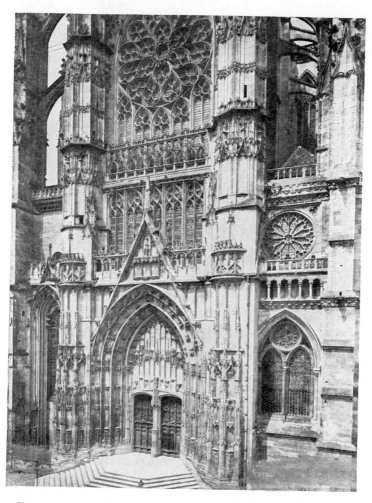

BEAUVAIS (XIII Century).   South transept of the cathedral.

asked the men in the street to furnish them with the
most characteristic faces.   The cathedral trembled
with the noise of the crafts and the forges.   Here are
the peasants sowing their wheat, reaping their grain,
pressing out their grapes or their apples.   Here are
horses, asses, and oxen breaking their furrow, or
dragging their cart.   The goats and the sheep show no
astonishment when, at the turn of a pillar, they meet
an elephant, a rhinoceros, a hippopotamus, or a king
or the Magi on their camels.   Gothic sculpture is an
image of freedom, uniting man's future with the
far-away memories which he had saved from the shipwreck of the ancient world.   Whether the cathedral
remains awake or goes to sleep, these memories are
ever-present and living, with a confused and murmuring life full of the songs of birds, of the sound of springs,
and of the swarming of the creatures under the moss.
About the capitals, the whole plant world sprouted
with great buds, then with leaves of pure outline which
earthy hands laid on the half-dressed stone;   then
came the overflow of vine branches with their leaves,
and thick tree stems bearing all the leaves of France
and sending forth their sound in the wind that animated
the organ of the towers: the vine, the rosebush, the
strawberry plant, the willow, the sage, the mallow, the
clover, the celery, the cabbage, the thistle, the parsley,
the watercress, the fern—the leaves of France dug out
from matter in such a transport of the senses that they
changed at every moment into vague moving forms—
lips, breasts, and folds of flesh where universal life
hesitated in its primitive appearances.   The bas-reliefs
that grew out of the walls seem the very flower of the
stone;   they seem to make concrete and visible, little
by little, the forms that it contains in germ, so well does
the image mingle with its surroundings, with its background of misty space.

There is nothing that more clearly reveals the futility of the old opposition between architecture and the so-called imitative arts than the French cathedral, where the living surfaces cover a living skeleton. There is nothing more superficial than the ordinary definition of plastics, whose function is not to imitate the world of

AIGUES-MORTES (XIII Century). Ramparts.

forms, but to seize in it the relationships which architecture precisely expresses most abstractly. It is not only its sculptured or painted ornamentation which causes architecture to re-enter the life of earth and sky, it is its first origin, the instinctive repetition that it presents of the great architecture of nature from which the human mind gathers up the elements of logical revelation that we call invention. All the vaults have evolved from the forms that were taught us by the cupola of the heavens and the droop of the long branches; all the columns are trees, all the walls are

rocks or cliffs, and the roof is spread out only to permit the people dwelling beneath it to shelter themselves
from the winds of the night—it slopes only to carry

ALBI (XIII Century).　The cathedral.

off the rain to the earth, which drinks it.　The northern
countries, which are wooded and whose light is diffused,
impose ornate façades on our imagination; the southern
countries, which are bare and whose light is dazzling,

dictate long, pure lines: the Romanesque endured in the south. Water penetrates the stone of the north, changes it, mingles it with the damp mold, with the mosses and rotten leaves. The marble of the south is

SENS. Rose window of the transept of the cathedral.

so saturated with the sun that little by little it becomes a focus of light, a source of heat as life-giving as that which concentrates autumn and summer in fruit. Everything attaches to a soil the edifice built of the stone which was drawn from that soil; it belongs to it

as the waters and the winds and the color of the sky
and the crops and the accustomed rhythm of the seasons. Under the pavement of the naves we get the
forest underground, the thick columns plunge to the
darkness of the crypt, to permit the vertical sweep of
their shafts and the spreading of their branches and
leaves to take root in the earth. In the French cathedral, in its long, pale columns, we get the tremulousness
of the forests of alburnum and of birch, the light airy
forests of Picardy and Champagne, and we see their
illumined branches in the flames of the stained glass.
When twilight floods the nave, making the pillars seem
larger in its glow and thrusting back the solemn vaults
even deeper into the mystery which darkens the gold
of the waning light, one thinks of our oak forests. And
the light vapor of our skies, permeating the whole mass
of the air, mingling the confused movement of the
ornamental forms with the silence of their depths,
penetrating the openwork of the towers, and casting a
veil of blond smoke over the conflagration of the stained
glass, seems to lift the cathedral above the slopes and
the plains, as it carries the heavy water of the winding
rivers into the upper air, where we see the faint tremor
of the trees whose leaves, shorn by autumn, are merged
by the rain with the mud of the roads. Branches move,
sounds arise, and a whispering begins again when the
wind has died away. At Coutances, the lines of the
spires of the central tower and of the polygonal belfries are characterized by the ascending movement
with which they launch upward everywhere. They
penetrate space with a flight so pure and so bare that
their points are lost in it like voices. Laon, from its
base to the top of its towers, is green with moss and
wild plants, the buttresses of Beauvais, which spring
up to a height three times greater than that of the
woods of the country, have the sound of a forest in a

Coutances (XIII Century). Spire of the cathedral.

storm, and the old spire of Chartres is a golden flame hung in the mist.

VII

Nothing in this social and natural expression is foreign to the earth and to the people from which it came forth spontaneously. And the unity of the symphony is the more impressive, through the vast number of voices that entered it, for song and prayer,

CAHORS (XIV Century). The Valentré Bridge.

to murmur, to weep, and to laugh, and to combine the changing melody of the lacework of stone and glass and their rays of light with the intermittent thunder of the bells and with the hum of the sonorous naves, where the plain song rises and falls. The cathedral often sheltered the neighboring university[1] and never entirely relinquished to it the cult of the intellectual

---

[1] The councils of the University of Paris were held at St. Julien le **Pauvre.**

life, for the students met the artisans under its vaults to commune with them in the collective and confused elaboration of farces, mystery plays, and moralities; and so, even before the university, it presented a powerful summary of the idea of the century and of the images of life. It formulated for us those turbulent schools where four or five nations came for their instruction, where the overlapping elements of all kinds collaborate—the master with his disciples, the Greek philosophers with the fathers of the Church, and what is taught with what is learned. The immeasurable mind of Aristotle, from which revolutionary thought claimed its authority against the theologians, would have recognized in the disordered unity and the rich material of this time the irruption of the genius of the senses which every thousand years arises from the depths of the peoples to save the world from the dangers of pure abstraction.

Men had cursed the flesh,

AMIENS (XIV Century).
The gilded Virgin.
(*Cathedral.*)

disdained form, and repressed the desire to love them
for what they teach us. And they had continued
to do this for so long a time that on the day
when that desire could no longer be restrained, it

Tours (xiv Century). Corbel. (*Old cathedral.*)

changed the axis of life, revealed life to itself, and
finally stifled it. There was such an overflowing
of forms, men were so drunk with sensations, that
not only was the Christian idea of purification an-
nihilated, but the art which had come to protest
against that idea was devoured. It died because it
had satisfied, with too great a violence, the needs that
had given it birth. In less than three hundred years
the French mind followed the course that leads from
Sens or from Noyon, from Notre Dame, from Chartres,

from Beauvais—from naked logic, unity, harmony, and the ever-present impulse of sobriety and strength, to Rheims, the magnificent, sensual orgy, and to Rouen, the frail and flamboyant death struggle. Sculpture,

BOURGES (XIV Century). The Saved. (*Cathedral.*)

affixed to the walls at first, incorporated in the walls, later on, detached itself from the walls; and once the dissociation had begun, it accentuated itself rapidly, until the final anarchy. From the fourteenth century on, it expresses scarcely more than that which one finds in an individual portrait having such characteristics as penetration, health, cordiality, and self-confidence. And then the image maker knows too much, he handles his chisel with such ease that he can watch it toying with the material, and the force that once governed his heart has entirely passed into his hand. The lines of the cathedral become complicated and entangled; they lose their meaning; its vaults are encumbered with supplementary ribbing which will soon be cut up into fragments by useless ornament. The cathedral disappears under the profusion of the detail, its supports are weakened by being hollowed out with carving; every day its solid parts are diminished and a greater risk of a collapse is incurred by making room for the great windows that were invading it more and more. When it had appeared, the world was dying of darkness, of solitude and silence; the cathedral revealed light, form, and tumult to the world, and was to die as a result.

Hence the explosive and transitory character of the French art of the Middle Ages. The cathedral had crutches, as Michelet said in his reproach. Its flying buttresses are so pure because they bear faithfully the weight of a world, as a century gathers the effort of a thousand years into a single effort. And so the cathedral has that aspect of improvisation which renders it so alive and which also gives it its appearance of fragility. When we think of the haste with which the work was done, we are tempted to think that the French people, suddenly aroused from sleep to enter upon the intoxication of life, dazzled with the daylight, overrun by innumerable images, and overflowing with energy and joy, had a premonition that, between the theocratic oppression which had reached its death struggle and the military oppression which was coming, it would barely have time to express, in tempestuous confusion, that which it had understood of Nature upon its first meeting with her since the death of the ancient gods.

When the cathedral was vanquished, at the same time with the Commune and for the same reasons, there remained nothing—save itself—of the impulse from which it had come forth. The energy of the nation, at first enervated by its own growth, and then crushed under the renewed invasions and under what was perhaps the most atrocious misery that history has known —the energy of the nation gave way   Nothing was

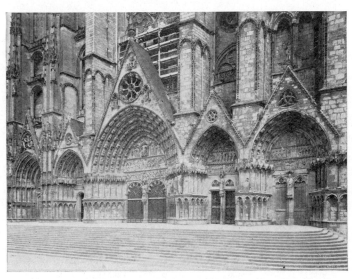

BOURGES (XIII to XVI Century). The five portals of the cathedral.

left in France but the growing monarchy and Catholicism, which, by working upon the disheartened spirits of the people, was regaining the ground it had lost. The upper clergy, the representative of political Christianity, took possession of the cathedral in order to oppose the doctrinal Christianity of the regular clergy against the human Christianity of the people. It is, thanks to the people, that Catholicism profited by the blows which the Middle Ages had dealt it and gained the fame for æsthetic greatness which has rendered it so alluring. It became for the future the sweet and terrible thing that we know, so powerful in its art, so powerful in its morality. It was diverse corresponding to the way in which it manifested itself in France, in Italy, in Flanders, in Spain, in Germany, or in England, and yet it was one in its dogma and in its authority. It was at once theological and popular, traditional and spontaneous, universal and national. Students have believed—the Catholic Church itself sincerely believed—that it had made the Occident of the thirteenth century in its own image. In reality, it was France and Europe, in the exaltation of their life, which, for one hundred and fifty years, caused Catholicism to assume their own appearance.

When St. Bernard, already anathematizing the stiff Romanesque sculpture which decorated the earlier temples, was at the same time combating the communal spirit and, in Abelard, condemning the spirit of the universities, he said, "so numerous and so astounding did the variety of the forms appear everywhere, that the monk is more tempted to study the marbles than his books and to meditate on these figures far more than on the law of God." The cathedral is Christian only for those who do not feel that all things human contain Christianity, and precede and survive it, as it is anti-Christian only for those who do not sense the way in which Christianity remains human.[1] The cathedral is human and traditional and revolutionary, and profoundly opposed to the principle of authority in

---

[1] Stated in the modern form, the problem is without meaning. People are still discussing as to whether the builders of the cathedral were not "anticlerical." When will they begin to understand that every rise of life in the breast of the masses shatters the dogma of yesterday, even when it celebrates it? Whether they are freemasons or not is of no importance. The image makers of the Middle Ages are not freethinkers. They are free instincts.

moral matters set forth by Christianity when it claimed to be definitively organized; we see this opposition in the way that Gothic art expressed moral ideas in the form most accessible to our senses and translated

POITIERS (Palais de Justice) (end of the XIV Century). Jeanne de Boulogne, detail.

into the language which is most purely that of the senses, the dogmas which affirm the majesty of pure spirit. It rehabilitates the nature of man, it rehabilitates nature itself in the world where he lives. It loves man for himself, weak and filled with an un-

bounded courage, and it describes his paradise with the
trees, the waters, and the clouds which he sees when he
raises his eyes or when he goes forth from the gates of
his city; it tells of the vegetables full of earth and the
fruits that are brought to him from the fields on
market days by the domestic animals who share
his lot.

The cathedral, indeed the whole art of the ogive,
realizes for a moment the equilibrium between the
virgin forces of the people and the metaphysical
monument whose mold Christian philosophy had been
preparing for a thousand years. But these forces
break the mold when they have attained their full
expansion. The masons and the image makers, in
opposition to the Church, consecrate the entrance of
the ever-dying and ever-renascent form of the world
into our spirit and our flesh. The desire of the people
sweeps on into its movement all the inert matter of the
prohibitions and the formulas in which the mechanism
of theocracy claims the right to imprison it. Undoubtedly, the clergy imposed on the decorators an
obligation, which they, however, very cheerfully accepted—that of respecting in the images a rigorous
hierarchy, an inflexible and symbolic method of writing,
over the arrangement of which the Church kept surveillance; "the art alone belongs to the painter, the law
to the Fathers," said the council of Nicea.[1] The
council of Nicea was not aware that the art is everything
and that the law without it is only an empty garment,
for at the moment when art springs from the hearts of
men it is passion, will, suffering, religion, justice, life.
What did it matter, therefore, that the edifice was the
cross, that the apse was the crown of thorns, that the
choir was the head of Christ, that the fire of the stained

---

[1] For everything that concerns the external relationships in the art of the
cathedrals, consult *L'Art Religieux du 13e Siècle en France*, by Émile Mâle.

Avignon (xiv Century). The palace of the Popes.

glass was celestial light, and that the towers were arms in prayer? The crowd in the Middle Ages expressed itself symbolically because the symbol summarized the higher moral realities which it did not discuss, so that it might remain the freer to discover its spiritual realities and because it found within itself an inexhaustible pretext for giving voice to the thing that was stifling it. In the Middle Ages, symbolism and theology were bound up with life, and their life was the real one; they were only one element in the formidable symphony in which all the forces of that period met, responded to each other and were associated one with another. Society, unconcerned as to the elements which constituted it, allowed its equilibrium and its activity to be organized spontaneously by the fiery life of these elements.

When we stand at a distance or on a height, it seems as if we could not apprehend the history of a great race save in the general characteristics which mark that race for us. It then seems to us to be contained entirely in one particular work and to take on a form that is, so to speak, visible or tangible, wherein all the adventures of its intelligence and its sorrow appear, as if sublimated. It seems to have lived, bled, carried on war and commerce, cultivated the soil, and wrought in iron, only that this work may be born, that it may contain, summarize, and exalt the obscure lives and the unformulated feeling of the billions of its living and its dead. And thereafter, each time that we evoke the spirit of a people, the name of a man who most obviously represents it in its most decisive hour comes to our lips. Beethoven brings us Germany, Shakespeare England, Michael Angelo Italy, Cervantes Spain, Rubens Flanders, Rembrandt the Netherlands. When we think of France, we hesitate. Montaigne is the hero of the eternal intelligence, standing above the destiny of the peoples, above their language, above their passion. Pascal has not the divine joy that mounts with the blood of the people in its acts, even when these are the acts of injustice and despair. In those who have best told our story, Rabelais, La Fontaine, and Molière, there is lacking that kind of

LISIEUX. House of the xv Century.

mystic passion which renders the human soul heroic and which makes it possible that, through a single man and at a single moment, there may be concentrated and epitomized within the human soul all the powers of life, which, at that particular moment, define for our eyes the course of destiny and of the world. Hugo puffs up his power with programs and sermons. Well then! the cathedral has everything we love in Hugo or Pascal; everything of ourselves that we find in Rabelais, Molière, or La Fontaine; everything that, in Montaigne, rises above time and place.

But by its vaults and by its towers it elevates all this in so lyrical a passion, that it lifts the French crowd up to the supreme conceptions which the greatest of our artists have almost never attained.

The French hero is the cathedral.

LUBECK

Chapter VIII. THE EXPANSION OF THE FRENCH IDEA

I

T HE "French miracle" was such a miracle indeed, that it stupefied the people of the cities and compelled the poor of the countryside to come as often as they were able to see, rising higher every year above the slopes of the tiled roofs and the sharp gables, the blue and gold embroidery of the painted stones, the blood of the stained glass glowing in the light, and the massive or tapering sweep of the towers and the spires that vibrated with the throb of the bronze. Their work done, the masons and image makers looked upon it with as much astonishment as if they had come from the other end of the world to

view it. Each one had labored in his workshop, had
made fast a window, had cut a statue, or erected his
wall—stone on stone; each one had seen only a leaf
or a blade of grass in the forest; many had died, even,
without raising their eyes from the bud that had grown
under their hands, from the fruit whose ripening they
had guarded and not always had the time to gather.
And now that the scaffolding was removed, and the
trestles were torn down, here were tall, solemn vaults,
rays of light in cataracts, a slender mountain of columns and statues filling the familiar heavens. Whence
came this formidable unity in which the presence of
faith, of hope, of the living god who dwelt in the heart
of the crowds affirmed itself without anyone, not even
the master builder who had made the plan for the
edifice, dreaming of expressing it? Not one of them
knew that it pre-existed in him, not one of them knew
that his own humility and his neighbor's and his own
weakness and his neighbor's—proceeding in the same
direction, at the same pace, and with the same rhythm
—were fusing more and more each day to bring forth
the huge, anonymous power which should burst upon
history as the highest manifestation of collective
idealism. When they turned to view their work not
one of them remembered that he had set his hand to
it, but they knew that that way was paradise.

And so people came from the country, and even from
a greater distance. They came to see, they came to
take lessons, they came to ask the master builders to
cross the sea or the mountains at the expense of the
rich cities, all of which wanted to have the most beautiful church or the highest rampart. For two centuries, moreover, France had been the great hearth of
the Occident. Through the Normans, it had conquered Sicily and England; under the ingenuous and
powerfully stimulating pretext of delivering the Holy

Sepulcher, it was incessantly sending forth colonizing expeditions to the Orient, covering Syria, Greece, and the islands with French settlements, and attempting to occupy Egypt and northern Africa. French barons were wearing the crowns of Athens, of Constantinople,

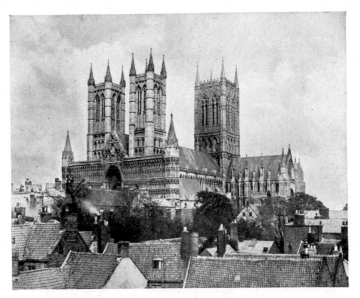

ENGLAND (XII Century). Lincoln Cathedral.

of Cyprus, and of Jerusalem. There emanated from the French soul that energy for expansion which permitted it each year, at a hundred points in France, to dig canals, to build bridges, aqueducts, and fountains, to open hospitals and schools, and to hang the pointed vaults, in majestic flight, a hundred feet from the soil. As it was to teach the world, five hundred years later, that the revelation of monarchy was outlived, so it ingenuously and joyously denounced theological revelation by sowing action, life, experience, and liberty everywhere.

23

Where the military men were unable to gain an entrance, thought still would penetrate by means of the merchants and the artists. On all the rivers of Europe, boats were carrying the material and the thought of the West. French romances sped all over the world. Almost all the heads of the foreign universities had passed through the University of Paris, where the nations maintained permanent colleges. Philippe Chinard, the French master builder, followed Frederick II everywhere. Charles of Anjou had called another, Pierre d'Angicourt, to Sicily. St. Louis, prisoner of the Saracens and spiritual king of the earth, was accompanied to Palestine by Eudes de Montereau, who fortified Jaffa. After the great Guillaume de Sens had broken his legs by a fall from the scaffolding in the nave of Canterbury, a hundred others had answered the call from foreign communes or vestry boards. Martin Ragevy and Villard de Honnecourt built churches in distant parts of Hungary. Companies of masons left for Germany. A master builder of Troyes built the temples, convents, castles, and commanderies of Cyprus. Mathieu d'Arras, who made the plans for the cathedral and the bridge of Prague, came from Avignon. The greater part of the Spanish cities, in the fourteenth century, called in French architects. Others went as far as Poland, and even Finland. The Benedictines, the Dominicans, and the Cistercians, above all, founded houses and orders that spread the vital thought over Europe. The Order of the Templars, the Order of Calatrava, and the Teutonic Order spread with a continuous activity in which, from one end of Christendom to the other, men recognized for an hour their sole and puissant hope. The great moral unity of Catholicism everywhere took on the appearance which the social idealism of the French communes irresistibly imposed on it.

Almost everywhere, at least in the beginning, the master builders would bring a first plan inspired by Amiens, or Rheims, or Chartres, or Notre Dame, or Beauvais. But the building of a cathedral often went

ENGLAND (XI and XII Centuries). Ely Cathedral.

on for two or three centuries, native architects succeeded the French masters, the masons, and image makers, who were recruited in increasing numbers from the local corporations, took root in their soil. The sky

and its sun and its clouds, the surrounding plain, the
bare or woody mountain that rose at the gates of the
city and the age-old forces established in the race by
the regime of the seasons, by the nature of the work
done in the country, its trade, peace, war, and food—
all took form, little by little, in the profile of the naves
and of the towers, in the disposition of the bays, in the
transparence of the stained glass, and in the projections which distributed light and shadow on the front
of the monuments. But the fact that the style was
originally a borrowed one was always a drawback to
the work; never, or hardly ever, did any town or country again have the impulse from which, for an hour,
there issued forth the spontaneous agreement of the
French crowd with the enthusiastic creation and the
logic of the artisans who expressed it.

II

England, however, barely missed participating in the
miracle at the same time with northern France, when
the latter country lived through that moment which,
until then, has never occurred more than once in the
history of a people and which France, the India of the
Middle Ages, and the Ancient Empire of Egypt alone
have known. England discovered the ogive at the
same time that we did, if not some years earlier. Why,
therefore, could she not, by making use of those powerful faculties for generalization of which, from Roger
Bacon to Newton, she has given as great a proof as we
have from Abelard to Lamarck—why could she not
systematize the use of the ogive, hang the stones
of her soil in the air between two diagonal lines of
ribbing, articulate the gigantic limbs of the great
body, and cause the flying buttresses to rise from

ENGLAND (XIII Century). Litchfield Cathedral.

the pavement of the cities as if to support the weight
of the towers? [1]

It was because the English cathedral was principally
the luxury of a certain class of society, because it did
not translate one of those surges of idealism in which
the French crowd sometimes offers a meeting place—
for ten years, for a month, for an hour—to the poor
and the rich, to those who do nothing, and to those
who work, to those who suffer, and to those who are
happy. As in France, to be sure, the English middle
class had, in the eleventh century, secured the rights
that were confirmed by Magna Charta in 1215. But
in order to maintain these rights it was not obliged to
struggle constantly as did our communes, which were
menaced incessantly by the Church and the barons. In
the freedom of the English commune, the solidarity of
the social organs was not so necessary, and the fierce
pride of the corporations, which the political powers
always treated on the footing of equality, set them up
one against the other without danger to themselves.
The cathedral was an expression of the wealth they had
in common and not of their brotherhood.

It is egoistic, exclusive, and close to the great current
of humanity; its formula is stiff and dry, seldom animated—and then always timidly—by the confused and
swarming life of the bas-reliefs and the statues through
which the French artisans brought to the framework
of society, like fruits on an altar, the tribute of their
love. For five hundred years the aristocratic arts of
priests and soldiers had been carried on in the shelter
of the ramparts of the military strongholds and the
walls of the monasteries of these mystic islands, and

---

[1] And why did she send over to France for Guillaume de Sens if this
builder, and perhaps the architect of Saint-Denis, were not the first in
Europe to use the broken arch as the determining principle of the whole
architecture of the ogive?

from such arts nothing of the people, or of life itself, could come forth. Ireland, with its dripping humidity buried under its green leaves, could not pass on to England, when transmitting Christianity to that country, anything more than the miniatures patiently composed in its monasteries while the eternal rain

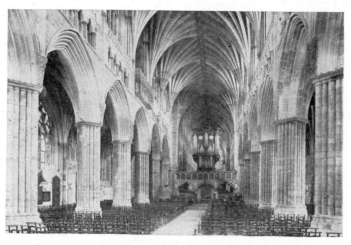

ENGLAND (XIII Century).   Exeter Cathedral, the nave.

drenched the windowpanes.   The weapons of the Saxons, the carved prows of the Scandinavian barks, and the importations from Byzantium were only so many separate elements for which the flame of a homogeneous people, that could weld them into a unified force, was lacking.   When the Normans arrived they appropriated the Roman tradition imported from France in the course of previous centuries, and built many powerful churches in which a square and crenelated tower rose from the center of the nave, as if to impress upon the mind the idea of military domination. But they were camping on British soil.   They were to furnish to the English people only the unshakable foundation of temples and strongholds. Cathedrals, abbeys, castles, ramparts, illuminated manuscripts, funerary statues of alabaster—all was an art of the classes, from the beginning until the hour when Shakespeare frees and spreads over the world the torrent of emotions and images sealed up in the heart of the crowd by all those somber stones and those carved sepulchers.

As one descends the valley of the Seine, the spires that appear above the towers become sharper and frailer. In Normandy, the life that creeps about the side of the French cathedrals and thoroughly imbues them with movement, becomes fixed and already tends to lose movement, even while it becomes slighter and more abundant, while the mass becomes airy and is cut into more and more by openings. The mighty poem of the people becomes complicated, mannered, and inclines toward the attributes of the art object. We are midway between the social art of France and the stiff rich monument, that we see when the mist rises, lifting above the lawns and the trees the symmetrically pointed spires and the parapets of the central tower that weighs heavily upon the long, low nave. Already at Rouen and at Coutances the tower is placed over the cross of the transept. And if the living decoration of the French provinces still animates the Norman churches, their sharply cut and voluntary movement gives us a foretaste of the geometrical decoration of England.

The diadem raised by the merchants of the British Isles above their rude industrial cities seemed to be made by the hands of goldsmiths and, in contrast with the enthusiasm expressed in the monuments which on the other side of the Channel derive their life from the houses and the fields in order to exalt it, the English cathedral is very obviously conceived as a proud hom-

age to the emancipation of a hard and egoistic class.
Whereas wings spread out above the naves of the Continental churches in which the vibrant columns rose
from the soil, here a wooden roof supported by corbels
dominated the low naves, which were arrested on all
sides by implacable horizontals. Often, tight sheaves
of parallel ribbing choked all the lines of the nave whose

ENGLAND (XIII Century). Carnarvon Castle.

profiles and curves disappeared among the tense clusters which they formed—a forest composed of a thousand dead branches without the leafage of the vault
and without space and without air above them. In the
apse, where the French builder allowed the darkness to
deepen, where the wall was rounded like a cradle
about the living god that it inclosed so lovingly, the
wall fell away like a portcullis, permitting the light to
pass through the straight-lined colonnades as if they
were iron railings.

The supreme expression of the English ogival style,

the perpendicular, appeared at the time when, among
us, the flame of stone, crackling as it launched skyward,
was announcing the last flicker of the exhausted life
around which a fatal twilight was rapidly gathering.
On the one hand we have the end of a dream, on the
other an affirmation of the will; on one side the abrupt

GERMANY (XI Century).   Cathedral of Speyer.

dissociation of the social forces, the defeat that comes
day by day, even as man's illusions recommence each
day, the mad charges, the feverish plunging of a civilization at the point of death—and on the other side the
concentration of all the means of conquest: method
in warfare, a definite goal to attain, victory, the practiced and steady rigor of a civilization that is determining and establishing itself.   Whereas on the one
side there is no longer anything more than ruins or
abandoned works, we find pinnacles arising on the
other side and spires shooting upward, the wrinkled
façades that appear to be made of frost and glass,

ALSACE (XII and XIII Centuries).   Strassburg Cathedral.

and the close-set latticed tracery of stone stalactites. For the spectral, aërial, and vague poetry of the English people to have its full effect in these icy and magnificent monuments, one should see them under a blue veil of moonlight or see the sharp spires rising out of the wet leaves and the mist. The art of the north demands the complicity of the vapor that spreads through space, of the foliage, of the sleeping water, and the uncertain illumination of the night. The rectangular manor houses lift up above the lakes the formidable profile of their polygonal towers, and as we view them we feel their whole bulk, and yet something more than their bulk, weighing upon the sinister history of the Middle Ages in England. They would not become a part of the mighty dream of this people— whose will has all the power that dwells in the lines of its towers, a people as resistant as their walls, this people whose soul, when it peers to its depths, is as steeped in fog and moonlight as they are themselves —they would not become a part of the dream of England, I repeat, if a mantle of ivy did not cover them from top to bottom, if blood did not filter between their stones, and if the echo of falling axes were not heard when one traverses their black corridors, where wandering specters brush by one in passing. The soul of the north has not been able to define itself by the visible lines of the world; and only poetry and music are vague enough to receive it in their embrace.

III

The sea with its ebb and flow carries the thought from one shore to the other. England, which owed so much to the Scandinavians, in its turn carried Anglo-Norman art to Norway, whereas Sweden, whither Etienne Bonneuil had come with his companions from

ALSACE (XIII Century). Strassburg Cathedral, a face.

France at the end of the thirteenth century, to build the cathedral of Upsala, received a mingling of German and French architecture by way of the Baltic. Indirectly, it is still French art that fertilizes the eastern slope of the northern peninsula, for German art came in a straight line from the masons of Champagne, of Ile-de-France, and of Picardy.

That is not to say that Germany had not attempted repeatedly, from the darkest moments of the Middle Ages onward, to create a national art for herself from the elements which she received from without, or that she evolved from within. Charlemagne had created a mixed civilization—Ancient, Byzantine, Germanic, and Christian—whose plastic expression has practically disappeared. It was the work of monks and scribes, a crude and false thing that had to die. When the Romanesque appeared it found, on the contrary, a social and political soil perfectly adapted to give to it a very powerful, clear-cut, and pure character. The Holy Roman Empire, the clergy, and the feudal lords meet there for an hour and bind those enormous stones with a moral cement so hard that it did not seem possible that mystic and warlike Germany would ever cease building the red walls that are stained by the rain and seldom animated by statues. As a matter of fact, it was late when she ceased, and she did so with bad grace. And when Bohemia desired a national architecture and sought solid materials for it near-by, it was in the nervous and sober combination of the massive German Romanesque and of the French ogival style that she found the formula for her art. The temples on the banks of the Rhine combined round and octagonal forms in the apses, in the transepts, in the four towers at the corners, and in the short curved steeples. Doubtless, they never expressed the living emotion of a people any more than did the other architectural forms of Germany; they expressed the power of the affiliated military and religious castes, who nevertheless recognized the spontaneous expression of the popular classes, faithfully and strictly disciplined. The real soul of the German crowds was never in the stone. The men of this period, who revealed the German soul to the future, were the wandering minstrels who sang the tale of the Nibelungen as, later on, it was to be heard in the voice of the master singers of the industrial cities and the hero musicians of the hours of hope or of despair —Luther, Sebastian Bach, Beethoven, and Richard Wagner. The German cathedral is forever being built up and pulled down. A few men come together; suddenly cries ring out from all their breasts and float above them; anon the sounds have found their echoing form in aërial vaults for which all the hearts are pillars. And when the men are no longer assembled, the cathedral has disappeared.

GERMANY (XIII Century). Cathedral of Naumburg, Countess Baba.

Despite the Hansa, despite the league of the Rhine towns, despite the wealth of the free cities of Germany whose rise was assisted by the struggle, in the thirteenth century, between the Pope and the Emperor, despite the strength of the Teutonic Order which covered Bavaria and the Sieben Gebirge with square towers flanked with sharp-pointed watchtowers, Germany of the Middle Ages had no original architecture.[1] The German cathedral does not resemble the living monuments of the French provinces or the marvelous goldsmith architecture of England or the mighty markets of Flanders or those accumulations of stone over shadowy depths in which we get a gleam of gold, as in the Spanish churches. It remains quite itself by the pedantic complications of its lines, the tangle of its ribbing, its stiffness, and its bristling, narrow, and metallic movement. But it is especially when it frees itself from the formula which it extracted little by little from the ogival edifices of Picardy and Burgundy that it almost invariably sacrifices its law of internal structure to the abstract and confused sentimentalism of the ornamented surfaces.

It was the wise and foolish virgins of the French portals who came to Strassburg to bring the good news to Germany. The definite balance of ensemble and the grace of the smiling statues in which, however, there is already the mark of the good-natured sentimentalism of the Teutons would not have surprised a master builder of the valley of the Seine. But the hard red façade, with its resemblance to rusty iron, already showed the tendencies of the German style through the abundance and the stiffness of the vertical lines, the long, pious parallels, the dry spindling forms of the

---

[1] The cathedral of Cologne, which was for so long a time considered the type and the masterpiece of Gothic architecture, is a turgid, thin, and dry amplification of the cathedral of Amiens.

colonnettes, and despite the magic life of the whole work which reminds one of a windowpane in winter when it is enriched by the fern shapes of the frost. Such a building was the necessary step between the mighty animation of Amiens, of Rheims, of Notre Dame de Paris, and the dogmatism of Cologne in which the

GERMANY (XIV Century). Gate at Neubrandenburg.

letter of the theological law had reigned two centuries earlier and which for a hundred years presided over the severe development of Romanesque architecture.

When the German cities had associated themselves to regulate the movement of all the treasures of Europe, the cloths of Flanders, the wines of France, the spices of the Orient brought by ships to the mouth of the Rhine and transported along its tributaries to the center and heart of the Teutonic continent, when by reason of the foreign war between the Papacy and the

24

Empire, the currents of activity that circulated everywhere had brought to all the cities workmen from the
Rhenish provinces, French image makers, wood carvers
from the Black Forest, and bronze workers that the

GERMANY (XIV Century).   Rathaus of Stralsund.

honest and powerful Roman school of Bishop Bern-
ward of Hildesheim had been educating for two centuries, a fertile mingling of all these confused forces
developed in the German soil the revelation of its desires.   To be exact, the process went on for a century,

the thirteenth, during which the statue makers of
Naumburg, before they reverted to the complication
and the honest sentimentalism of German sculpture,

GERMANY (XIV Century). Cathedral of Ulm.

made a vigorous effort in the direction of the monumental style whose qualities of love, strength, and simplicity the masters of Rheims were at that moment
revealing to France and to the world. But this cen-

tury sufficed to define the dominating tendencies of
Gothic-building in Germany before the mind of the
workman in the industrial cities had seized upon it
and developed in it, with meticulous ingenuity and
patience, the complications which, while it all contributed to lead architecture away from its true function, prepared Germany for the Renaissance by indi-
vidualizing little by little its industries and crafts.

Beside the cathedrals of our northern provinces,
square to the very base of their towers, established so
powerfully on their horizontal lines and deriving all
the elements of their incomparable lyrism from the
life about them and from the need to fulfill a definite
purpose, the German cathedral is subjective and con-
fessedly sentimental; clearly, it aims to rise as high as
possible at all costs and to attain its objects by abstract
means.   Everywhere we find hard lines mounting
straight upward and giving all the more sweep to the
edifice because its pyramidal form is indicated in them
from the ground to the top of the spire that is planted
full in the center of the façade, on a single tower which
gathers together the elements of the ensemble in order
to carry it still higher by prolonging the lines of the
pointed steeples which shoot up from all sides.   It was
of German Gothic that those writers were thinking
when they defined the Catholic architecture of the
Middle Ages as an impetuous aspiration toward heaven.
It is above all a moral aspiration, and it never attained
so perfect an expression in balance of structure as to
make it comparable with that which gives to the
towers of Rheims their aërial lightness, to the old
spire of Chartres its pure and infinite movement, and
to the towers of Notre Dame or Amiens the tremendous
power to lift the pavement of the cities to the very
bosom of space where, every day of spring and summer
and autumn, it is caressed by the gold of the last mo-

ments of the sunlight. It is a noble effort, none the less, a mighty and mystic elevation of human sentiment toward the poignant love for that unknown thing which the sense of life is, and which the great music

FLANDERS (XIII and XIV Centuries). The market of Ypres.

will stir up, in the depths of our hearts, five centuries later.

In the north of Germany, over which war passes less frequently, where the bare plains that descend to the seashore contrast with the overhanging rocks, the trailing mists of the Rhine, and the forests of black pines of the mountainous regions of Bavaria and Austria, where the most powerful Hanseatic cities of the Empire, Lubeck, Bremen, and Hamburg claimed the commerce of all northern Europe, from the counters of London and Bruges to the fairs of Nijni-Novgorod, the pyramidal thrust of the churches was far less wild.

Representing wholesale commerce and maritime life, the solid Rathauses were set up with walls as high as cliffs, lightened by circular openings between pointed turrets, to withstand the salt spray which forms a green coating on the copper steeples that rise above the red roofs. The blue-and-black coating of the bricks gave them an oily varnish, and the fishermen with their boots of seal hide, returning from the ice flows, found again their slaty sky, their greasy waters, and the dull luster of the tar on their boats. Here the soil and the water took architecture back to themselves, and the ogive restored its original significance by adapting it to its function.

More profoundly rooted than the great Catholic idea, as a result of which Europe was to be covered with temples that should be of the same type everywhere, the local use of the edifice, at least in the countries of very marked character, weighed down the idea until it touched the earth at every point. The Dutch, a practical, moderately idealistic, and spontaneously balanced people, preserved the essential principles of their first monuments until the period when, in Germany and in France, the growing complication of ogival architecture marked the end of mediæval society. The independence of Holland and the Reformation are announced by the bare naves, the massiveness and the roundness of the pillars which support them, and the sturdy gathered strength that is a quality of their mind, the mind of serious business men, of engineers, and of the solid soldiers that the Dutch make upon occasion. We see their quality everywhere—in the thick, low dikes that hurl back the sea, in the slow, full-bellied boats that come up to the heart of the pasture lands, as well as in the buildings of to-day which continue to embody the unshakable good sense of the Dutch amid the architectural anarchy of Europe.

Flanders is nearer the soil on which the cathedrals rose. There, from the end of the twelfth century onward, the cities of workmen where the trade in hides and woolens

FLANDERS (XIII to XV Century).   Market and
belfry of Bruges.

centered, where cloths were woven and dyed—Bruges and Ypres especially—built formidable markets whose vertical walls, pierced by two regular rows of windows, have the sureness that comes of necessity.   They unhesitatingly express a categorical ideal, thanks to "a

century of friendship."[1]　Here the admirable heroism
of popular need triumphs over all narrow interests and
belies the systems that endeavor to bring it back to an
abstract, universal, and dogmatic form.　Ogival art
was so little the language of Christianity when the
latter is stripped of everything which binds it to a
given locality and to matter, that if its social expression in France assumed an externally religious form, the
principle which it carried with it engendered commercial buildings in Flanders, as, in the Italian city, it
brought forth sober fortresses and proud municipal
palaces.　The Flemings built these also, to be sure, but
it was to defend their warehouses and their looms.
Their finest monuments were born of their mercantile
spirit, as the finest Italian monuments were born of the
passionate individualism which characterizes Italy,
and as the finest French monuments sprang from the
social idealism which has been the life of France and
which passes, through Rabelais and Diderot, from the
Gothic cathedral to the Revolution.

IV

Perhaps in all Europe during the Middle Ages of
Christianity, mystic Spain was the only country that
was unable to attain the summarized architectural
expression of the desire of its multitudes.　Two centuries of incessant warfare between the natives and the
Moors, a violent confusion of races and languages, a
soil cut up by ravines, by mountains, and by inaccessible plateaus which stony deserts isolated one from
another, were enough to prevent a collective soul from
defining itself there.　Spain underwent the influence of
Roman architecture, Arab architecture, Romanesque

---

[1] Michelet, *Histoire de France.*

SPAIN (XIII Century). Cathedral of Avila.

architecture, and French architecture, one after the
other, until the hour of political unity revealed her to
herself, but too late for her to escape the influences of
nascent European individualism, which at least en-
couraged her to release the brutal and subtle energy
that she possessed even though she did not recognize

SPAIN (XV Century). Façade of the palace of Guadalajara.

it. For four hundred years the little Christian monarchies of her northern provinces had to send for the
architects and sculptors of France, of Burgundy, of
Germany, and the Netherlands to build and decorate
the alcazars and the churches. The sculptors of the
school of Toulouse invaded Castile, Galicia, Navarra,
and Catalonia whither, in the thirteenth and fourteenth centuries, the image makers and the architects
of the valley of the Seine repaired in their turn. In the
sixteenth century, in the full tide of the Renaissance,
when Italy was already pressing upon her through her

Spain (xiii to xv Century). Cathedral of Burgos.

Mediterranean provinces, Spain was still calling in French and Burgundian masters.

From the time when the Cistercians and the Clunisians introduced Romanesque sculpture into Spain, the art, upon contact with this people that loves picturesque projections and brutal contrasts of light and shade, assumed a character of exuberance and of decorative profusion in which architectural line was lost. It was in vain that the hell which caused the capitals and tympanums to bristle with monstrous beasts retreated before the invasion of the saints and the Virgin which the French image makers brought with them when the building guilds in France were too rich in workmen to employ them for the construction and decoration of the churches. The native pupils of the visiting artisans were men of a different type: half-warriors, half-peasants, whom the fire of the sky had rendered as hard as their flints, and who chopped away the trees so as to have no shade in which to cool their blood; such men could not accommodate the mystic fever that consumed them to the profiles of the churches whose sculptured stone lent animation to the work without in any way impairing its power, even as an undulation passes over the mass of leaves at the edge of a forest. At the same time the memory of the Moorish leather workers, armorers, and goldsmiths pursued them at their labors. They chiseled stone as though it were a metal that one can cast, twist, and emboss from within. When Gil de Siloe, the fifteenth-century master, received the manifold heritage from the French statue makers, from the Spaniards whom they had educated, and from the Berber decorators who sawed the lacework of the paneling and the railings of the mosques out of wood —the tombs and the altar screens, enormous jewels of the lapidary which came from his hands, seemed to be incrusted with gems and to bristle with stalactites; they were fluted and warty like an embossed copper.

When Spain had only Granada to recapture from the Moors, when the dust and the rocks of the peninsula had been reunited under the Catholic scepter, there was really an hour when, if moral fellowship was not

SPAIN. Mausoleum at Miraflores, by Gil de Siloe

attained in order to reach great architecture at a single bound, there was, at least, a fever that infected the whole land in common; something funereal, cruel, and frenzied fired all the somber hearts and spurted forth from them like jets of blood thickened with black clots, like furious torrents of gold and stones. What need there was for order and harmony! The naves built by the French and the mosques built by the Mussulmans were torn open so that in the middle of them, between gratings of gold, a choir filled with golden ornaments might be installed, a mountain of gold that gleams in the shadows. Without the lamps it would have been impossible to see the clothed idols, the crucified corpses with the bleeding knees, or the crust of gold which covered the tangled ribbing of the vaults, or the night that swallows up everything. The golden orgy of the Flemish altar screens encumbers the whole nave, enormous golden staircases descend into the churches which are crushed by heavy lacework of stone. Here is a forest of heavily built belfries, here are thick traceries of closely worked embroidery in which the flame of the Gothic twists like an arabesque and under which the Arab arch breaks the ogival arch and causes it to become round and undulating. Here is an ocean of enervated sculptures wherein the most mystic of peoples offers the fearful testimony of its submission to the purposes of the most mystic of centuries. We are made to think of the crackling of the fires that burn victims at the stake, of their charred bodies, and of the frightful immolation of the human being to the savage powers that he can neither control nor understand and obey.

Between the sublime instinct of the crowds who accepted all the symbols so as to permit their creative force to reach its goal without weakening, and the new-born reason of the individuals who discussed all the symbols in order that they might try to penetrate the mystery of nature, there was a separation that tore men's flesh, and it was here that the expression of this tragic period reached its apogee of confusion and disorder. Spain must have felt that she was born to the collective life too late and that she was no longer in time to be the first to expound the shaken idea of Catholicism; and it was perhaps because of remorse over the fact that she had not lived it through until after the others had done so, that she remained attached

Spain (end of the xv Century). Detail of the façade of San
Gregorio at Valladolid.

to it the most fiercely of all, and that she was the last.
In her fever, she heaped up all the stones wrought by
the sculptors who, for five hundred years, had been
living on her lean flanks, the Visigoths, the French, the
Flemings, the Germans, the Moors, the Jews, and the
Iberians, and it was with furor that she affirmed her

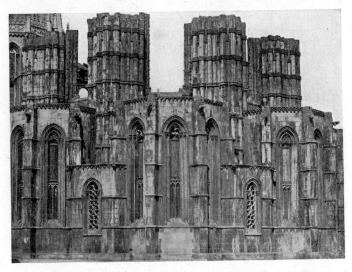

PORTUGAL (XIV and XV Centuries). Façade of the chapel of
Batalha.

irreducible fanaticism at the hour when the workmen
of the north, in the countries torn by war, were con-
fessing their despair.

However, nothing was lost. Man, goaded by doubt,
was commencing once more his climb toward the inaccessible summit. While the last masons were setting
the last and the highest spires over the last and the
highest naves, there sallied forth from a port of that
same Spain three caravels that were to plunge into the
west. In barely a hundred and fifty years, at a time

when there were no other roads than the rivers, when the cities were surrounded by walls, when several months of dangerous navigation were needed to go

PORTUGAL (XVI Century). Window of the abbey of Thomar.

from the coasts of France to the coasts of the Levant, the thing which had enabled the men of the Middle Ages to establish over the whole of Europe one of the densest and yet one of the most coherent and deeply

25

rooted civilizations in history—their obscure solidarity
—was now suddenly expanding as if the life of a too-
powerful body had burst its armor, as if its blood, its
glance, and its thought were spreading on all sides
through the rifts in the metal. The Portuguese architects were already asking the great mariners, who were
colonizing Africa and India, to tell them how the Indians decorated their temples, and to bring back to
them from their voyages the things that they would
group in the last flowerings of Moorish art and of ogival
art: keels, anchors, cables, the fauna and flora of the
seas, octopuses, madripores, corals, and shells. . . . The
conquest of the sea and the sky was to cause the spirit
to leap when once it was stripped of its ancient beliefs,
and bring it to the threshold of new intuitions where
new beliefs elaborate themselves little by little.

YPRES

ASSISI

Chapter IX. THE MISSION OF FRANCIS OF ASSISI

I

ITALY did not know the centuries of silence into which the annihilation of the Latin world plunged Gaul. Visited, as Gaul was, and more frequently than Gaul, by invasion, Italy retained, nevertheless, the memory of a well-ordered world of imposing aspect, one which resembled her own desire. The world of the ancient Mediterranean was to enter the modern world along the slope of her natural genius. Rome installed in the basilicas its rebaptized gods. The old races called upon the old civilizations to furnish them the means of awaiting the return of life.

The Barbarians overthrew the temples, their Italianized sons set them up again. And nothing is changed. From the ruin of yesterday still another basilica comes forth. The role of the conqueror is not to teach new processes, but to infuse new energy. He offers his virgin senses to the revelation of the glorious landscape. Thus was Greece rendered fecund by the Dorians. New generalizations are born from the melting of the

LUCCA (XI Century). The cathedral.

human material from the north in the Greco-Latin crucible.

We know it well. We must tell it. The greatest men have confessed it to us. Montaigne will ask Italy to approve his wisdom, Shakespeare invokes her name daily to justify his passion. Goethe lives through her,

and Stendhal, and Nietzsche. Byron dies through her.
In the days of Rembrandt's affluence, Giorgione reigns
over his studio, and when he becomes poor there is
always something of the Italian flame at the center of
the ray of light which follows his descent into the
shadows of the mind. It is Italy that organizes the

SIENA (XII and XIII Centuries). Fonte Branda.

tumult of Rubens, that reveals space to Velasquez, to
Poussin the architecture of the earth, to Claude Lorrain the architecture of the sky. As soon as one touches
Italy, one feels oneself overwhelmed by the intoxication that comes of understanding. Intelligence and
instinct merge, the scientist agrees that the artist shall
take possession of mechanics and of geometry, the
artist willingly grinds the colors and mixes the mortar.
The most atrocious voluptuousness is only a step from
sainthood; chastity burns like an orgy. Here love is
as funereal as death; death has the attraction and the

mystery of love. The ambition to dominate increases the thirst for conquest and knowledge, and yet knowledge and conquest are never definitive enough to make him who desires them worthy to command. Here pride is so strong that it will invariably abase itself before the things it still must learn in order that, with them, it may affirm itself before the world. Nowhere do crime and genius approach so closely to each other. Cain and Prometheus may be divined in the curve of every brow, in the depths of all eyes, and in all the hands that clutch the handle of the dagger or the tool of the workman. The earth trembles, and yet one feels something eternal in the profile of these mountains and the curve of these shores. Everywhere in Italy the world incorporates the mind with its form, and demands insatiably that the passion of men's hearts shall tear it forth. Italy! There is something that pains in the love that we have for you; we are afraid that we shall never know fully what you desire to teach us.

The potential force which is there must impose itself despite everything. Byzantium itself contributes less than is generally believed. Save at Ravenna, a colony of the Greek empire, save at Venice, where the Orient lives, save in Sicily, a Greek country where the Byzantine elements mingle with the Arab and Norman elements developing, in the Middle Ages, a voluptuous, cruel, paradoxical, and barbarous style that is impossible to define and difficult to recognize, Byzantium does not furnish Italy with a single idea which, on being transplanted, can originate a new architectural order. Italy accepts the cupola only because it already covers the Pantheon. In the middle of the thirteenth century, when the French image makers, the masters of Occidental sculpture, are in demand everywhere, Nicola Pisano studies Roman sarcophagi to learn the working of marble; he cuts, as if with a hatchet, his

SAN GIMIGNANO (XIII Century). Palace of the Podesta.

crowds of figures, glowing with life, rough and tense
from brutal effort; and so he sets up the trenchant
claim of the primitive Latin genius as opposed to the
claims of the artists of the north. Italy does nor forget, because she remains Italy.

Too often people look upon the perpetuation of
certain essential forms as the result of a traditional

VOLTERRA (XIII to XV Century). Fortress.

desire transmitted by the schools, when in reality the
forms are only an expression of the desires of a race
and of the indications of its soil. In all the Mediterranean countries, where palm trees, pines, and yew
trees detached their smooth trunks against a hard
sky, the column which reappears on the front of the
churches and which is used from the top to the bottom
of the towers of Romanesque Italy was a natural
expression that could not disappear. Antiquity and
the new Italy are in accord in these lines of galleries
bordered by arcades which spread their carved tracery
over the round baptisteries, the bare façades of the

temples, and the square campaniles. The basilica has called to its aid the trees whose clearly marked foliage allows the transparence and the limpidity of the world to shine through their overhanging branches, and it is

NICOLA PISANO. The Crucifixion, bas-relief. (*Baptistery of Pisa.*)

with their grace and pride that it covers the great Roman vessel.

The daily needs and the riches of Italy required this architecture. The image of her powerful cities and her villas, scattered over the sides of the hills among the cypresses, is imprinted on the hearts of those who cannot forget the educating power of her severe and melodious contours; it is in the hearts of all those who retain the clear memory of the white arcades and of the sheathings of black and white marble which from afar mingle the cathedrals with the blurred reds of the roofs. At the hour when the theocratic Romanesque was defining architectural

dogma in the north and west of Europe, Pisa and Lucca
and many other cities of continental Italy were already
passing beyond the towers and the temples to the
popular expression that suited the Italians, as the

TREVISO (1310).   San Nicola.

French Commune was to pass on, a century later, to
the popular expression that suited the French.   The
Italian Romanesque derives from the living spirit of
the race with perfect ease.   Italy will not have to rise
up throughout its whole extent, as the north of France
had to, in order to claim the right to assert its vision.

CIMABUE. Madonna with angels and Saint Francis of Assisi, fresco. (*Lower Church, Assisi.*)

Catholicism here never ceased to employ external
magnificence as an expression of political domination,
which, if it does not leave freedom of thought to man,
at least permits him complete freedom of sensation.
The gallery with colonnades defines the church and
the loggia, and the city house and the country house
which the Tuscans and Lombards would still be building
to-day, had they been left to their own devices. Along
the streets paved with their broad flagstones, it is still
the gallery with colonnades that shelters the crowd
from showers and sun, and supports the pink or white
façades whose rows of green shutters rise to the line
of the roof. Under the pines shaped like parasols, it is
the gallery that detaches its profiles against the straight-
lined terraces of the Florentine villas. And at the
gates of the cities, it protects the cool Campo Santo,
paved with marble, where one walks over the dead.

II

In contrast with what occurred at the decline of the
ancient civilizations, life reappeared in the north of the
country. The south had not been so deeply plowed by
the successive invasions. The Norman barons, in
southern Italy, had had to defend themselves against a
climate very different from their own and against a
race that had been enervated by an effort reaching
back farther into the past than did that of continental
Italy. Moreover, they asked the protection of the
Pope in repressing the conquered provinces. The
whole of the feudal organization was used in breaking
down the activity of the native population.

In the north, on the contrary, the cities profited by
the struggle between the Pope and the Emperor in
order to gain their autonomy and to fortify it by a
system of alternative alliances with one or the other of

the two powers that were fighting for the domination of Italy. Guelphs and Ghibellines, Blacks and Whites, Pisa, Florence, Lucca, Siena, Parma, Modena, Bergamo, Mantua, Milan, Pavia, and Cremona, took now the one standard and now the other, to live their life

GIOVANNI PISANO. Nativity. (*Museum of Pisa.*)

of incessant warfare either under the cross of the Church or under the flag of the Empire. They had, indeed, to choose between death—at a moment when the passion for living was rising in floods—and a life which depended for its strength upon active vigilance, unwearying curiosity, and a continuous physical and moral effort. Hence, the energy of the Italian Republic, out of which the modern mind has evolved, whether we like to admit it or not.

If, amid all these rival cities which were ready to fall

upon one another on the morrow of their violent recon-
ciliations, the rise of Florence was the most violent—
to the point of absorbing Tuscany in two centuries, of
playing a mighty role in the life of Europe, and of
inscribing herself upon our memory with lines of steel
—it was because she was at the crossing of the roads

MONTEPULCIANO (XIV Century). Cathedral.

that connect Rome with Germany and that connect
the two seas which border the peninsula. The whole
commercial, military, and moral life of the Italy of the
Middle Ages traversed her. The grace and the vigor
of the country that surrounds her were to make of her
senses, tense and burnt by fever, the natural mold
into which life was poured that it might be cast into
well-characterized and clear images. We must remember that Tuscany, when it called itself Etruria,
had already played a role in history analogous to this
one. Many of the Etruscan painters have the bizarre

Volterra (xiii Century). Palace of the Priori.

elegance which will characterize the art of the Tuscans two thousand years later.

Italy received the Gothic from France, at the dawn of the municipal life of her northern cities. She did not understand it. The forest of the cathedral was not made for her sky. In their silent shadows the immense naves extinguished the fever of her spirit. France is a country united by planes and rivers. Italy is a country divided by mountains. From the north to the south her cities of bronze menace one another from the tops of high hills separated by sudden ravines. The Italy of the Middle Ages could not have a religious architecture, because religious architecture, at that moment, received its grandeur from the social desires which created it and because, the soil being too cut up and the sky too clement to make men feel the necessity for aiding men, Italy had greater need for passion and intelligence, the instruments of the individual, than for instinct and faith, the instruments of the race. We must face the fact that, save for the Romanesque churches of the earliest period, with their pride, their warlike power, and their façade with its patina of gold, the Italian cathedrals are ugly. To be sure, they borrow a singular charm from the hard and lusty cities which mount tumultuously like an army rushing to the attack of the campanile that stands as straight as a mast in a hurricane. It is a bewitching, perverse charm and one from which we cannot tear ourselves without making an effort to dominate its superficial sensations. But when the Gothic appears, the cathedrals are overloaded with decoration and become mannered and grandiloquent. The Romans had made the same error in the old days when they emerged from their utilitarian architecture to erect temples to political parvenus. The Italians did not see that the use of ornament is to define the indispensable organs of the architectural

SIENA (XIV Century). Sansedoni Palace.

body by making them more slender or lighter—
heavier or broader, and that this must be done by ac-
centing directly along the lines of their function. When
ornament exceeds this role it becomes a source of ugli-
ness. It masks the bone structure of the building whose
characteristic projections are the only things that can
justify it. There is no monumental architecture without social cohesion. Here the bones come through the
skin, there the garments hang loosely. All the architecture of the Italian Renaissance, all the architecture
of Europe since that period has been engulfed in a mis-
understanding of this fundamental principle. And the
misunderstood art of ornament of thirteenth-century
France avenged Gothic architecture by invading a
school which had no other reason for existence than
that of combating its own magnificent precepts.

The municipal palaces were created for precise needs
and defined the violent and free personality of the city;
the private palaces defined the whole isolated and
devouring personality of the lord who lived in them and
who brought into the cities, where Italy concenters,
the feudal world which had been driven from the
countryside. And it is in these palaces that the Italian
architect again finds himself, as the Roman architect
found himself when his problem was to open roads, to
build circuses, thermæ, and aqueducts. Here he is at
home, and he affirms the fact. Immediately he becomes
strong, sober, precise, and definitive. One receives the
impression that the great pavement on which people
walk and which is reddened by their blood on days of
rebellion, has been set up straight toward the sky,
perpendicular with the street. The fierce palaces follow one another, almost solid like blocks, without any
other ornament than the brass fists that stick out of
the walls as hitching posts for the horses. As the palaces
start up from the soil their line is a little oblique, it

bends backward, like the spine of a bowman. Higher up it becomes vertical. At the top it leans forward, like the square shoulders whose mailed arms are about to send down lead and iron. Thus the whole façade is concave, impossible to scale. And two hermetical

SIENA (XIV Century). Salimbeni Palace.

walls on each side of the street defy and menace each other, with the sinister melody of stone that has been set in place with a certainty of its practical function, even as a geometrical theorem is inscribed in the logical functioning of the brain. These crenelated cubes dominated by a square tower, these perfectly bare walls pierced by pairs of narrow windows between which stands a colonnette as stiff as an iron bar, and these profiles as hard as axes rise from the paved lanes of Siena, Perugia, Volterra, Florence, and Mantua and never seem more than half open. When the standard bearers unfurl the banner of the unions in the public square, the gates of bronze are closed against the insurrection of the people. Civil war continues. Let there be two different plumes on men's hoods, let a glance be given or a gesture made and the dagger leaps from its sheath. The tocsin sounds, men are ambushed at the cross streets, pursued under the vaults and murdered in the churches while the fortified houses pour down boiling oil and pitch upon the tumult. There is Italy, and nowhere else. When the illustrious Brunelleschi, right in the fifteenth century, built the Pitti Palace, piling two bare floors on almost unhewn blocks, when, after his journey to Rome, he broke with the disfigured architecture of the French to return to the positive art of his ancestors and abandoned the unreal lyrism of the religious architects of his country to set, on its eightfold ribbing of stone, the dome which rises above the roofs of Florence with a sweep so powerful and so firm, he was accomplishing a more radical revolution against the artists of the Italian Gothic than that which the men of the French Gothic had accomplished, three centuries earlier, against the monks who built in the Romanesque style. He rendered to the genius of his race the homage of recognizing that genius in himself.

III

And so at the hour when northern France was lifting up, amid the tremendous vibration of the bells, sonorous poems of stone and glass that hover and sway over the cities, Italy was defining herself in the violent, straight-lined palaces by the quality which, much later, will define her Renaissance. Already, here in the Middle Ages, she was affirming the rights of the individual. The Romanesque architects of Italy often

signed their works and all of Tuscany knew Nicola
Pisano, the sculptor, when not one of the image makers
of France had thought to tell his name. The Scaligers,
erect on their war horses, were already stamping the
dust. It was not possible for popular Christianity to
take on the form
in the Italian im-
agination which
French sensibility
had given it. Only
few individuals
could, without be-
ing consumed by
it, embody in their
lives the poetry of
exalted sentiment
which marked the
character of the
Christianity of the
people. There is,
indeed, a cathedral
in Italy. But all
the crowd could
do was to cherish
an ardent desire
for it. It did not

PISAN ART (XIV to XV Century).
Virgin, detail, wood. (*Louvre.*)

set its hand to the work. The body of the cathedral
is Francis of Assisi. Its towers are Dante and Giotto.

The foundation of the century is violence. The
feudal Church, here, weighs down more heavily than
in other places. The tiara and the miter are bought,
when they are not taken by assault. Through the
fear of hell the priest obtains obedience of the poor,
among whom furious feeling obscures the sense of
social duty, even as it does with the priest himself.
Remember with what rage the tortures of the in-

ferno are painted on the walls of the Campo Santo
of Pisa.

It was by a reaction that gentleness was born. It
was as absolute as the preceding violence because,
like the latter, it set fire to minds whose passion refused
to stop short of full surrender to their insatiable instinct. Francis of Assisi was transported by love as
other men were by the frenzy of killing. If he lived
under the rule of the men whose corruption and violence had provoked his coming, it was because he felt
in himself a gentleness, an invincible power, capable of
cleansing and reviving the world. When he caused
the human spirit to re-enter nature, from which primitive Christianity had torn it away, he restored to it the
nurture of its dignity and strength. His pantheism
protested against the Christian dualism which defines
the discord between the soul and the flesh, and brutally
cuts off access to the great harmonies. Dying, he
repented of having practiced asceticism, of having
"offended his brother the body." The profound and
charming word! He was, in Italy, in the realm of
sentiment, what Abelard had been in France and what
Roger Bacon was to be in England in the domain of
reason. The whole of pagan humanity, which he bound
up with the spirit of Christ, revived in his love for universal life. And this love led him, where it had led
the last thinkers of the pagan world, to the inner
negation of property, which is to say—to freedom.

He did not preach moral sermons to the men of his
time, to weary them without changing them. With a
poetry so passionate that, while he spoke, he trembled,
he laughed, he wept for joy, he told them that everything
that was in him spoke of love for what is on the earth.
He never ceased loving. He fell asleep and awoke
under the trees. He called the beasts to him, he sang,
warbled, and whistled with them, he begged alms for

GIOTTO. Saint Francis speaking to the birds, fresco.
(*Upper Church, Assisi.*)

them, and the beasts followed him. He asked counsel
of the crickets and they gave it to him, and he did not

Giotto. The Virgin and Saint Anne, fresco.
(*Arena, Padua.*)

hesitate to follow it. He did not know theology, but
he left this prayer:

Praised be my Lord God, with all his creatures, and especially
our brother the sun, who brings us the day and who brings us the

GIOTTO. Jesus insulted by the Jews, fresco, detail.
(*Arena, Padua.*)

light; fair is he, and he shines with a very great splendor. O Lord, he signifies to us thee.

Praised be my Lord for our sister the moon, and for the stars, the which he has set clear and lovely in heaven.

Praised be my Lord for our brother the wind, and for air and

GIOTTO.   The confession of Saint Francis, fresco.
(*Santa Croce, Florence.*)

clouds, calms and all weather, by which thou upholdest life in all creatures.

Praised be my Lord for our sister water, who is very serviceable to us, and humble and precious and clean.

Praised be my Lord for our brother fire, through whom thou givest us light in the darkness; and he is bright and pleasant, and very mighty and strong.

Praised be my Lord for our mother the earth, the which doth sustain us, and bringest forth divers fruits and flowers of many colors, and grass.

(Translation of Maurice Francis Egan.)

When he died, the cities of Umbria fought around his coffin for the possession of his bones. Such is the understanding of men. No matter. Even this again was passion. And he left in the piety of the multitudes and in the imagination of the strong a memory so resplendent that it illuminated Italy until the end

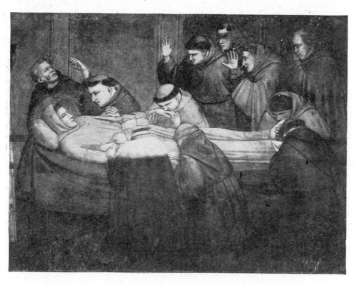

GIOTTO. Death of Saint Francis, detail, fresco.
(*Santa Croce, Florence.*)

of her evening. He restored to her the love of forms, and on that love she lived for four hundred years.

The greatest poet and the greatest painter of the Middle Ages drank from the well of his memory. At one bound the towers sprang up from the nave. The one rough and thickly growing, shot through by flames, full of the sound of the organ and of thunder—is upheld by iron ribbing. The other is calm, a ray rising from the world of the senses to follow in a straight course to the light of the spirit. Dante and Giotto. The two faces of the Middle Ages. The Inferno and

Paradise. Above all, the two faces of Italy, loving and
violent, as she is charming and savage in her luminous
bays and in her harsh rocks. It is the first of the great
contrasts which we shall find up to the end of her
heroic life, contrasts that are enveloped in the same
harmony of passion and of intelligence; Masaccio and

GIOTTO.   The descent from the Cross, detail, fresco.
(*Arena, Padua.*)

Fra Angelico, Donatello and Gozzoli, Luca Signorelli
and Ghirlandajo, Michael Angelo and Raphael. The
same heaven harkens to the voice of the prophet and
to the song of the shepherd as their sound rises to its
sparkling spheres.

Giotto is not a primitive, any more than Dante. He
is the conclusion of a long effort. If he revealed the
language of forms to those who came a hundred years
after him, it is slightly in the manner in which Phidias

GIOTTO. The descent from the Cross, fresco. (*Arena, Padua.*)

can still reveal it to those who love him enough to refuse to follow him. Guido, Cimabue, Duccio himself, the noble Sienese who recovered, through Byzantine tradition, the real soul of Greece and for the first time translated the drama of the Passion into terms of

SCHOOL OF GIOTTO. The massacre of the innocents, fresco.
(*Lower Church, Assisi.*)

humanity, had not been able to force open the hieratic mold offered by the painters of Ravenna and the mosaicists sent by Constantinople. With Giotto everything invades the forms at once—movement, life, intelligence, and the great architectural calm. Because he was almost the first one to arrive, the means he used were limited, but with them he was able to translate a perfectly mature conception of the world and of life. His epoch permitted him to give only one expression to them, and he gave it, completely and con-

Perugia (xiv Century).   Palazzo Pubblico.

sciously, with the freedom and the sobriety of the men
who bear within them one of those decisive moments
that humanity sometimes expends several centuries in
attaining. He was one of those after whom dissociation and analysis must inevitably begin again.· Renaissance Italy is separated from him by an abyss, and we
shall have to wait until Raphael sketches and Rubens
completes, for the modern spirit, the synthesis that
Giotto made for the mediæval spirit.

He had that genius for the symbol which mediæval
Christianity imposed on its poets as, upon those who
cultivate the soil, Nature imposes the rhythm of her
seasons. Since life for these poets symbolized the
divine idea, they were unable to find their symbol
save in the material of life which was passionately
loved and passionately studied for what it contains
and reveals. The symbol came to Giotto in the attitudes of men, in the humble movement of the beasts
which grazed or hopped about at the level of the soil, in
the prodigious blue carpet that day spread across space,
and in the innumerable fires that night revealed there.
Although he had within him only the potential forces
accumulated by the unsatisfied needs of the men who
had gone before him, although practically no one before
his time had observed the life of forms, he could see at
once that all our desires, and all our dreams, and all
that is divine in us comes to us from our meeting with
living forms, from the rough or charming places amid
which we have lived, from the majestic bodies which
we have seen bowed with weeping or raised again by
hope, from the hands that supplicate, or that open, or
that part the long hair over faces attentive, dolorous,
or grave. His sense of all this was so pure that the
image of it all, which he has made to live on the walls
of Assisi and of Padua, passes directly into us like a
process of life, without our having the time to perceive

that the thing before us is neither sculpture, in the exact sense of the word, since the profiles and the groups, though disposed sculpturally, are projected on a painted surface—nor is it painting, since the role of the values, of the reflections, and the passages is barely

SIMONE MARTINI. Two saints, detail, fresco. (*Lower Church, Assisi.*)

suspected. This rudimentary form is traversed by a lightning flash of the soul which instantly causes it to stand erect.

In Italy he was, in himself, the incarnation of the Christianity of the people which, in that period, covered with its thick tangled growth the field of sen-

27

sibility of the French crowds. Like them, he could
easily feel the meaning for everyone of the birth, the
life, and the death of the Man whom the poor had
caused to be deified that they might the better recognize themselves in Him; and he told the story in that
language both of the intellect and the heart which his
race and his sky alone could dictate to him. In the
ingenuousness of his heart he found the loftiest drama
of man. And as he saw only the essential direction of
the gestures of those who enacted that drama, he made
them more direct, more exact, and more true in order
to bring its scenes before men who, after his time,
would need only to close their eyes to feel the drama
living within them.

It comes over us gently, in calm and incessant waves.
Like a leaf that has fallen on the great waters of a
river, we follow the movement of irresistible gentleness
which is within men and women and which causes them
to prostrate themselves around the dead hero that is in
their hands as they support the bloodless head and the
broken feet and arms; it spreads like a steady light
over earth and heaven which become tranquil round
about Him. No one before Giotto, not even those who
had turned to woman to speak their farewell through
her, no one had ever quite grasped her role in the
inner life of humanity, no one had ever seen her thus
forever surrounded by passion, ceaselessly torn by
maternity and by love, and crucified at all times.
Never had anyone said that she, unlike the living gods
that we nail to the cross, has not the consolation of
pride, that she allows herself to be tortured, and yet
does not lose faith in her executioners, who are her sons
and the fathers of her sons, and that she asks of them
no other recompense than the right to suffer for them.
The world had not yet observed all that there is in a
face where the eyes are hollow under the agonized lines

SIMONE MARTINI. Calvary, detail. (*Spanish Chapel, Florence.*)

of the brow, in a head that rests on two knotted hands, or in the gesture of two outstretched arms. This work is the greatest dramatic poem in the history of painting. It is not to be described, it is not to be explained, it is not to be evoked, it must be lived through. One must have seen, at Assisi, how those burning harmonies cause the shadows to tremble, one must have seen the heaps of murdered children, the mothers who die or supplicate or gaze at the little limp body across their knees, one must have seen the soldiers who look like butchers. And in Florence, one must have seen the friends of Francis who bow over his death under the wave of sorrow of the last moments. At Padua, one must have seen the kneeling women, those who open their arms and those whose clasped hands make a cradle for the divine corpse, and the Christ among the hideous men who insult Him, and the men who suffer and the ones who pray and the ones who love. And when one has seen this, it is like a strong and gentle wine that one bears away within him forever.

Giotto had picked up the echo of French art in the illuminations in the books, and had certainly met, in Italy, masons and image makers from the banks of the Seine. The son of the old sculptor of Pisa, Giovanni, who came but a short time before him, had touched him by his Nativities, full of animation and tenderness, where one sees the enchantment of the actors in the scene as they hear the cry of the child, as they see the beasts cropping the grass, and as they surprise life at its dawn with the charmed mother who bends over the cradle. Giovanni had left him speechless with his scenes of murder, his crucifixions, and his massacres of the innocents, dramas so burning and so full of move-ment that they seemed to fill the stone with their passion and to hurl it in gusts of flame before the spec-tator. He had roused him to enthusiasm by the surety of his language, as powerful and flexible as a long sword that one bends double and that flashes lightning as it springs back. Through the Sienese painters, he had got back to Ravenna, where, before the splendor of the polychrome of the shining mosaics, he had surmised, beyond Byzantium, the calm of the Panathenaic processions that still took their course around the Parthenon. He had seen the architecture of antiquity at Rome, at Naples, and at Assisi, where Cavallini, the painter, brought to him the tradition of the Roman mosaicists. Standing before the frescoes of Cimabue, that were still fresh, with their blue and the gold that reddened in the glow of the torches,

TADDEO GADDI. The Annunciation.
(*Santa Croce, Florence.*)

he had worked in the darkness of the lower church where all the mystic skies have accumulated in the plaster their azure, their twilights, and the stars of their nights. The line of the mountains had called to him everywhere, likewise the bays and men. Behold those figures that stand out, pure and with a single movement, those harps and those violins that are played upon, those palms that are waved, those banners that are bowed, and those noble groups around the beds where there is a death or a birth. Something is quivering there that the Greeks did not know, a sadness in the mouths, a gentleness in the eyes, the confidence that man for a moment had in man and in the hope that suffering might cease. Something shines there that the Middle Ages of the Occident no longer knew, a re-echoing of forms in other forms, a harmony of movements that answer one another, a line which by its rhythmic undulation connects the torsos which bend over with others that are prostrate and still others that stand erect.

I cannot, for my part, imagine a man more intelligent than Giotto. And I am sure that this intelligence is nothing else than the progressive and logical refining of the most direct thought and of the most unstudied emotion. When he had seen how his friend died, and had seen his wife giving birth, or his child suffering, he knew the spontaneous organization among the attitudes of those who weep or those who act in and about the drama, all of them having the drama itself as the sole center of attraction. Without effort, as it seems, and to express this drama and the circumstances of it directly and naturally, the living masses obey the secret laws that have presided over the harmony of the groups since the beginning of time. It is because each one of the beings who takes part therein acts according to the character of his sentiment which he contributes to the more general character of the ensemble—the artistic, or if you will, metaphysical character that reproduces the mysterious eurhythmy of the worlds with an instinctive, musical, and yet close fidelity. Beside the old Florentine master, Raphael seems to have perceived the mere externals of action, Michael Angelo gives the impression of a desperate effort toward that perfect equilibrium which, in Giotto, is an essen-

The Church Militant, fresco, detail. (*Santa Maria Novella, Florence.*)

tial function; Rubens seems to force into theatrical
attitudes the inner movement that arranges and dis-
tributes; and Rembrandt, at times, seems to be seeking
effects. The order that all of them feverishly pursue
in the sudden intuitions, the tempests, the revolts, or

ORCAGNA. Paradise, detail, fresco. (*Santa Maria Novella,
Florence.*)

the sustained tension of the spirit enters into Giotto
with the emotion itself, and he acquires an architectural and plastic character through the harmonious
meeting of the mind and the heart. And, considered
in this way, the "composition" of Giotto is perhaps
the greatest miracle in the history of painting. I say
"miracle," because a miracle is the most spontaneous
realization in action of the desire that is most inaccessible in the mind. These clasped hands, these fingers
that clutch at the breast, these bodies kneeling or

ANDREA DA FIRENZE (?). The sick imploring Saint Dominic,
fresco. (*Spanish Chapel, Florence.*)

arising or half-bowed or erect, this progressive building up in steps of human forms, all the outer attributes of the despair, of the supplication, of the adoration, and of the prayer that make up this pathetic work enter like a flood into the unity of thought to demonstrate the well-defined accord of our moral requirements with our æsthetic needs. A powerful and contagious melody runs through and sways all the violent actions. . . . This poet of sorrow possessed the joy that belongs to the epochs of life in which everything reaches a climax and unites and agrees in all minds, so that it may one day comfort those who will seek the traces of these minds, whatever the faith and the life of the seekers, whatever the cause of their suffering and the form of their hope. It was not Giotto who brought about the unity of his work: it was the unity of the time that created him. And Unity, which is a hymn, raises us above tears. Giotto does not weep over the Christ or over woman, nor do we, as we look at his work. With Giotto we are in the presence of an unspeakable gentleness, an unspeakable hope. He understands, he bends over, he reaches out a strong hand, he lifts up the man who has fallen, and, to sustain him and carry him along, he intones a magnificent chant; his great severe line undulates, rises, descends and reascends, like a voice.

Profoundly Italian though his idealistic, dramatic, and decorative genius, and containing, although he epitomized only a single moment of Italy, the whole Italy that was to come, even fallen Italy, the universal quality of humanity that Giotto possessed brings him into communion with all the heroes of painting, through the piety with which he welcomed life, through the passionate feeling he had for the burdens that it laid upon him, and through the divine desire that caused him to transfigure the world and support the celestial blue of the half-opened paradise on the grave human

accents of the reds, the greens, and the blacks. . . .
His hope never rose higher than his courage as a man.
On the day when he re-assembled, around the crucified
Jesus, angels half emerging from heaven on their wings

PISA (XIV Century). The triumph of death, fresco.
(*Campo Santo.*)

made up of rays of light, he recovered the supreme
symbol, that Æschylus had imagined, to fortify our
courage when he saw in flight around Prometheus the
swarm of the Oceanides.

IV

In itself, then, this work is a social monument wherein
radiant painting groups sculptural volumes in an architectural rhythm. When the man had disappeared, it
crumbled rapidly. Those who came after him could

do no more than gather up the debris for the building of isolated edifices which, in the anarchy of the century, were only provisional sanctuaries, frail and exposed to

Siena (xiv Century). Via Golluzza.

all storms. The disquieted and disunited soul of Italy could no longer find in them more than a shadow of the heroic certitude wherein the great spirits of the Middle Ages had imagined her hope. It was after Giotto that the veritable primitives appeared, but

primitives who had lost the great impulse—the end of
an epoch. That dull dawn that illumined from within
the great serious faces of the virgins of Cimabue, with
their great eyes to whose depths we can never look,
any more than we can those of the figures painted on
the sarcophagi of Egypt, on the cupolas of Constanti-

DUCCIO.   Christ in the Garden.   (*Opera del Duomo, Siena.*)

nople, and on the walls of Pompeii, that nascent force
that was beginning to sculpture the flat skulls of the
Byzantine idols, to lift up, in confused animation, the
choir of the saved, to the accompanying tones of the
harps of heaven, all of that obscure flame of life which,
in the flash of the mind that we call Giotto, suddenly
revealed man to himself, sank to earth together at the
same time, and its light diminished till nothing was
left but a few hesitating gleams that went out in smoke.
As the Italian artists could not re-create the magnificent
equilibrium of soul which had covered the walls of
Assisi and Padua with those austere lines through

which the order of the universe inscribed itself for a moment, and as they saw only two divine works behind them, they sought their refuge in the more despairing one, the only one, indeed, that gave them the liberty to speak as they pleased. Giotto

Duccio.   The miraculous draught of fishes.
(*Opera del Duomo, Siena.*)

being inaccessible to them, the Dantesque cycle opens at the moment when the plague in Tuscany justified the visions of the poet. In Florence, Orcagna, the man of severe imagination, the painter who shows us visages ennobled by meditation or contracted by grief, saw all about him the gathering of crowds who raised their eyes to heaven and who bowed their great forms in prayer. Taddeo Gaddi, in the gentleness of his despair, nailed the Christ on all the walls. The Spanish chapel was covered with painting over whose fervency passed a wind of terror, where the cripple and the sick man crept out of their hovels to stretch forth their hands. At Pisa, abandoned to the terrible Dominicans in its political decadence, it was now only the walls of the cemetery that were decorated, and then with rotting corpses, with worms, with demons and

PIETRO LORENZETTI. The descent from the Cross, fresco. (*Lower Church, Assisi.*)

tortures—we witness a veritable furor of remorse. . . . Siena obstinately allowed herself to sink deeper and deeper into a sickly resolve to die without a struggle.

Of all the Italian cities she had always been the most violent, the one that had known the greatest suffering in civil war and had been most frequently devastated by the military conflicts of the north and south, between which she was caught. She retained the hardness of the age of iron in Italy. Her artists

saw Giotto, but touched him no deeper than his skin,
and allowed him to penetrate no deeper than theirs.
Duccio played the same role among the painters of
Siena as Giotto did among the Florentines. They
were of the same age, but doubtless they knew little
of each other. In any case, far more than Giotto, he

AMBROGIO LORENZETTI. The Pope and the Franciscans,
fresco, detail. (*San Francesco, Siena.*)

remains engulfed in the Byzantium which, be it said,
he animates with an expressiveness of great power
and charm. He has, to the highest degree, the gift of
giving life and movement to his crowds. They are
active and busy, without great actions, but with a
movement in the ensemble that clearly reveals the
meaning of the scene at our first glance. He has but
the slightest intuition of that sublime "composition"
which, with the great Florentine, is no other than a

perfect balance between the moral element and the descriptive element. But he goes straight to his goal of relating the emotion aroused in him by the life and death of the Lord, and he expresses his ideas in living forms; his speech is marked by nobility, tenderness, verve, and archness, even when he is impassioned, and

AMBROGIO LORENZETTI. Landscape, fresco. (*Academy, Siena.*)

in these qualities he has scarcely a superior throughout the whole of Italian painting, save Giotto himself. His immediate successors, Barna, for example, make a melodramatic travesty, though an ardent and highly colored one, of this power for passion which would suffice to define, outside of the genius of Giotto, the genius of Italy itself. All her heroes have possessed this dramatic soul, and for five centuries all her false artists have shamelessly used it to calumniate, before the eyes of men, the ideal that she has poured forth so generously. Barna and Spinello Aretino disfigure the

28

death struggle of the Middle Ages of the Latin world, as the Bolognese school was later on to disfigure the death struggle of the Latin Renaissance by turning into theatrical declamation the spiritual realities that had been wrested from the unknown by Masaccio, Da Vinci, Michael Angelo, Raphael, and Titian.

And yet in this retrograde city which, amid the disorder and the anxiety of all minds, was possessed by the desire to protect its gods under its armor, the slow fading of the last flower of the Gothic had a penetrating perfume. We meet with something here that has a certain resemblance to the end of French architecture. . . . It is like the dying poetry of the stained glass with which a sick people irritates its fever, after the living poetry that had resounded in stone and bronze with the voices of strong men. Siena goes to her death in the burning shadow of the marble cathedral whose black and white campanile mounts from the rock under the pitiless sky. She sinks in the mystic fervor of the pure blues and the golds brought to her painters by the Byzantine mosaicists. Simone Martini withdraws his gaze from the military cavalcades and the high crenelated towers that arise and threaten one another over the wave of the roofs, only that he may listen the better to the vibrating of the celestial harps in the space that no eye can penetrate, but from which comes the wind that sways the lilies he paints. With him all the walls of the palaces and the churches tremble with profound voices, as if the pale virgins who cover them from top to bottom and who, amid the gold and the palms, raising the great oblique eyes in their long pure faces, were together making audible, in the poignant accents of chanted suffering and gentleness, the noble protest of the consoling legends against the noble effort of the time. In the heart of the fifteenth century, when round them a renewed ideal is tormenting Tuscany, Bartolo di Fredi, Sano di Pietro, and Lorenzo di Pietro are still obstinately listening to distant voices which for the other Italians are lost in silence. Only Ambrogio Lorenzetti, the powerful decorator whose frescoes sing, vibrate, weep, and become calm again and swell like the tone of the choir

SIENESE SCHOOL (end of XIV Century). Crucifixion, fresco, detail. (*Subiaco.*)

of violoncellos, only Ambrogio has heard the confused murmur that rises from the streets and the countryside and from the little hills covered with vineyards and pine trees—the murmur that announces a new awakening; and at the same time his brother Pietro imprints a new unity upon the plastic splendor that he discovers in the drama of the Cross. A marvelous animation peoples his august landscapes, where the labors of the husbandmen and scenes of war cover the serried hills

and cut into the hollow valleys. It is a vast poem, epic
and intimate, teeming with imagination, as if a world
foreseen were fermenting in the furrows of the plow,
in the seed, and in harvests. And then, more profoundly than any one of the Florentines of his time,
Ambrogio scrutinizes and characterizes faces. His

SANO DI PIETRO or SASSETTA.
Charity, Poverty, and Humility.
(*Chantilly.*)

great effigies, as firm and pure as the portraits of the
Chinese, seem graven in the wall, seem outlined and
cemented with stone. Slowly and powerfully their
eyes awaken and look out from the hard faces, they do
not move, but are terrible in their severity, their concentration, and their silence. Their drawing is so
concise and so completely a result of the will of the
artist, the expressive lines and curves are so closely

linked that we already behold a first and almost complete realization of the desire to determine by geometrical means the least abstract characteristics of
life when it moves us most; and later on, it will be in
an art conceived in this manner that we shall find the
meeting place of the heroes of the following century,
Paolo Uccello, Andrea del Castagno, Piero della Fran-
cesca, Luca Signorelli. But even so, Ambrogio, almost
as truly as his brother Pietro, remains a man of the
Middle Ages in the strength of his moral philosophy—
already quite strained, it is true, and too voluntary,
through his uncompromising and precise sense of the
just and the unjust expressed in the beautiful dark
harmonies, red and black, in which there resounds, with
a painful sharpness, the supreme appeal of the past.
Siena dies of her desire to maintain, in the face of new
needs, the worn-out principle that had caused her to
live. While she is shutting herself up in her narrow
independence, Florence absorbs Tuscany, and subjects
it to her spirit.

SANCHI (III Century B.C.).   Detail of a door of the Stupa.

ALPHABETICAL INDEX

OF THE NAMES CITED IN THIS VOLUME[1]

[1] The names of the artists who are directly in question are printed in italics.

AFRICA. Dance mask (Gaboon). (*Guillaume Collection.*)

SYNOPTIC TABLES